T0313161

Putting Partnerships to Work

Strategic Alliances for Development between Government, the Private Sector and Civil Society

Edited by Michael Warner and Rory Sullivan

Putting Partnerships to Work

STRATEGIC ALLIANCES FOR DEVELOPMENT BETWEEN GOVERNMENT, THE PRIVATE SECTOR AND CIVIL SOCIETY

EDITED BY MICHAEL WARNER AND RORY SULLIVAN

Routledge
Taylor & Francis Group

LONDON AND NEW YORK

First published 2004 by the American Planning Association

Published 2017 by Routledge

2 Park Square, Milton Park, Abingdon, Oxon OX14 4RN
711 Third Avenue, New York, NY 10017, USA

Routledge is an imprint of the Taylor & Francis Group, an informa business

Cover by LaliAbril.com.

British Library Cataloguing in Publication Data:
A catalogue record for this book is available from the British Library.

ISBN: 9781874719724 (hbk)

Contents

Acknowledgements

This book marks the culmination of four years of applied research into the art and science of developing partnerships for sustainable development between government agencies, civil society and community groups, and companies from the extractive industries. An extraordinarily wide range of individuals and organisations were engaged in formulating and contributing to the case studies and other materials that have formed the basis of this book. We would like to express our thanks to them all, in particular the authors of the chapters presented here. Finally, we wish to acknowledge and thank the original programme sponsors: the World Bank Group, CARE International UK, Department for International Development (UK), Shell International, BP, Rio Tinto, Anglo American, Placer Dome, Norsk Hydro and WMC Resources.

Preface

Michael Warner and Rory Sullivan

The World Summit on Sustainable Development held in Johannesburg in September 2002 clearly identified the corporate sector as one of the key actors in the delivery of national and international poverty reduction targets in developing countries. 'Partnerships' between government, civil society and business were proposed as one means whereby these poverty reduction targets were to be achieved. Despite the rhetoric, there was less consideration of how such partnerships could work in practice, the outcomes that could be achieved or the relative merits of partnerships over other, more traditional, approaches to development.

This book is about partnerships between the private sector, government and civil society. Its objective is to share practical experiences in establishing and implementing such partnerships and to show how partnerships work. The focus is on the oil, gas and mining industries, as these sectors have tended to be the primary drivers of foreign investment in developing countries. Corporations in these industries increasingly operate in regions characterised by poor communities and fragile environments. A more effective use of external relationships to ensure these investments contribute more fully to poverty reduction and local environmental management is critical, for the companies, for government and for the poor.

Putting Partnerships to Work is about how partnerships work, the types of outcome that can be achieved and the necessary conditions for partnerships to be successful. The material presented is based on the authors' experience working for the Secretariat of the Natural Resources Cluster (NRC) of Business Partners for Development (BPD). This major research programme, which ran from 1998 to 2002, aimed to enhance the role of oil, gas and mining corporations in international development. The programme objective was to produce practical guidance, based on the experience of specific natural resource operations around the world, on how partnerships involving companies, government authorities and civil-society organisations can be an effective means of reducing investment risks and of promoting community and regional development. The programme encompassed partnerships in Colombia, Nigeria, India, Venezuela, Bolivia, Zambia,

Azerbaijan, Indonesia and Tanzania. The specific projects that were implemented included not only 'traditional' development projects such as the provision of water, healthcare or infrastructure but also themes as diverse as conflict prevention, regional development, micro-enterprise development and the management of oil-spill compensation. Based on the experience of establishing and implementing effective partnerships, the NRC identified good practice and developed replicable guidelines, tools and training materials.

This book is not only about good practice. It is something of a 'warts and all' look at partnerships, presenting the positive outcomes and the lessons from the programme as well as the risks and costs if things went wrong. The book also provides evidence not only of the viability of partnerships (i.e. that partnerships 'can work') but also evidence that partnership approaches can provide substantially better outcomes for all parties than can the more traditional approaches to development or corporate social responsibility. For example, a road in India was constructed at 25% of the cost to government; it took just 11 months for a community health centre in Venezuela to become operational and with its long-term financial future assured; and primary education enrolment rates in the vicinity of a gold mine in Tanzania have jumped from a historic level of 60–80% to almost 100% (as a consequence of improved infrastructure and community awareness of the importance of education).

These development and public-sector benefits have been accompanied by substantial business benefits, including significant reductions in the cost of community development initiatives and/or the leverage of additional resources, greater sustainability and viability of development projects and significant improvements to corporate reputation and their local 'social licence to operate' with communities. Our experience has been that to achieve these benefits requires all parties to invest time and effort in first exploring the best design for the partnership, in understanding the motivations of their potential partners and, once the partnership has been established, in continuing to actively support the partnership and ensure its ongoing viability.

Our view is that partnerships that engage the strengths of companies, government and civil society can, under the right conditions, yield better (and more sustainable) results for communities and for business than can traditional approaches to development. It is also our view that, because it is built on the central idea of each partner 'doing what they do best', the partnership approach offers an opportunity to rethink the way in which companies view they contributions to the livelihoods of local communities. Through partnerships we hope that local social and economic development will be seen less as an 'add-on' or 'cost' to the company and more as an integral part of business strategy providing significant commercial and other benefits.

Perhaps most importantly, partnerships offer the potential for regional operating companies to change the perceptions of government and of civil society that the company will take the primary responsibility for local development. Rather, partnerships enable companies to locate themselves as one of (but not the only) agent of development in the local region. Partnerships enable communities to take charge of their own development needs, interacting with government to jointly design and maintain public services. They also allow government to fulfil its proper role of carrying out its public mandate, delivering necessary services and ensuring the quality and sustainability of development impacts.

The challenges of poverty reduction in the developing world are so great that no one sector can solve them on its own. Partnerships between business, government and civil society are a means of addressing this most fundamental of truths. We hope that this book will provide a roadmap for all those working towards making the elimination of poverty a reality.

Michael Warner and Rory Sullivan
December 2003

1
Introduction

Rory Sullivan and Michael Warner

In today's world, 2.8 billion people live on less than US$2 a day, 1.2 billion people lack access to clean water and about twice that number have no sanitation. In Africa, half of the continent's children either do not enter primary school or drop out before finishing. By 2001 an estimated 40 million adults and children around the world had AIDS, of whom 28 million were in Sub-Saharan Africa, and 6 million in South and South-East Asia. AIDS is estimated to kill 3 million people a year, 80% of whom are in Africa.

The recent World Summit on Sustainable Development (Rio + 10) held in Johannesburg clearly placed the corporate sector at the centre of international efforts to reduce poverty. Although the language of partnerships was all-pervasive at Rio + 10, there was less of a sense of how precisely companies could contribute to these new social partnerships, the manner in which such partnerships would or could be structured or the outcomes that could be achieved (or how these outcomes compared with those of other approaches to development or poverty alleviation). The overwhelming sense was of a concept that had been wholeheartedly embraced but where little consideration had been given to what that concept could mean in practice, or how it could be taken up to scale.

The purpose of this book is to contribute to the understanding of partnerships—specifically, of three-way (tri-sector) partnerships combining partners drawn from government, civil society and the business sector—and of the way in which partnerships can contribute to poverty alleviation and development. The focus is on the oil, gas and mining industries, as these sectors have tended to be the primary drivers of foreign direct investment in developing countries. The material presented is based on the Business Partners for Development (BPD) programme. This programme ran from 1998 to 2002 and looked at the experience of specific natural resource operations around the world. Its purpose was to assess how partnerships involving companies, government authorities and civil-society organisations could be an effective means of reducing social risks and of promoting community and regional development.

1.1 Why look at the extractive industries? The importance of foreign investment

The capital flows to developing countries include official aid, portfolio investment and foreign direct investment (FDI). This book is about the last of these: that is, the flow of capital to developing countries and emerging economies, where the investors retain a controlling interest in the business operations. Developing countries and emerging economies[1] received approximately a quarter of world FDI flows over the period 1970–2000. Since FDI flows vary considerably from one year to the next, focusing on flows in any particular year conceals important long-run trends. A better measure is therefore the overall 'stock' of inward FDI, which is sometimes measured as the accumulation of flows. Figure 1.1 shows the regional share of global FDI stock.

FDI flows around the world have experienced two principal waves. From 1975 to 1981, flows were dominated by commercial bank lending, involving a high proportion of 'petro dollars'. Between 1981 and 1984, this lending declined as the banks lost confidence in the financial stability of the borrowing countries, linked in part to the fall in oil prices and related debt crisis. A second wave emerged as markets and financial institutions integrated and countries moved towards economic liberalisation in trade and investment. The recent economic slowdown in South-East Asia signalled a subsequent decline in flows, though this time less pronounced, but with flows to the developing world remaining fairly constant.

It is well known that, cumulatively, FDI is the largest source of external capital flow for all developing countries taken together. In particular, FDI is larger than official (multilateral and bilateral) development assistance. However, this broad analysis oversimplifies the situation. In reality, FDI flows to developing countries are concentrated in only a handful of emerging markets (e.g. China, Brazil, Mexico, Singapore, Thailand). For example, in 1999, 11 emerging markets (see Fig.

---

1   These are defined by the United Nations Commission on Trade and Development as countries not in the Organisation for Economic Co-operation and Development, but including Mexico, Korea and Czechoslovakia. The rationale for this classification is as follows: 'There is no established convention for the designation of "developed" and "developing' countries or areas in the United Nations system. In common practice, Japan in Asia, Canada and the United States in northern America, Australia and New Zealand in Oceania, and Europe are considered 'developed' regions or areas. In international trade statistics, the Southern African Customs Union is also treated as a developed region and Israel as a developed country; countries emerging from the former Yugoslavia are treated as developing countries; and countries of eastern Europe and of the Commonwealth of Independent States (code 172) in Europe are not included under either developed or developing regions' (UNCTAD 2001).

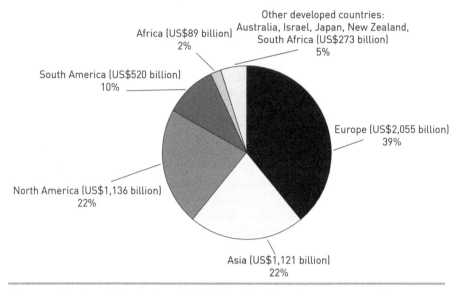

Figure 1.1 Regional distribution of global foreign direct investment stock

Source: UNCTAD 2001

1.2) attracted 80% of FDI flows to developing countries. In contrast, over the same period Africa, including South Africa, attracted less than 5%.

However, the proportion of FDI stock is not the critical factor. More important is the volume of stocks or flows in relation to the size of the host country or region. On this measure, for example, Angola, Equatorial Guinea, Lesotho and Liberia all received more FDI than does Singapore (Velde 2002). For many countries in Sub-Saharan Africa, the extractive industries dominate the flow of FDI. For example, in 1999 nearly two-thirds of US FDI stock was in the petroleum sector, and over 40% of UK FDI stocks were in the mining sector. Across the developing world as a whole, it is the oil, gas and mining industries that generate the majority of tax revenue and export earnings (see Table 1.1).

Despite the significant capital flows implied by this data and the substantial revenues generated for governments, there is growing evidence that mineral-dependent developing countries often experience low economic growth and high poverty rates (Power 2002; Ross 2001a, 2001b). The consequence has been that the potential contribution of the oil, gas and mining industries to economic develop-ment and poverty alleviation has increasingly been challenged. This challenge has been reinforced by the criticisms of the manner in which companies have man-aged issues such as environmental impacts (e.g. on water resources), resettlement, human rights and contributions to conflict.

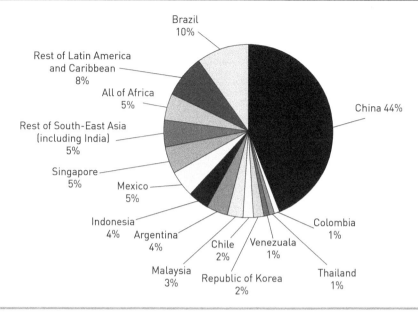

Figure 1.2 Foreign direct investment flows to developing countries in 1999

Source: UNCTAD 2001

1.2 Social issues and the extractive industries: the role of partnerships

While the management of environmental issues is well understood by the oil, gas and mining industries, social issues are a relatively new area of management focus. Because of the multitude of stakeholders involved, social issues are frequently complex and require approaches and solutions that go beyond the traditional technical 'fixes' and contingency planning approaches of the extractive industries. Examples of the social issues that are faced by these industries include:

- Securing a social licence to operate
- Maintaining community relations during periods of investment uncertainty
- Contributing to community development
- Creating local employment and managing retrenchment
- Contributing to long-term regional development
- Preventing and resolving disputes with communities and non-governmental organisations (NGOs)
- Managing the closure of projects

Country	Percentage of merchandise exports		
	Ores and metals	Fuels	Total
Nigeria	0	99	99
Algeria	0	96	96
Libya	0	95	95
Yemen	0	93	93
Saudi Arabia	1	85	86
Venezuela	4	81	85
Kuwait	0	79	79
Oman	1	77	78
Guinea	71	0	71
Azerbaijan	1	69	70
Syrian Arab Republic	1	68	69
Niger	67	0	67
Zambia	66	0	66
Kazakhstan	22	42	64
Mongolia	60	0	60
Norway	7	50	57
Trinidad and Tobago	0	54	54
Russian Federation	11	41	52
Peru	40	5	45
Chile	43	0	43
Colombia	1	40	41
Egypt	4	37	41
Democratic Republic of Congo	40	0	40
Mauritania	40	0	40
Australia	17	19	36
Papua New Guinea	35	0	35
Tajikistan	35	0	35
Ecuador	0	33	33
South Africa	21	10	31
Bolivia	23	6	29
Indonesia	5	23	28
Jordan	27	0	27
Senegal	10	17	27
Togo	27	0	27

Table 1.1 Mineral dependence in the structure of exports

Source: MMSD 2002

Failure to effectively manage social issues can affect the core business interests both of individual operations and of the industry as a whole (Sullivan and Frankental 2002). Conversely, those organisations that successfully manage social issues can both create competitive advantage for themselves and help ensure the longer-term viability of the extractive industries.

The most common approach to managing social issues has been for corporations to adopt a company-led, compliance-focused approach, with an emphasis on meeting legal and contractual requirements (such as the conditions imposed by the state regulators and/or investing institutions). As an alternative, in response to community expectations for tangible benefits (frequently fuelled by the failure of tax revenues and wages to deliver improvements in the lives of the majority of people living in the regions of operations), some corporations (in particular state-owned enterprises and the oil or mining 'majors') have established comprehensive programmes of local community development that exceed the compliance requirements of government regulators and investors and which are focused on those communities worst affected by operations.

These social investment or community development programmes have been implemented through a variety of vehicles: through outsourcing to consultants; through the establishment of company-led local foundations or trust funds; and through in-house community development or corporate social responsibility teams. Such programmes generally mimic the practices of development NGOs.

There is, however, another alternative method of implementation: that is, to share the responsibility with government and civil society. This approach can result in more manageable costs and risks for the company, increased effectiveness of actions in the community and reduced long-term dependence of communities on the company. At its heart lies the exploitation of synergies that comes when non-traditional parties decide to collaborate. Tri-sector partnerships are, in essence, a new form of strategic alliance. The approach can be defined as a voluntary collaboration to promote sustainable development based on the most efficient allocation of complementary resources across corporate business, civil society and government.

Table 1.3 provides a broad assessment of the advantages and disadvantages of the different approaches that can be adopted for managing social issues. Given the increasing expectations of communities for mining, oil and gas companies to provide public goods, some criticism of the quality and sustainability of community programmes and the rising awareness at the boardroom level of the long-term liabilities of creating community dependence, the low rates of return and/or the high transaction costs associated with social investment, corporations are beginning to investigate whether and how they can manage social issues more efficiently. It is within this context that there is now real interest in partnerships.

The approach is innovative because it requires companies to move away from the conventional 'command-and-control' approaches to community development and to enter into voluntary arrangements with non-traditional parties. It also signals a willingness to go beyond public consultation and stakeholder dialogue and allows participants do something practical together.

The partnership approach involves the 'pooling' of resources, competences, capacity and expertise, thereby achieving outcomes that add value to what each

Option	Advantages	Disadvantages
Compensation	Defines who is responsible and limits financial exposure of company	Usually implemented by government authorities, creating the potential for inefficiency and corruption
Paternalism (i.e. the company provides all public services)	Company has control of outcomes	Creates dependence of communities on the company High cost to company Potentially undermines public-sector governance
Employment	Meets community expectations and may reduce the risk of sabotage or theft	Can create inter-community and intra-community jealousies The number of jobs is unlikely to be sufficient to meet demand May reduce opportunities for local people owing to poor skills, unions and 'turn-key contracts' (i.e. subcontractors may source labour from outside the local community)
Company–led voluntary community projects	Company has control Costs limited by targeting the project-affected people	Often fuels community expectations May lead to risk of future liabilities for company Undermines role of government
Company-led local foundations	Company transfers responsibility to foundation Company gets the credit Provides a 'good-news story' for social reporting	Frequently focuses only on 'project-affected' people Transaction costs are high May present the risk of future liabilities (e.g. community dependence). May exclude competent parties May be difficult to access funding from the wider donor community

Table 1.2 **Assessment of the different options for managing social issues**
(continued opposite)

Option	Advantages	Disadvantages
Outsourcing of community projects to non-governmental organisations	Shifts risk and responsibility Allows cost savings Provides potential for an enhanced reputation	Range of company competences are under-utilised Potential clash of cultures Sometimes has a poor fit with government and donor agency strategies
Outsourcing of community projects to consultants	May meet initial compliance requirements (e.g. as specified in development agreements)	Entails higher costs Sustainability of community projects is lowered There is no long-term protection against social risk or 'visible' damage to reputation
Partnership approach to voluntary community projects	Allows risks to be shared Aids resource leverage Allows better management of the social licence to operate during investment uncertainties	Core business is exposed to uncertainties Loss of control

Table 1.2 (continued)

party could achieve by acting alone. The approach builds on the idea that each sector in society has core competences and resources that, if appropriately arranged, are complementary to one another. In the context of managing social issues, these include:

- Government authorities:
  - Provide strategic co-ordination through local development plans
  - Provide new decentralised powers (to regional and local governments)
  - Give access to budgets for providing public services
  - Play a role as a broker or capacity builder

- Oil, gas and mining companies:
  - Provide employment
  - Share knowledge of procurement and supply chain management
  - Build local infrastructure
  - Provide capital equipment, technical skills and logistics management
  - Have a performance-led work ethic
  - Give access to best international practices
  - Have a capacity for advocacy

- Civil-society organisations:
  - Have local knowledge
  - Have the capacity to mobilise community participation, tools and methods to ensure relevance to local need
  - Offer independent monitoring

Bringing these unique yet complementary resources together into a partnership can lead to a range of benefits. These can include new channels of communication between companies and local communities, which increases the opportunities to prevent local disputes and manage social risk and offers a more durable local 'social licence to operate'. Partnerships can also help close the gap between the expectations of regulators and investors and the social performance of operations 'on the ground'.

However, the partnership model of corporate social responsibility is not without risk. For example, the reputations of the partners may be damaged if one or other partner fails to deliver on its commitments. However, these risks can be managed, and value added for all parties, if the proposed partnership is first assessed to determine its relative merits against the alternatives for managing social issues or delivering developmental impact, if the process of building trust and reaching agreement between the partners is properly managed and if partners can be found that have complementary resources and that are willing to the share responsibilities.

1.3 Business Partners for Development

The Natural Resources Cluster (NRC) of Business Partners for Development (BPD) was an applied research programme aimed at enhancing the role of oil, gas and mining corporations in international development. The programme objective was to produce practical guidance, based on the experience of specific natural resource operations around the world, on how three-way partnerships involving companies, government authorities and civil-society organisations can be an effective means of reducing social risks and of promoting community and regional development. The NRC comprised the World Bank Group, the UK Department for International Development, CARE International and private-sector corporations (Anglo American, BP, CESC/RPG, Norsk Hydro, Placer Dome, Rio Tinto, Royal Dutch/Shell and WMC Resources). The three-year programme actively developed practical examples of how business can act in tri-sector partnerships to generate business, public-sector governance and development benefits. The programme studied tri-sector partnerships in Colombia, Nigeria, India, Venezuela, Bolivia, Zambia, Azerbaijan, Indonesia and Tanzania, covering a range of community development projects. BPD provided four essential types of input to these projects, namely:

- A role as a convenor (i.e. acting as a catalyst to mobilise disparate parties to enter into collaborative negotiations)

- Facilitation (to help manage processes of partnership-building, building consensus between non-traditional parties around areas of complementarity and creating innovative tri-partner structures, roles, responsibilities and financing mechanisms)

- Capacity-building (i.e. providing training in the principles and tools of partnership-building and conflict management, building the institutional capacity required to implement agreements and ensure quality in social development activities)

- Learning (i.e. acting as a conduit for knowledge networking and sharing, identifying good practice and developing replicable guidelines, tools and training materials)

1.4 Structure of the book

The overall aim of this book is to communicate the lessons learned and outcomes achieved from the NRC. This encompasses the specific lessons from the partnership projects that were established as well as the more general or cross-cutting lessons on partnerships that have emerged from the projects as a whole. The book is divided as follows.

In this chapter we have provided an overview of the drivers for partnering in the oil, gas and mining industries. In Chapter 2 the analytical framework for looking at partnerships is presented, encompassing issues such as the types of outcome that may be achieved, the potential partners and partnership structures.

Part 1 (Chapters 3–11) consists of the detailed case studies that have been the focus of the NRC. The case studies are summarised in Table 1.3. The material presented in these chapters covers the period 1998–2002 (i.e. the lifetime of the NRC). Unless otherwise indicated, the material presented was current to the end of 2002. Each of the chapters follow a broadly similar structure, starting with an overview of the business and social context within which the company was operating, including an assessment of the drivers for partnership. This is then followed by a description of the process followed to explore, establish and maintain the partnership. The partnership outcomes for business, government and civil society are then assessed, both quantitatively (e.g. financial costs and benefits) and qualitatively (e.g. benefits to reputation). Each chapter also includes an assessment of the specific lessons learned from the case study for tri-sector partnerships more generally.

Part 2 (Chapters 12–14) is a more detailed discussion of the mechanics of partnering, synthesising the lessons learned from across the case studies. Chapter 12 develops the material presented in Chapter 2 to provide more detailed guidance for those considering establishing tri-sector partnerships, including a discussion of the resources and skills required and the key elements of partnership. Chapters 13 and 14 provide specific guidance on monitoring and measuring the performance (or effectiveness) of partnerships.

Chapter	Company	Country	Subject of partnership
3	Shell Petroleum Development Corporation (SPDC)	Nigeria	Improving environmental and social impact assessment
4	Integrated Coal Mining Limited (ICML)	India	Livelihoods assessment, road construction, healthcare
5	Placer Dome/Corporación Venezolana de Guayana	Venezuela	Healthcare
6	Transredes	Bolivia	Management of oil-spill compensation
7	BP and others	Azerbaijan	Conflict prevention
8	Kahama Mining Corporation Limited (KMCL)	Tanzania	Infrastructure provision, water supply, community healthcare, primary education, adult education
9	Konkola Copper Mines Plc (KCM)	Zambia	Local business development, economic diversification
10	Kelian Equatorial Mining (KEM)	Indonesia	Mine closure
11	BP Exploration Company	Colombia	Regional development

Table 1.3 Case studies

Part 3 (Chapters 15–20) can be loosely described as covering issues around partnering. In the course of the three years that BPD operated, a number of common questions were raised about partnerships. These were:

- What are the costs and benefits of partnering?

- Who should own (or claim credit for) the outcomes of partnerships?

- Do partnerships have a role to play in conflict situations?

- Can local foundations use the partnership model to enhance their effectiveness?

- Can partnerships enable community expectations to be managed?

- Has the partnership concept been successfully institutionalised in other industry sectors? Are there lessons that can be drawn for the oil, gas and mining industries?

Chapters 15–20 consider these questions, building both on the experience with the NRC case studies and on the published literature on partnerships.

Finally, the NRC has enabled some conclusions to be drawn regarding some of the key business issues faced by the international oil, gas and mining industries; that is, regarding:

- Maintaining community relations during periods of investment uncertainty
- Contributing to community development
- Securing the social license to operate
- Preventing and resolving disputes with communities and non-governmental organisations
- Creating local employment and managing retrenchment
- Contributing to long-term regional development
- Managing the closure of projects

These conclusions are presented in Chapter 21. Appendices A–E provide some specific tools and documents which complement and expand the material presented in this book. These are: an example of a grievance-resolution process (Appendix A), an example of a partnership memorandum of understanding (Appendix B), an example of a partnership charter (Appendix C), a comprehensive list of indicators for assessing partnership performance (Appendix D) and an example of the application of these indicators to a specific partnership (Appendix E).

Finally, it is pertinent to note that this book is just one of the many publications from the NRC. Over the period 1998 to the present, the NRC published a range of detailed case study reports, working papers, progress reports and other documents. Readers wishing to obtain more information on specific case studies or issues raised in this book are referred to the publications listed in Appendix F and to the wealth of material available on the NRC website: www.bpd-naturalresources.org.

References

MMSD (Mining Minerals and Sustainable Development) (2002) *Breaking New Ground* (London: Earthscan Publications).

Power, T. (2002) Digging to Development? *A Historical Look at Mining and Economic Development* (Washington, DC: Oxfam America).

Ross, M. (2001a) 'Does Oil Hinder Democracy?', *World Politics* 53 (April 2001): 325-61.

Ross, M. (2001b) *Extractive Sectors and the Poor* (Washington, DC: Oxfam America).

Sullivan, R., and P. Frankental (2002) 'Corporate Citizenship and the Mining Industry: Defining and Implementing Human Rights Norms', *Journal of Corporate Citizenship* 7 (Autumn 2002): 79-91.

UNCTAD (United Nations Commission on Trade and Development) (2001) *FDI in Least Developed Countries at a Glance* (Geneva: United Nations).

Velde, D. (2002) *Foreign Direct Investment for Development: Policy Challenges for Sub-Saharan African Countries* (London: Overseas Development Institute).

2
Building blocks for partnerships

Michael Warner

This chapter presents a framework for thinking about partnerships between the business units of major corporations, government authorities and development agencies and civil-society organisations. The framework is designed for use by any party involved in, or affected by, the oil, gas and mining sectors and presents a way in which corporations can play a partnership role in social investment and sustainable development.

The framework promotes a systematic view of the key building blocks of partnerships, including: their characteristics; the outcomes for business, public-sector governance and community development; their role within the operational phases of an oil, gas or mining project and at different levels of society; their integration with conventional project management activities; the range of partners involved; the social investment or community development theme around which the partnership is built; and the detailed structure and management of the partnership. The framework is presented diagrammatically in Figure 2.1.

2.1 Characteristics

The partnerships that engage corporations in social investment can be wide-ranging, covering the spectrum from knowledge-sharing to joint responsibility. The characteristics that are common to partnerships include voluntary engagement, mutually agreed objectives, distinct accountabilities and reciprocal obligations, and 'added value' to what each partner could achieve alone. Partnership

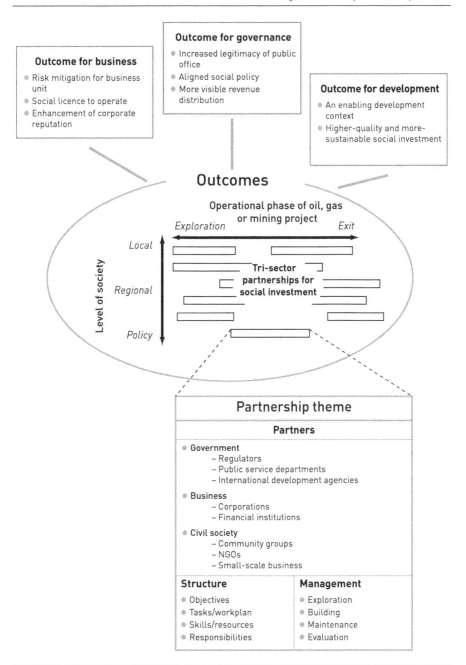

Figure 2.1 The partnership framework

approaches to development are distinctive because they can provide a new model for converting the wealth generated by the private sector in developing countries into sustainable local development while also creating broad consensus on a more efficient distribution of responsibilities, incentives, regulations, costs, risks and benefits between business, government and civil society, building, protecting and re-creating long-term relationships between multiple, non-traditional, parties and delivering a higher level of development impact and business benefit than could be achieved by bi-sector partnerships where business works with either government or civil society. Box 2.1 presents a typology of partnerships involving corporations in social investment

- **Knowledge-sharing:** long-term voluntary agreement between parties to share studies, proposals and evaluations (e.g. due diligence studies, technical feasibility studies, risk assessments, community development strategies, monitoring reports).

- **Dialogue:** medium-term voluntary agreement between parties to consult with each other during the preparation of regional plans and policy, environmental standards, reporting requirements and so on.

- **Informed consent:** voluntary agreement between parties that any one party will not proceed with an action without prior consent by all parties, on the basis that each fully understands the implications of the proposed actions.

- **Contractual:** medium-term voluntary agreement between all parties for one or more party to provide services under contract to another.

- **Shared work-plan:** medium-term voluntary agreement between parties for each to implement an independent set of tasks that, with the tasks of others, build towards a common goal. Accountability and responsibility rests with each party separately.

- **Shared responsibility:** long-term voluntary agreement between parties to share the overall responsibility for implementing tasks and to be jointly accountable to stakeholders.

Box 2.1 A typology of partnerships involving corporations in social investment

2.2 Outcomes

2.2.1 Outcomes for business

For the oil, gas and mining industries, partnerships for social investment are a new type of 'product', offering the potential for the development of a unique set of relationships that, if properly maintained, can increase rates of investment return, create social capital and produce a continuous flow of benefits. The business outcomes from these partnerships can be divided into two: namely, outcomes for the individual operational business unit and outcomes for the global corporation.

For the business unit, the outcomes can include:

- An increased likelihood that communities and households adversely affected by operations will be satisfied that the business unit is responsive to their concerns (thereby granting the unit a 'social licence to operate')

- The reduced dependence of local communities on the business unit (e.g. as a result of the greater empowerment of communities to manage their own development, or the more visible distribution of tax and royalty revenues)

- A basis for resolving local disputes that threaten delays to financial approval or operations

- The availability of new social capital for the business (e.g. in the form of partners willing to sustain social investment activities at times when operations are delayed, subject to temporary 'downsizing' or suspended)

- The unit becoming the 'company of choice' by increasing the appeal of the business to governmental authorising agencies (or by reducing political objections to mine site expansion or exploration and production ventures)

In terms of corporate reputation, the outcomes can include:

- Reduced risks to marketing, sales and share price associated with perceived poor management of social impacts

- Evidence to stakeholders of the effective implementation of company policy on sustainability and corporate citizenship

- Reduced risk of negative public reaction (e.g. on contentious issues such as those relating to indigenous peoples, human rights, resettlement and sustainable development)

- An increased attractiveness of the company to prospective employees

2.2.2 Outcomes for community development

Those oil, gas and mining companies showing leadership in the field of corporate citizenship acknowledge that they are not (and never can become) wholly independent development agencies. Even in remote rural areas, where government services are poor and civil society unorganised, there is a limit to the extent to which a single oil, gas or mining business unit can be the sole development catalyst for the local community.

The problem is not simply that community development is external to a corporation's core competence; it is also that many countries have experienced a 'step-shift' in public awareness concerning the huge wealth-creating potential of oil, gas and mining operations. Coupled with new government policies for citizen participation and economic decentralisation, and with revenue streams visibly bypassing the region of operations, leading corporations are increasingly 'invited' to take on ever more responsibility for social investment.

Until recently the social responsibility of an oil or mining business unit ended with its formal obligation to compensate local populations for the operation's negative social impacts (e.g. loss of land and homesteads and, in remoter rural areas, loss of access to wildlife and forest products). Commonly, this meant cash compensation for lost assets, combined with jobs on the project, vocational training in alternative income activities and (in some cases) the construction of community infrastructure (schools, health clinics, water supply and so on). Today, the demand from many quarters is for companies to be part of a 'smarter' type of social investment, one that reflects the complex relationship between mitigating negative social impact and promoting community development. For example, it may be inappropriate to provide vocational training in marketable vegetables if the only available market for produce is ten hours' walk away, if credit for agro-chemical inputs is unavailable to those without capital assets or if protection from roaming cattle means an end to labour-efficient grazing. In short, if the alternative livelihood on offer cannot be readily adopted into the household economy, and if there is no 'enabling' development context to provide technical, financial and marketing support, the efforts of oil, gas and mining corporations to mitigate social impacts will be less effective than they otherwise might be.

Adopting a 'smarter' social investment strategy that links social impact mitigation to community development seems essential. Such a strategy should address both the household economy (i.e. to ensure that the economy of those impacted by operations is restored in ways that afford an equal or greater level of welfare, income, subsistence and security, that are independent of handouts and long-term maintenance from the oil, gas or mining business unit and that are sustainable beyond the life of the business operation) and the community and regional development context (by providing the technology, finance and markets necessary for new assets and skill-sets to be transformed into sustainable livelihoods and by engaging the winners and the losers of compensation alike). However, the complexity of such strategies means that it is not only unrealistic but also inefficient to expect the community relations teams of individual business units to be the sole development partners of local communities.

2.2.3 Outcomes for public-sector governance

The contribution of an oil, gas or mining corporation to a country's wealth through tax and royalty revenues is frequently disproportionate to the influence that the company has over revenue management. Targeted partnerships are one way to begin to address this anomaly. For example, a closer alignment of social investment objectives and practices, both among oil companies operating in the same region and between these companies, municipal governments and official development agencies such as the World Bank, can begin to provide the political incentive to redirect revenues back to the region of oil, gas or mining operation.

Some strategies for improving revenue management through tri-sector partnerships could include:

- Business units and official international development agencies collaborating with central government to agree revenue distribution mechanisms 'prior' to commencing operations (e.g. dividing revenues between state, municipal government, local trust fund and affected communities and establishing mechanisms for independent auditing)

● Business units promoting dedicated revenue-management programmes of their own (using, for example, a local foundation as the vehicle and concentrating efforts on those management procedures that are least politically sensitive, such as public accounting)

● Business units collaborating with municipal government agencies and civil-society service providers in imaginative public–private partnerships to design, build and operate public facilities (with government providing leadership on public policy and entering into 'lease-back' arrangements using revenue streams, with the private sector and development agencies absorbing the financial risks and with civil society taking responsibility for facilities management)

Partnerships can impact on public-sector governance in other ways. Greater complementarity between the social impact mitigation and community development activities of oil, gas and mining corporations, and the regional development policies and plans of municipal authorities, can improve the responsiveness of government to community needs and increase the perceived legitimacy of public office. The legitimacy of public office is increasingly important at the level of municipal government. With the trend around the developing world moving towards decentralised budgets and local policy formulation, new mechanisms are needed to strengthen the capacity of municipal authorities to deliver improved public services in line with growing local expectations. Partnerships have a facilitating role to play in this area.

2.3 Partnerships at different operational phases and levels of society

Partnerships can come and go throughout the life of an oil, gas or mining operation, can change shape, organisation and function over time and can develop at and between different levels of the project–society interface, from the operational to the policy level (see Fig. 2.2).

The ephemeral nature of some partnerships points to the importance of the need for companies to engage in continuous consultation with stakeholders throughout the life of a project. If relationships with government agencies and civil-society organisations built during the feasibility stage of a project can be maintained over time, subsequent processes of partnership-building can be significantly shortened.

It is unlikely that processes of building and managing tri-sector partnerships will take place in isolation from existing processes of strategic planning or project management. It is more conceivable, for example, that in the future the terms of

Phase of project

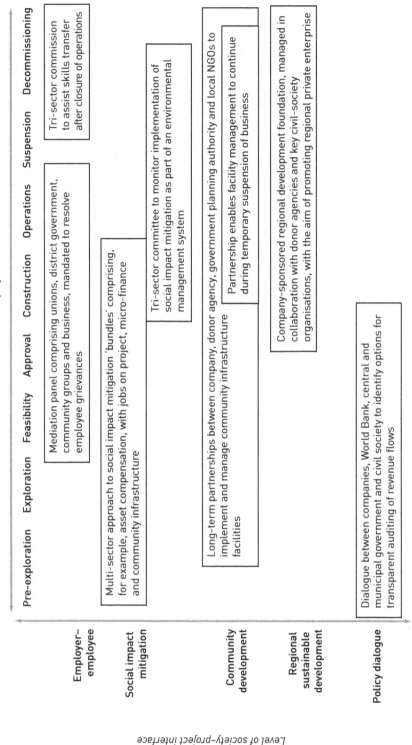

Level of society–project interface

Figure 2.2 Examples of tri-sector partnerships in the oil, gas and mining sectors

reference for project feasibility studies, monitoring reports and closure strategies prepared by business, government agencies or civil-society organisations will include requirements to explore partnerships for social investment.

2.4 The partners

Central and municipal authorities, development assistance agencies and non-governmental organisations (NGOs) all, at one time or another, prepare strategic plans for social investment. These are often targeted at specific geographical areas or social groups and are implemented by a combination of field staff and specialist advisors. For example, municipal authorities are guided by district or regional development plans and are supported by various extension services; central government ministries and multilateral development agencies allocate budgets to strengthen particular development sectors (health, water supply, road infrastructure and so on); bilateral development agencies periodically prepare country strategies encompassing geographically specific multi-sectoral programmes and often action these through NGOs; and many NGOs facilitate community-led strategies and implement these through community-based organisations. Furthermore, many of the above agencies are mandated to work in the same remote rural areas that are of interest to oil, gas and mining companies. In conclusion, either by way of geographic priorities, budget allocations or development expertise, there are numerous actors in society with the necessary incentives to work with the same communities that are currently the focus of social investment by oil, gas and mining corporations.

2.5 Partnership structure and management

As with any type of human organisation, partnerships need to incorporate both structure and management. A key difference between a partnership and other forms of human organisation is that, in a true partnership, the structure and management rules are agreed (and changed) by mutual consent. The key issues in partnership structure are the partners and their legitimate representatives, the geographic boundaries and/or target population, the vision and objectives for the partnership, the activities, tasks and resources to be contributed, the specific responsibilities of the partners and mechanisms for communications, resolving grievances, performance monitoring and risk management. Partnership structures are discussed in greater detail in Part 2, in Chapters 12–14.

The idea of proactively formulating partnerships between companies, government and civil society in developing economies is relatively new. There are cases where such partnerships have fallen together, driven by overriding mutually perceived benefits, but there is little experience of partnerships between business,

government and civil society being intentionally brokered and actively maintained over time. It is this process of 'partnership management' (i.e. exploring the
costs, benefits and risks of forming a partnership, building the trust necessary to
structure the partnership and maintaining the flow of benefits over time) that is
critical to whether a partnership is ultimately successful.

The operational problem for any organisation intent on building such partnerships is that the various parties arrive at the negotiating table with very different
experiences, perceptions, aspirations, objectives, values, relative power and capabilities to negotiate. It is, therefore, unsurprising that a carefully planned and
facilitated process of consensus-building is often pivotal to structuring effective
tri-sector partnerships. The key underpinning principles for managing tri-sector
partnerships are listed in Box 2.2.

- **Partnership exploration:**
    - Find the most practicable strategy
    - Be purpose-driven
    - Build on simple ideas
    - Make available 'room for negotiation'
    - Have realistic expectations
    - Undertake prior consultation
    - Joint process-design

- **Partnership building:**
    - Appreciate that perceptions matter
    - Integrate cultural norms
    - Build trust and confidence
    - Build in the capacity to negotiate
    - Ensure the negotiation is interest-based
    - Encourage joint problem-solving
    - Widen and prioritise options
    - Test for feasibility

- **Partnership maintenance:**
    - Recognise reciprocal obligations
    - Have clear work-plans
    - Maintain internal communications
    - Adapt to internal and external 'events'
    - Measure 'added value'
    - Reflect on and learn from the experience

Box 2.2 Principles for managing partnerships

In the partnership exploration process, the parties identify their social investment and sustainable local development 'needs' and weigh the risks, costs and
benefits of addressing these 'needs' through a tri-sector partnership. The parties
should also assess the wider context in which the partnership would commence

(e.g. prior relationships, underlying motivations and interests of potential partners, external political and economic environment, security risks), including developing a joint understanding of the risks, costs and benefits of the proposed partnership. Based on this process of exploration, the potential partners agree to enter into negotiations.

The partnership-building process requires that be a degree of trust and confidence between the partners and, where necessary, a strengthening of the institutional and human capacity for partners to negotiate 'on a level playing field'. The negotiation process should lead to consensus being reached on the detailed structure of the partnership (vision, objectives, tasks, responsibilities, contractual arrangements, grievance mechanism and so on), and measures should be put in place to maintain and extend the flow of benefits over time.

Partnership maintenance requires that measures be implemented to manage the way in which the partners communicate, make decisions and resolve grievances and the way in which they respond to changes in internal structure (e.g. to changes in personnel) and external environment (e.g. to economic or political events).

Part 1
Case studies

3

Shell Petroleum Development Corporation, Nigeria

Partnering and environmental impact assessment

Rory Sullivan and Michael Warner

This case study examines the efforts of the Shell Petroleum Development Corporation Limited (SPDC) in Nigeria to revitalise its environmental impact assessment (EIA) procedures, with the aim of improving the company's informal social licence to operate and of 'fast-tracking' environmental clearance.

The 'SPDC EIA Improvement Project' is being implemented at a time of significant political and social change in Nigeria. These changes include the ongoing process of transition from a military to civilian government and an influx of funds from multilateral and other donor agencies. Thus, many of the preconditions for successful partnering around community development projects are now in place. However, the legacy of under-development in the Niger Delta, environmental degradation and human rights issues continue to leave a sense of grievance within the affected communities. This has complicated the process of building effective partnerships around the EIA process.

SPDC has used the proposed redevelopment of an oil and gas field in the Utapate Region of the Niger Delta as a pilot project to investigate the possibility of partnering in the EIA process. At the time of writing, the EIA studies have only just commenced and therefore many of the likely outcomes from the partnering approach have yet to be seen. The evidence that is available suggests that EIA offers a potential 'hook' for introducing tri-sector partnering into the upstream operations of oil and gas companies, not least because the EIA process is a statutory requirement, activated automatically for all major new investment projects.

Past grievances, high community expectations of benefits and a lack of experience in this type of public consultation within SPDC seem to be the main obstacles to engaging communities in partnership arrangements around the EIA studies. Workshops held with local non-governmental organisations (NGOs), government agencies (including environmental regulators) and research institutes concluded that these non-community parties were willing to work with SPDC on improving the quality of EIA. What is not clear, however, is whether partnering arrangements at the time of the EIA studies would add value beyond best-practice public and stakeholder consultation. The main purpose of building such partnerships at this early stage of EIA is essentially to develop notions of trust, joint responsibility and shared risk that can then be carried forward. The intention of SPDC to develop partnership arrangements that link the emerging environmental and social management and mitigation plan for the Utapate project to broader community development programmes offers the potential for significant added value to community development.

3.1 Social context

Since Nigeria gained independence in 1960 the allocation of oil revenues has been a source of political debate and conflict in that country. Most of the revenues have either failed to reach the oil-producing areas or have been used to extract political benefits. Widespread corruption has further diluted the development potential of oil revenues. The consequence is that Nigeria is one of the most under-developed countries in the world. Life expectancy at birth is only 51.4 years, the adult literacy rate is just 57% and the proportions of the population without access to safe water, health services and sanitation are 50%, 49% and 43%, respectively. In the 1990s, protests relating to the environmental damage caused by oil production and the failure of local people to realise economic benefits escalated in the Niger Delta. The international concerns about human rights infringements by government authorities in Nigeria have included alleged instances of harassment, unlawful detentions, beatings, torture and killings.

In 1999 the first civilian government for 16 years took power in Nigeria. The new government has committed itself to returning 13% of oil revenues from the Niger Delta back to the region of operations. With the change in government, international non-governmental organisations (NGOs) and multilateral and bilateral development assistance agencies are starting to re-establish themselves in Nigeria. It appears likely that the success of the democratic process in Nigeria will, at least within the Niger Delta, require tangible benefits for affected communities and for populations in the wider region.

3.2 Business context

The Shell Petroleum Development Corporation Limited (SPDC) is the largest oil and gas operating company in Nigeria and is responsible for 40% of Nigeria's total output. SPDC is the operator of a joint venture involving the Nigerian National Petroleum Company, which holds 55%, Shell (30%), Elf (10%) and Agip (5%). The company's operations are concentrated in the Niger Delta and the adjoining shallow offshore area, covering a combined oil-mining lease area of approximately 31,000 square kilometres. The facilities in the area include over 6,000 kilometres of pipelines and flowlines, 87 flow stations, eight gas plants and more than 1,000 producing wells.

The key social issues affecting SPDC are the potential disruption of new and existing oil and gas development projects (as a consequence of community protests, sabotage or theft), competition for access to new oil and gas concessions in the Niger Delta (e.g. SPDC recently lost out on access to a new concession, in part because one of the other tendering companies promised more community development benefits) and the recognition that, despite the large sums invested by SPDC in community development (between US$50million and US$60 million per annum), the task of providing infrastructure, livelihood opportunities and of building local institutions is beyond the capability of the company alone, and that SPDC need to share the costs, risks and, above all, the long-term liabilities for community development with others.

In March 2001, SPDC held its annual two-day stakeholder consultation conference in Port Harcourt, as part of the company's ongoing commitment to consult on its performance on social and environmental issues with communities, civil-society groups, NGOs and governments across SPDC's area of operations. In her address to the conference, SPDC's Corporate Community Development Advisor Dr Deidre Lapin made the following observations:

> A revolution is . . . sweeping the globe. Called the partnership movement, this revolution builds alliances across the traditionally separate sectors of business, government, funding agencies, development organisations, civil society and—of course—communities . . . Last July, the United Nations Development Programme and SPDC jointly held a small roundtable here in Warri to begin defining partnering strategies for sustainable development in the Niger Delta . . . people and organisations must co-operate—as genuine partners—in remaking the physical infrastructure, the basic services, the natural resources and the civic institutions that have grown weak with neglect. Now Nigeria's forefathers fully understood the idea that working in partnership with others is not an option; it is a civic obligation . . . Partnering puts consultation into a new light. It converts consultation into dialogue, it affirms equality between the partners, it identifies shared goals, deepens co-operation, creates a sense of mutual benefit and mutual respect, generates willingness to pool resources and reduces risks. At the end of the process we are all winners.

The concept of multi-sector partnering pervaded many of the discussions during the conference. For example, the 14 syndicate groups at the workshop reflected on the opportunities for using partnership to resolve each of the issues under consideration and, both in SPDC's Managing Director's closing address and in the formal closing remarks of the workshop, the principle of partnership was affirmed. In particular, it was noted that:

> Partnering was discussed throughout the workshop as a powerful means of increasing the overall investment in environment and community development in the [Niger] Delta. By drawing together a

wide range of community, government, donors and business partners, it will be possible to multiply the inputs provided by SPDC.

3.3 Environmental impact assessment in Shell Petroleum Development Corporation

In Nigeria, environmental impact assessment (EIA), encompassing both social impact assessment and health impact assessment, is a statutory requirement for all categories of petroleum exploration and production development projects. SPDC undertakes around 20 EIA studies each year. The EIA process is meant to enable SPDC to design out and/or mitigate potentially significant negative environmental and social impacts, enhance positive impacts and document the results so as to meet government regulatory requirements.

Traditionally, the practice of EIA by SPDC has not been particularly effective as a tool to manage the negative social and health impacts of projects. The physical presence of an oil or gas company in communities raises expectations and concerns over issues such as employment, resettlement, the effect of the project on the local means of livelihood and community development planning. The difficulties in handling these issues effectively often resulted in only partial acceptance of projects by the affected communities. This, in turn, led to local disputes between the company and communities, disruptions to construction or production and increased risk and financial expense for the company.

In response to these problems, SPDC has recently revised its EIA procedures and practices to address some specific limitations such as the late initiation of EIA in the project cycle, the fact that little or no social and health assessment elements have been included in EIA deliverables and the poor follow-up of environmental management plans (EMPs) during project execution. SPDC has an ongoing programme of EIA improvement. The current focus of these activities includes the quality and breadth of baseline studies, the range of public consultation and infor-

There is so much anger and frustration in the Delta and, as a consequence, communities do not respond positively as not all of their basic needs are being met.

Olukayode Soremekun, Shell Petroleum Development Corporation Limited

mation disclosure, the accuracy of impact assessment and the linkage between the resulting EMP and the community development programmes.

3.4 The partnering process

One of the improvements being investigated by SPDC is the potential for building multi-sectoral partnerships around the EIA process. SPDC is using the planned redevelopment of the Utapate–Greater Utapate Field as a pilot project for this. The priority social, health and environmental issues identified for the Utapate project are presented in Box 3.1.

* Community priorities:
    - Continuing adverse health and safety effects of redundant oil facilities in the project area on local communities
    - Procedures and impacts of land acquisition and land use in the project area
* Priorities of the EIA consultants:
    - The effect of the construction, siting and routing of new facilities on surface and groundwater bodies and aquatic resources
    - The effect of the influx of migrant and contract workers on cultural values
* Priorities of the project proponent, Shell Petroleum Development Corporation:
    - The effect of construction, siting and routing of new facilities on water systems and aquatic resources
    - The effect of pressure on the limited capacity of existing community facilities and infrastructure from the influx of migrant and contract workers
* Other priority issues and impacts:
    - The effect of oil spills and other pollution incidents on the quality of drinking water and on fisheries
    - The influx of migrant workers, potentially leading to increases in teenage pregnancy and sexually transmitted diseases in local communities
    - Increased competition from migrant workers for employment
    - The effect of migrant workers on social issues such as alcoholism and prostitution

Box 3.1 Priority social, health and environmental Issues for the Utapate redevelopment environmental impact assessment

The partnership-building process around the EIA for the Utapate project has centred on three key meetings, namely a scoping workshop held in Port Harcourt in September 2001, a meeting of working-group members in Iko Town in October 2001, and a public meeting at Okoroete community in April 2002.

3.4.1 Scoping workshop, Port Harcourt, September 2001

The aims of the September 2001 scoping workshop were to identify who should be consulted in the EIA studies and to identify and prioritise an initial inventory of social, health and environmental impacts from the project development and operations that might be significant to the affected communities. The workshop invitees included the principal chiefs of Iko Town (the main settlement affected by the siting of the flow station and gas plant facilities of the project), representatives of women's groups in Iko Town, federal, state and local government, SPDC (the environment, occupational health, community development and engineering departments) and local NGOs.

The meeting agreed to establish two working groups (on natural resources and on community issues) that would contribute to the EIA process. Outline partnering agreements were negotiated for each group. It was expected that the partnering agreements would be further developed, finalised and ratified by the group members at meetings to be held in Iko Town in early October 2001.

3.4.2 Working-group meeting, Iko Town, October 2001

In October 2001 the provisional members of the Natural Resources Working Group met in Iko Town. The objective of the meeting was to reach consensus on a partnering agreement for stakeholder involvement in the EIA studies of the Utapate project. The meeting was disrupted by some of the 'youth'[1] from the village. A series of concerns were voiced, including, *inter alia*, that the youth of Iko Town had not been formally invited, that the provisional members of the two working groups did not fully represent the communities as a whole, that the past effects of oil production had caused hardship and suffering to the communities and that these impacts had not been taken seriously by SPDC, and that SPDC had failed to complete community projects already started in the community. Such a range of issues are not uncommon in the Niger Delta. They have been provided here to illustrate the extent of outstanding grievance that SPDC (and, indeed, other oil, gas and mining companies) face when seeking to redevelop an area that has previously been affected by mining, or oil or gas production. Some analysis is needed here to unpack these grievances.

First, all over the developing world, tensions between chiefs and elders and the youth and men of communities are increasing. As the young gain economic power, the status of traditional leaders is gradually being undermined or eroded. These changes are exacerbated by the changes in governance structures, in particular the establishment of local or regional government structures as part of the government's decentralisation policies. An example is the Niger Delta Development Corporation, which has been established to manage the return of 13% of the oil revenues generated in the Niger Delta to the Niger Delta. Such structures represent a new locus of power and further cloud the confusion regarding who are the legitimate representatives of communities.

Second, there exists a culture of self-interest in the Niger Delta that, on many occasions, overrides the wider good of the community. The causes are both cultural and economic, the economic causes involving a link between the presence of a cash-rich oil industry and the success achieved by many 'youth' in realising both individual and group benefits from companies through extortion, the threat of

---

1   The term 'youth' encapsulates males from teenagers through to 40. It predominantly refers to young men (i.e. not elders). Many men in this age group are unemployed or under-employed.

violence and actual violence. These tensions, together with the changes in the status of traditional leaders, have distorted the lines of representation which, in the past, were undisputed.

Third, there is the issue of past environmental damage caused by oil development and the continuing threat to people's welfare from redundant facilities. In the 1970s the environmental quality standards applied to oil and gas development in the Niger Delta were much lower than is the case today. Furthermore, the responsibility for cleaning up or compensating for past environmental damage is defined, in part, by state law in relation to the ownership structure of the company that caused the damage. These two issues (i.e. changing environmental standards and the responsibility for clean-up) complicate, at least in a legal sense, the question of liabilities for past environmental damage.

Despite these caveats, it is clear that more could have been done to prepare the youth of Iko Town for this meeting, to secure their buy-in to the idea of working groups to oversee the EIA studies and to encourage the attendance of other relevant community chiefs, leaders of the key youth groups in Iko Town and the chairmen of the relevant local government areas. In response to the demands of the youth, the Secretariat of the Natural Resources Cluster of BPD made proposals to put the partnering agreements back on track. The key elements of the proposal were to:

- Broaden the stakeholder analysis undertaken at the September 2001 scoping workshop, with the aim of ensuring that the 'strategic' set of stakeholders necessary to move the EIA process forward had been identified and engaged with

- Through dialogue with these 'strategic' stakeholders, design an acceptable process of dispute resolution to manage the grievances of the youth and others; the process would need 'buy-in' from SPDC senior management, with agreed 'limits to negotiation'

- Begin the process of resolving the grievances, starting with agreement on the mechanisms through which different types of grievance would be resolved (e.g. legal, SPDC joint-venture partners, Shell as operator, local courts, state-level government, the chief system)

- With the grievance process having begun, review prospects for establishing and running the EIA working groups

The full proposal is presented in Appendix A to this book, as the proposal provides a broad framework for dispute resolution and grievance management and is likely to have more general application outside the specific context for which it was developed.

3.4.3 Public meeting, Okoroete Community, 24 April 2002

In April 2002 a second attempt was made by the SPDC EIA team to engage, *en masse*, with the affected communities. The objectives of the meeting were to explain SPDC's oil and gas development to all communities in the Utapate and Greater Utapate area, to inform a wider audience of the results of the scoping workshop held in Port Harcourt in September 2001 and to consult communities on how the scope of the EIA might be amended. Whereas in the September 2001 scoping workshop the participants had been willing to focus on the environmental and social effects of the proposed project, on this occasion nearly all the comments raised addressed either the anticipated developmental benefits of the project (such as employment and scholarships) or grievances relating to the impact of past development. Examples of the grievances raised at the meeting are presented in Box 3.2.

Chiefs

• What will happen when our rivers are destroyed?'

• What is Shell giving us? We want you to develop us and to give us employment.'

• We now have a big hope. We want our people to work with Shell. But not as labourers but in good jobs.'

• We are not happy to see Shell here. They have destroyed our farmland and our rivers. If Shell is ready to drill, then Shell must be ready to compensate our community. We assure you that the very peaceful relationship that you want cannot go ahead without compensation . . . we don't want the same old study.'

• We are not happy with Shell here. They have destroyed our forests and our fisheries. They should be prepared to provide compensation . . . Leave the oil there.'

Women

• What will Shell do for us? What did Shell put in our water? If Shell live with us, what water will they drink? We are suffering too much. We have cholera because of poor water.'

• When Shell was here before, people did not get work and so the community did not benefit. If Shell pays money to the Federal government and then expects them to do development, then Shell should stop paying the Federal government and should do development themselves.'

Youth

• We know the problems that Shell can bring. We have seen the experience of the Ogoni people. The youth want to work with Shell and we hope that Shell wants to work with us . . . Shell uses contractors and must now tell contractors the youths' conditions . . . local youth must be employed, even if they are unskilled . . . they must be trained.'

• Shell must choose the correct people to negotiate with and who represent the community. Shell must maintain good relationships with the community and must not allow the political leaders to decide on employment or compensation.'

Box 3.2 **Community grievances and issues raised at the public meeting at Okoroete, 24 April 2002: statements by chiefs, women and youths**

3.4.4 Integrating partnering into environmental impact assessment studies

From the experience with the Utapate redevelopment EIA process, conclusions were reached on where partnering concepts could used to improve the EIA process. Figure 3.1 provides an overlay of these options on the EIA process. The options are around seven areas, as follows:

- Partnering prior to contracting consultants

- Partnering to manage baseline data

- Partnering during scoping

- Partnering to manage impact assessment

- Partnering to link the EIA and the EMP to community development

- Partnering in the SPDC review of the draft EIA report

- Partnering during implementation and monitoring of the EMP

3.4.4.1 Partnering prior to contracting consultants

This approach is not really a partnering process per se but a multi-stakeholder dialogue to agree the criteria for 'certifying' EIA consultants (i.e. as the basis of a list from which 'call-off' contracts will be granted by SPDC) and to agree the rules by which competitive bids will be judged by SPDC. The aim of this process would be to improve transparency and accountability in the contracting process.

3.4.4.2 Partnering to manage baseline data

This would involve partnering between different organisations with complementary competences in data-gathering, data analysis and data management, with the aim of improving the accuracy, reliability and credibility of environmental and social baseline data across the Delta Region in terms of its relevance to EIA studies.

3.4.4.3 Partnering during scoping

This would be a short-term partnership between the internal SPDC EIA team, consultants, representatives of affected communities, and other relevant parties from government and civil society. The partnership would be convened to more accurately target the inventory of impacts in the EIA, to agree those impacts that are most likely to be significant and to agree the methods and standards to be used. The partnership could also be tasked with designing the subsequent programme of public consultation, as well as identifying opportunities to partner in the management of different impact assessment topics (see also Section 3.4.4.4).

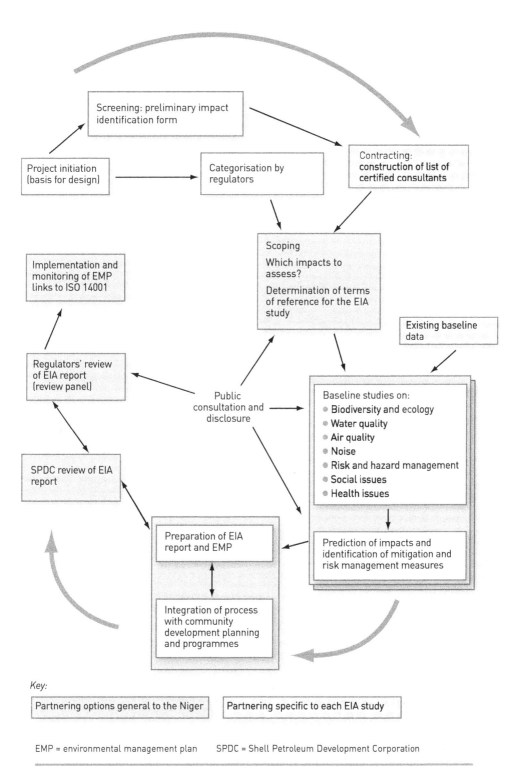

Key:

Partnering options general to the Niger | Partnering specific to each EIA study

EMP = environmental management plan   SPDC = Shell Petroleum Development Corporation

Figure 3.1 Partnering options in the environmental impact assessment (EIA) process

3.4.4.4 Partnering to manage impact assessment

Topic-specific working groups drawn from affected communities, civil society and government authorities could join the SPDC EIA team and their consultants to provide greater credibility to the prediction and mitigation aspects of EIA, in particular in relation to biodiversity and ecology, natural resource, socioeconomic and community impacts. The approach is likely to work best where different stakeholders contribute different core competences to the EIA studies. For example:

> *In the past we just relied on consultants to complete EIA studies. However, we are now looking at broadening the number of departments [within SPDC] that are involved. We are also identifying the key people in the community . . . for example, traditional doctors may be a valuable source of information on community problems.*
>
> **Chinyere Nkele, Shell Petroleum Development Corporation Limited**

- Consultants contribute 'best-practice' methods, quality standards and experience of successful mitigation from similar projects.

- Communities contribute local knowledge about sensitive environs and whether mitigation measures will be sustainable.

- Government departments contribute their existing survey data.

- Universities contribute predictive models and students to undertake surveys.

- SPDC supervises and co-ordinates the assessment, with SPDC specialists validating the working group's findings.

3.4.4.5 Partnering to link environmental impact assessment and the environmental management plan to community development

Although it has been acknowledged that the EIA process should not substitute for community development planning, it has also been recognised that the EIA process, particularly the identification of mitigation measures and the preparation of the EMP, might trigger community development planning (where none is already taking place) or be integrated with aspects of existing community development programmes. SPDC already partners with many types of civil society, government and donor organisations on various community development programmes. Partnering at the time of EMP preparation would, at a minimum, bring together two sets of resources: those of SPDC allocated for mitigating potentially adverse social and health impacts from oil and gas development, and those from the SPDC community development budget. This in turn would provide an incentive for international development agencies, NGOs and government authorities at federal, state and local levels to contribute their resources. As an example, this could see the transformation of a programme aimed at construction workers regarding awareness of sexually transmitted diseases (STDs) into an area-wide programme of STD awareness and prevention.

3.4.4.6 Partnering in the Shell Petroleum Development Corporation review of the draft environmental impact assessment report

There is a need for SPDC to validate the findings of each EIA study, prior to submitting the EIA report and EMP to the Ministry of Environment and the Department of Primary Resources. A formal dialogue process with external parties from communities, civil society and relevant local government authorities might improve the final quality of the EIA report and reduce the likelihood that the report will be rejected by the regulators.

3.4.4.7 Partnering during implementation and monitoring of the environmental management plan

Stakeholders at both the September 2000 workshop and the SPDC Annual Stakeholder Consultation Workshop in March 2001 raised the issue that SPDC has a poor record in ensuring that mitigation measures agreed in the EIA report are effectively implemented or that the intended effect of these measures on avoiding or reducing the risk of negative environmental and social impacts are realised in practice. Establishing a partnership to periodically monitor and verify EMP implementation—for example, involving the project line or asset manager, SPDC environment, social and health staff, representatives from the affected communities and external interested parties from civil society and local government—is one way to improve performance and address this concern.

3.4.4.8 Success factors

From the experience with the Utapate project, a number of success factors for integrating partnering at the stage of the EIA studies were identified (see Box 3.3).

- Partners must be selected on the basis of the unique and complementary resources they can bring.
- Partners must be prepared to jointly manage the environmental impact assessment studies on an ongoing basis (otherwise there will be little difference between partnering and public/stakeholder consultation).
- Since partners are being asked to contribute resources to help mitigate the adverse effects of one party, the company may have to fund the inputs of each party.
- Prior one-to-one discussions with potential partners are essential to establish trust, explore the potential roles each will play and to agree the process by which the partners will negotiate the partnership.
- The negotiated partnering agreement should be built around the design and management of a public consultation and disclosure plan.

Box 3.3 **Success factors for integrating partnering into environmental impact assessment studies**

3.4.5 Linking the environmental management plan to community development through partnering

As a consequence of the difficulties in establishing partnerships around the EIA studies, SPDC decided to wait until the stage of EMP preparation before trying again to develop formal partnership arrangements with the affected communities. At this later stage of the EIA process there are likely to be greater synergies from integrating social and environmental impact mitigation measures into wider community development (be that implemented by SPDC, NGOs, governments or international donors) as well as building these new arrangements into the memorandum of understanding that SPDC signs with each affected community to clarify expected benefits.

SPDC already has multi-sector partnering experience associated with its community development programmes, such as in healthcare, infrastructure and local business development. An example is provided by SPDC's involvement in the establishment of a Fisheries and Skills Development Centre in Iko Town. The project encompasses fish processing (smoking, and freezing and storage), the provision of credit and skills training in areas such as cassava processing, boat and engine repair, and reading and writing. A village electricity network installed by the youth powers the centre. The project has involved a range of partners providing resources to ensure the effectiveness of the project. The project partners (and their contributions) included SPDC (which provided financial support), Voluntary Service Overseas (VSO; which provided two volunteers to assist in community capacity-building), the youth (who installed and maintain the village electricity network), local teachers (who gave basic literacy training and encouraged local schoolchildren to establish and maintain school fish ponds), the local university (which provided support for training and skills) and various NGOs (which offered project management skills and participatory rural analysis studies to identify community capacities and needs).

3.5 Outcomes

3.5.1 Overview

Box 3.4 summarises the 'added value' of the partnership in SPDC's process from three perspectives: business benefits, community development impact and good governance. The benefits for which there is already evidence from the Utapate redevelopment project are marked with stars. The remainder (marked with triangles) are 'anticipated' benefits. Some of the specific outcomes are considered in greater detail below.

Business benefits

- Cost-effectiveness of the environmental impact assessment (EIA):
  - ▲ Potential leverage of resources to secure synergies between implementation of the environmental management plan (EMP) and community development: the Department for International Development, UK (DFID), the European Union and the US Agency for International Development (USAID) all have resources dedicated to the Niger Delta; furthermore, the Niger Delta Development Corporation has been established as the strategic body for returning the 13% of oil revenues to the Delta region
  - ▲ Possible funding from international donor agencies to add development value to the infrastructure required for oil and gas projects; for example, donors might be willing to meet part of the costs of electricity generation in return for the company rolling this out to local communities

- Community development and social investment:
  - ▲ Encouragement of the alignment of community development activities built on the back of EMP preparation with state-level and local-level government policies and development plans
  - ▲ Expansion of the existing use of memoranda of understanding (MOUs) of Shell Petroleum Development Corporation Limited (SPDC) with affected communities to help to attract partners and reduce the likelihood of additional demands from communities at later stages in the project

- Reputation:
  - ★ Demonstration of SPDC's commitment to community development and democracy, through its efforts to partner in the EIA process with international NGOs and donor agencies
  - ▲ Demonstration of enhanced community development benefits when bidding for access to new concessions

- Social licence to operate:
  - ▲ Reduced likelihood of sabotage, ransoms and theft arising from greater interdependence between communities and the oil project (e.g. for electricity)

Community development impact

- Improved quality of EIAs and EMPs:
  - ★ More accurate prediction of significant environmental, health and social impacts, and greater sustainability of impact mitigation measures
  - ▲ Reassurance for communities that EMP monitoring is being managed not only by SPDC but also by independent third parties

Note:
▲ Anticipated benefit
★ Benefits for which there is already evidence

Box 3.4 **Added value of partnership process** (continued over)

- Violence in the communities:
  - ▲ Reduced inter-community and intra-community tensions (as a result of bene-
    fits being spread more equitably)

- Community capacity:
  - ★ Use of the EIA process as the starting point for communities to define their
    development needs
  - ★ An improved ability of communities to negotiate with SPDC, government, donor
    agencies and others on community development issues

Public-sector governance

- Visibility of public offices:
  - ▲ Enabling of government to meet the goals specified in local, state and federal
    development plans through harnessing private-sector and other agency
    resources
  - ▲ Provision of a framework of accountability for government by enabling com-
    munities and other stakeholders to track government expenditure

- Political stability:
  - ▲ Enabling of elected officials to demonstrate that election promises on develop-
    ment issues are achieved and, more generally, to demonstrate the benefits of
    democratically elected government over other forms of government

- Government capacity:
  - ▲ Improvement of government capacity to manage community development
    projects (through shared monitoring and learning processes in negotiating and
    implementing MOUs)

- Cost-effectiveness of government expenditures:
  - ▲ Provision (through EIA) of an entry point for resources from companies, donor
    agencies, community and government to be used for community development,
    thereby offering potential cost savings for government

Box 3.4 (continued)

3.5.2 Cost-effectiveness of the environmental impact assessment

The cost to SPDC of the EIA process can be considered in two main areas: namely,
the cost of the EIA study (i.e. up to the preparation of the EIA and EMP) and the cost
of implementing the EMP. EIA studies are a relatively low financial resource activity
(relative to, for example, the costs of construction and operation). It is likely that a
partnership approach to the EIA process would marginally increase the costs to

SPDC, as some additional resources would be required to negotiate and manage the partnership process. These incremental costs may be seen as necessary to ensure that there is a better-quality EIA and EMP and, more relevantly, to facilitate the process of obtaining environmental permits and clearances. There may be some cost savings (e.g. through harnessing pre-existing research capacities), but these are likely to be minor.

It is EMP implementation that offers the greatest potential for the leverage of resources into community development. There is significant donor agency and NGO interest in Nigeria, and a number of international bodies have already committed significant funds to development activities. For example, the UK Department for International Development (DFID) has committed approximately US$40 million, and the European Union has offered US$80 million over a four-year period. The US Agency for International Development (USAID) is proposing an investment of a similar order of magnitude. The proposed return of 13% of oil revenues to the Delta region is likely to add somewhere between US$100 million and US$200 million to the funds available for development in the region. From SPDC's perspective, these additional funding sources offer the potential to (a) release funds from SPDC for other projects or initiatives, (b) enable community development projects to have a greater reach (e.g. the incremental costs of rolling out a specific project or initiative to other communities may be much less than the initial set-up costs) and (c) provide economies of scale. SPDC has already met with a number of the donor agencies and NGOs to discuss their activities and to identify potential areas of common interest where resources and capacity may be shared.

3.5.3 Community development and social investment

Involving other partners offers the potential for SPDC to reduce its exposure to long-term liabilities or community dependence. The first way in which this can be achieved is through explicitly defining the responsibilities of SPDC and of other parties for the implementation and maintenance of community development activities. The second is through ensuring that training and capacity-building are an integral part of all community development activities.

The issue of longer-term community dependence is complex. Despite the criticisms of SPDC, it also appears that communities are reluctant for SPDC to withdraw from the provision of community development benefits. Apart from the financial value of SPDC's contributions (and the community expectation that SPDC will provide development benefits), it appears that there is a strong distrust of government and the willingness or ability of government to fill the development role that has been occupied by SPDC. For example, one of the comments made at the public meeting at Okoroete (see also Box 3.2) was 'If Shell pays money to the Federal government and then expects them to do development, then Shell should stop paying the Federal government and should do development themselves.'

> •Shell is seen as the government on the ground. However, Shell needs to identify the things that the government should be providing.•
>
> **Chinyere Nkele, Shell Petroleum Development Corporation Limited**

3.5.4 Reputation

Corporate reputation, at the global and national levels, represents a critical issue for SPDC. At the global level, Shell International has been heavily criticised for its role in the Niger Delta. Even though SPDC has invested significant time and resources in improving its social and environmental performance in the Niger Delta, these criticisms are likely to remain for some time. However, the transition from a military to a civilian government and the efforts by the civilian government to address issues such as corruption and the lack of development mean that the international debate around SPDC's role in Nigeria will, over time, move from issues such as Shell's role in supporting the military regime to an assessment of the contribution of Shell to development and to the quality of life of those living in the Niger Delta. This change presents significant opportunities for Shell, through enabling Shell to demonstrate positive contributions (to environmental quality and to development) rather than trying to justify actual or perceived negative impacts. Partnerships around community development offer donor agencies and international NGOs the opportunity to provide an independent assessment of SPDC's community development activities while also enabling Shell to build trust (with NGOs, communities, donor agencies and government), share responsibilities for development, communicate performance, provide an independent assessment of SPDC's contribution to development and create accountabilities for development (not only for SPDC but also for government).

The other element of reputation relates to SPDC's ability to access new oil and gas concessions in the Niger Delta. It appears that SPDC recently lost out on access to a new concession as one of the other tendering companies offered significantly more community development benefits (in particular, a new road) than did SPDC. Anecdotally, SPDC has recognised that it has not systematically maximised the benefits (either in terms of development outcomes or SPDC's reputation) from community development activities. Partnering should enable SPDC (a) to maximise the leverage of resources into its community development activities, (b) to develop and improve its relationships with government, donor agencies and communities and (c) to demonstrate its commitment and 'added value' to community development.

* In the past, when there were problems in the field and facilities were shut down, it could take two weeks for production to restart. Now, we find that problems can be resolved and facilities restarted within two days. In the future, we expect that, where there is a problem or issue, the community will come and talk to us before forcing our facilities to shut down.'

Olukayode Soremekun, Shell Petroleum Development Corporation Limited

3.5.5 Social licence to operate

Sabotage (and the attendant issues of the disruption of production and extortion) are major problems for SPDC. The potential contributions of a partnering approach to EMP implementation are to provide a mechanism for SPDC, government and communities to work together, to enable a shared understanding of development needs and solutions to be developed and to allow trust to be built. Despite the ongoing tensions in the Niger Delta, there is evidence that SPDC's community development activities are starting to provide tangible business benefits in terms of reductions in sabotage and disrupted production.

3.5.6 Violence in the communities

The lack of development of the Niger Delta has created a sense of grievance and anger in the community. The source of many of the tensions has been the manner in which the benefits of development have been distributed. Anecdotally, the benefits of development have not been distributed throughout the community but have been concentrated in the hands of a few. The causes are multiple but include corruption, the limited return of revenue to the Niger Delta from national government and the lack of transparent and accountable public bodies. The strong police presence (to keep the peace and to provide protection for SPDC's assets and infrastructure) in the Delta is symptomatic of the tensions in the region. Partnerships offer the potential to provide a framework for dialogue between SPDC and local communities and to help ensure that the benefits of oil and gas developments accrue to the community as a whole. These partnerships, in turn, may help create community ownership of development projects, build capacity, develop a sense of shared responsibility and ensure (or, at least, increase the likelihood of) an equitable distribution of the benefits of development as well as the more general benefits of partnership such as the leverage of resources.

A related issue is that of intra-community violence. Many of the tensions in the Niger Delta have been fuelled by the differences in wealth between different communities. At the moment, most of the benefits of development accrue to those communities where oil reserves or oil infrastructure (e.g. flow stations) are located, with limited development benefit outside these areas. This has led to competition between communities to have oil and gas infrastructure located in their communities. Partnership approaches to development can help to ensure that community development activities are aligned with regional development plans. This should help to ensure that the benefits of oil development are spread more equitably through the community (both within and outside the communities or areas with oil reserves). Partnership approaches also offer the potential for extending the scope of a specific project or of distributing the benefits more widely than would otherwise have been the case.

3.6 Conclusions

In the specific case of the Utapate redevelopment project, it appears that (as a consequence of the history of development in the Niger Delta and the level of grievances of affected communities) it may not be feasible to include community representatives in a partnering agreement built around improving the quality of the EIA studies. This is not a general recommendation to exclude communities from such studies. Rather, the specific context of the Delta means that effective processes for consultation and grievance resolution are necessary prerequisites before partnerships with communities around the EIA studies should be attempted. More feasible at this point in time are multi-sector partnerships (excluding communities), designed to pool information and resources to gathering baseline data and improve the accuracy of impact prediction. Although the incremental benefits of this type of partnership are likely to provide only marginal improvements over best-practice stakeholder consultation, one should not forget that the rationale for moving to a negotiated partnering approach to the EIA studies, especially in the Niger Delta, is as much to do with rebuilding trust and social capital as it is about the quality of the EIA studies themselves. Most importantly, EIA is a statutory requirement for new developments and therefore presents an opportunity for community development to be integrated into project design and project implementation.

It is perhaps at the later stage of EMP implementation that synergies are most likely to accrue from a partnership approach, for two reasons. First, there is renewed international donor agency and NGO interest in Nigeria and significant new funding has been committed to development activities. Second, outside of the EIA process, SPDC has multi-sector partnering experience associated with its community development programme, such as in healthcare, infrastructure and local business development.

4

Integrated Coal Mining Limited, India
Livelihoods assessment, road construction and healthcare

Rory Sullivan, Santiago Porto and Michael Warner,
with Amit Mukherjee, Rajat Das and Joydev Mazumdar

This chapter describes the partnership approach that underpinned a livelihoods assessment and a series of trust-building measures at the Sarshatali Coal Mining project, West Bengal, India, of Integrated Coal Mining Limited (ICML). The experience with the partnership approach subsequently led the company to form a partnership (in conjunction with the district government and the local community) to construct a 10.5 km link road from the mine to the nearest railway station. The district government authorities have provided 25% of the capital cost of the project, with ICML providing 75%. The collaborative process reduced the time required for land acquisition and the payment of compensation from over two years to around four months. The road is likely to significantly enhance the access of local communities to markets, the local hospital and school. In addition to the road link, a series of other partnership projects are now being initiated. These include projects relating to income restoration, community healthcare and afforestation of the mine site. It is clear that ICML, local non-governmental organisations and the district authorities are beginning to internalise the concept of tri-sector partnerships, having now developed the necessary skills to explore and negotiate complex partnership arrangements in a variety of settings, without external assistance.

4.1 Overview

Integrated Coal Mining Limited (ICML) has been established by CESC Limited to set up and operate a planned coal mine located near the village of Sarshatali in West Bengal. The Sarshatali Coal Mining project will be the first privately owned and operated coal mine in India. If successful, it is expected to create opportunities for CESC Limited to develop other coal resources and expand operations.

The experience with partnerships at the mine can be considered in two distinct stages. The first (described in Section 4.2) relates to the requirements of ICML's investors (in particular, the International Finance Corporation [IFC]) that ICML effectively manage resettlement (approximately 215 households would be affected by the mine development), the mitigation of social and environmental impacts and the distribution of benefits to local communities associated with the mine. This led to a partnership being established to complete a livelihoods assessment to prioritise social development needs in the mine impact area and to identify and implement trust-building measures during the period of uncertainty over the future of the mine project. Section 4.3 describes the manner in which the changes in the business context affected the implementation of the livelihoods assessment. The second stage (described in Sections 4.4–4.6) relates to the subsequent partnership projects that have emerged as a consequence of the experience with the livelihoods assessment and trust-building measures (LATM) partnership.

4.1.1 Social context

Eight communities lie within the mine impact area, comprising a total population of 10,600 people, 25% of whom are scheduled caste. Livelihoods are dominated by rain-fed agriculture, wage labour and illegal coal trading. Land holdings average one hectare, and half the population are landless. An average of 65% of cash income is spent on food, and there is evidence of seasonal malnutrition. Between 50% and 65% of households fall below the poverty line. The infrastructure in the area is poor, with no hard-surfaced access to markets, no electricity, and low and infrequent healthcare. One settlement, Diguli (which contains 57 households), is to be resettled as a result of the proposed mine.

4.1.2 Business context, 1998–2000

ICML contracted international environmental consultants to prepare a social and environmental impact assessment (released in 1998). The assessment included interim management plans for resettlement and rehabilitation, indigenous peoples and community development. At this time, ICML was faced with delays in the signing of financing agreements for the mine. These delays raised ICML's interest in an approach to managing social issues that shared the burden of meeting social obligations and helped to manage rising expectations within the affected communities. The delays in financial closure also meant that the timing of ICML's commitment to release funds for income restoration and community development was slipping. Such delays are not uncommon in the mining industry. However, early land acquisition combined with implementation of requirements by regulators and investors for public consultation and the early design of environmental and social management plans tend to raise community expectations. Two business objectives therefore underpinned the decision of ICML to explore the tri-sector partnership model, namely: (a) to close the gap between community expectations and company social performance (which was exacerbated by delays in securing finance) to the point where the company's 'social licence to operate' was secure enough to begin the development of the operation's physical infrastructure; and (b) to share the cost burden of beginning to implement the company's proposed income restoration and community development programmes during a period of uncertainty over the timing of financial closure. By April 1999, ICML's socio-economic baseline data (the basis for its various social management plans) was becoming outdated. The IFC had noted this and was encouraging the company to update its information. Given the financial uncertainties around the project, the cost of commissioning this update was an issue for the company.

At the time that a partnership approach to managing social issues was first discussed, the idea that updating the baseline socioeconomic data might itself be a vehicle for a partnership model was not considered. What was focusing the minds of the company was the urgent need to implement some type of programme of trust-building measures to manage community expectations in the mine impact area. The problem was identifying exactly what to do. The measures ICML chose to implement had to be low-cost and yet credible to the affected communities (i.e. something of genuine relevance to reducing poverty and developing livelihoods). Thus there were two other specific objectives driving ICML. These were the need to update the socioeconomic baseline data in the mine impact area as part of complying with investors' requirements, and the need to rapidly identify and implement low-cost trust-building projects that were relevant to achieving poverty reduction.

4.2 The livelihoods assessment and trust-building measures partnership

Over a four-month period in 1999 a partnership arrangement was brokered between ICML and CESC Limited, ASHA (the Association for Social and Health Advancement), a community development non-governmental organisation [NGO] based in Calcutta), Suchetana (a local NGO), the Office of the District Administrator, and community leaders (village- and 'block'-level Panchayat). The objectives of the partnership were (a) to complete a livelihoods assessment to prioritise social development needs in the mine impact area and to meet the requirements of investors for updated baseline socioeconomic information and (b) to identify and implement trust-building measures (including pilot income-restoration projects for those most affected by the acquisition of land, and outline designs for development projects that would bring community-wide benefits) during the period of uncertainty over the future of the mine project.

The key elements of the partnership development process were:

- Early exploratory workshops to develop mutual understanding and reveal potential complementarities in the social programmes and resources of the different organisations

- Independent third-party facilitation to manage early mistrust

- Selection of the NGO partners, based on a systematic process of consultation, with appraisal against transparent suitability criteria

- Negotiation of a memorandum of understanding (MOU) between the partners by using the techniques of 'interest-based negotiation' and 'joint problem-solving'

The consultation process was based on an equitable and joint exploration of the mutual benefits and risks of working in partnership. Through these open discussions, a degree of trust was built between the company and the consultees, and each party was able to judge whether it was in its interests to look for ways to work together. This open approach has since paid dividends. For example, even though CARE West Bengal declined to engage in collaboration with ICML in the mine impact area, the consultation process resulted in better communications between the two organisations. CARE appreciated that ICML was both serious about working with the NGO sector and, by opting for a partnership model, was not seeking to devolve itself of its social responsibilities. Since then, CARE West Bengal has taken a less critical stance towards the company. Furthermore, the manner of the initial consultation left the two NGOs still involved (ASHA and Suchetana) with the impression that subsequent negotiations with the company over roles and responsibilities within a partnership would be equitable and fair.

In contrast, a different aspect of the consultation process created future problems between the partners. This was the criterion that all partners should have the capacity (or be able to develop the capacity) to implement their likely roles. Whether, in hindsight, this aspect of the partnering selection process could have been handled differently is not certain. What is clear is that the criterion was critical to the eventual effectiveness of the partnership. As the partners began to implement their assigned roles, it became clear that one of the NGOs, Suchetana, had an insufficient number of staff experienced in the techniques of participatory data-gathering. Although this had been identified as a potential problem during the NGO selection process, and a programme of capacity-building designed and implemented at the outset of the partnership, the result remained insufficient to meet the needs of ICML. The problem was eventually overcome through ASHA (the other NGO in the partnership), together with ICML, taking on more responsibility. Understandably, residual tensions, particularly between the two NGOs, remained.

Two of the organisations involved in the partnership exploration process and development of the MOU declined to become signatories. The Additional District Magistrate (ADM)'s office did not become a signatory, raising concerns that the MOU might be interpreted as having legal standing and as such ADM was not empowered to sign. However, the office stated its support in principle for the MOU and agreed to be an active member of the partnership. This was subsequently demonstrated by the level of participation of the ADM office in a wide range of activities across the mine impact area. The IFC also declined to sign the MOU, preferring instead to stay out of the partnership altogether. The precise reason for this is unclear, but was thought to be linked to two factors: a lack of local IFC staff able to participate in activities, and a perceived potential conflict of interest between the role of the IFC as a partner in social investment and its role as enforcer of social conditionality in the ICML financing deal. The absence of the IFC from the partnership meant that it was not involved in the subsequent discussions over the direction of the LATM activities.

The two NGOs soon became involved in income restoration (in the formulation of self-help groups) and in planning for resettlement (by way of assisting negotiations over relocation). This led to problems with IFC where officers, not being privy to these discussions and the development logic that underpinned them, were concerned primarily with whether these activities might alter commitments made by ICML to the IFC with regard to the agreed project Resettlement and Rehabilitation Plan. This was illustrated by the development of self-help groups by ASHA in the three villages that were most affected by land acquisition. This necessitated a delay to the agreed schedule for the implementation of training for income restoration. From the IFC perspective, this was in danger of contravening scheduling commitments made by ICML to the IFC. However, recent experience in India points to the importance of the cohesion and leadership that develop in the process of forming self-help groups in providing for greater durability and adaptability of income-earning activities.

4.2.1 Partnership activities

The major activities that were completed as part of the LATM partnership were:

- A livelihoods assessment survey
- Income and livelihood restoration
- Trust-building measures
- Community development planning
- Resettlement planning

Building on the socioeconomic data gathered for the 1998 environmental impact assessment (EIA) study, livelihood baseline surveys were conducted in all eight villages lying within 5 km of the mine concession (approximately 1,400 households, encompassing 10,600 individuals). The survey process included field-based workshops to upgrade the skills of the NGOs in how to engage with communities, combined with training in techniques for data collection and community participation.

Regarding income and livelihood restoration, effort was concentrated in the three villages most affected by land acquisition (including the community of Diguli, which was to be resettled). The process was initiated with a meeting of all Panchayat leaders in the mine impact area and included representatives from the ADM office. The aim of the meeting was to ameliorate concerns over the threat of the proposed self-help groups to the formal community institutions. A subsequent six-month process of building self-help groups was co-ordinated by ASHA and ICML. Concurrent with team-building, communications and leadership training, participants' aptitudes were matched with the available markets. A range of economically viable livelihood options were concluded. These fell into two broad categories: on-farm intensification, to utilise the remaining land more efficiently (e.g. through the growing of new crops, and through improved animal husbandry) and off-farm alternatives (e.g. crafts and trading).

With respect to trust-building measures, through dialogue between the partners, measures were implemented to maintain and develop trust in the mine impact area during the period of uncertainty over the future of the mine project. The measures included a significant scaling-up of the rural 'health camps' (involving the examination of patients, medicine prescriptions, referral to health institutions for follow-up, data collection on illnesses and health behaviour) periodically organised by the local Health and Welfare Department, the provision of emergency drinking-water supplies (for areas affected by persistent drought), agricultural training and the repair of tube wells.

Regarding community development planning, the LATM partnership engaged in the identification and planning of community projects for longer-term and wider-benefit, including supporting the establishment of a training centre and the rehabilitation of local schools.

Finally, ASHA played an active role in assisting the company in developing an appropriate resettlement plan. The plan includes details on the design of new homesteads—in particular, sanitation facilities—as well as measures to prevent the Diguli community from splitting up following the resettlement process. ASHA also played a key role in facilitating dialogue between the affected villagers and the company.

An overview of the roles and responsibilities of the different parties to the partnership is presented in Table 4.1.

4.2.2 Partnership impacts

For all parties, the pooling of competences proved significant benefits for each of the partnership participants. Box 4.1 summarises the added value of the partnership from three perspectives: business benefits, community development and public-sector governance.

4.2.3 Key success factors in the livelihoods assessment and trust-building measures partnership

The key factors in the success of the LATM partnership arrangements in the Sarshatali coal-mining project were: a negotiated common vision and set of objectives for the partnership captured in a written MOU, each party proactively working to satisfy the needs of the others (e.g. ASHA's willingness to work on resettlement planning, which was a topic that lay outside the original terms of the MOU), and high levels of personal interaction and joint problem-solving.

Organisation	Compliance		Additional social investment	
	Socioeconomic surveys	Income restoration	Road infrastructure	Health services
Company: ICML	All costs Performance monitoring	All costs Co-ordination Performance monitoring	Cost sharing Construction equipment	Cost sharing Co-sponsoring
NGOs: ASHA and Suchetana	Implementation	Formation of 'self-help' groups Market research	Mobilisation of community participation	Co-ordination Implementation
Government: local government departments	Secure 'buy-in' from formal community institutions	Vocational training Mediation	Cost sharing Infrastructure maintenance	Promotion Cost sharing
Community: formal community institutions	Mobilisation of community participation	Mobilisation of community participation	Mobilisation of community participation	Mobilisation of community participation

ASHA = Association for Social and Health Advancement   ICML = Integrated Coal Mining Limited

Table 4.1 Division of roles and responsibilities

4.3 Business context, 2000 to the present

At the time that the LATM partnership was being implemented, mining was expected to commence by the end of 2001. Since that time the IFC has withdrawn its interest as an investor, and ICML is presently seeking funding for the project from its internal resources. Overburden removal commenced in May 2002 and mining scheduled to start in October 2002.

Since May 2001 there has been limited community development activity in the area. The financial uncertainty around the mine meant that ICML was reluctant to progress community development or income-restoration projects until coal production had actually commenced. ICML's reluctance to commit resources to community development activities meant that some of the momentum and enthusiasm generated by the LATM partnership was lost. Anecdotally, community expectations were raised by the LATM project but the lack of follow-through (with the exception of the repair of three tube wells) undermined some of the support for the partnership. ICML is of the view that the community is well aware of the

Business benefits

- Social licence to operate:
  - Increased confidence: the LATM partnership raised the confidence of the company to press ahead with the design and early construction work for the project, in the knowledge that its 'social licence to operate' was secure for the foreseeable future
  - Reduced risk that social tensions might affect the future reliability of coal supply from the mine
- Cost-effectiveness of community development expenditures:
  - Reduced compliance costs: the partnership enabled the company to meet its investor compliance requirements at a cost saving of 25%
  - Shared costs: during a period of prolonged investment uncertainty for the company, the costs of community development in the mine impact area were shared with government departments; over the course of the year, Integrated Coal Mining Limited (ICML) spent 89% less on community development compared with the budget that the company had originally allocated to this stage of project development
- Reduced community dependence:
  - Lower dependence: with the government acting as broker and non-governmental organisations (NGOs) contributing 'state-of-the-art' participatory methods, income restoration for those losing land was of a higher quality and more sustainable, leading to the prospect of lower community dependence on the company in the future.

Community development impact

- Local community development:
  - Improved community participation
  - Increased livelihood relevance
  - Improved sustainability
  - Improved time-to-benefit of community intervention
- Community capacity-building:
  - Improved civic leadership
  - Strengthened community institutions

Public-sector governance

- Cost-effectiveness of government expenditures:
  - More immediate and effective implementation of government social programmes
  - More effective 'joined-up' government between the Department of Health and the Planning Department
- Accountability:
  - Better access for community representatives to senior government officials
  - Improved government involvement: government authorities seen to be carrying out their civic responsibilities in a more consultative, responsive and transparent manner

Box 4.1 **Added value of livelihoods assessment and trust-building measures (LATM) partnership**

financial constraints under which ICML is operating and that the community understands that ICML will reactivate the income-restoration project as soon as the financial uncertainties around the mine project have been resolved.

4.4 Link road partnership

It was initially envisaged that coal from the mine would be transported by rail to the Barabani railway station. However, the construction of such a rail link would have been extremely expensive. Therefore, ICML decided to build a road link between the mine area and the railway station. There was already a road (of approximately 10.5 km) between the mine area and the railway station, but the road was not continuous and, in many places, was little more than a track and thus was not suitable for the extended volume and type of traffic from the mine site (estimated at 25 trucks per hour between 6 am and 6 pm). ICML recognised that upgrading the existing road to the required standard would be the cheapest option for the company, through allowing at least some of the pre-existing stretches of road to be used, and also potentially reducing the time required for land acquisition and compensation.

Building on its experience with the LATM partnership, ICML decided to investigate the possibility of a partnership approach to the link road construction project. The potential advantages to ICML were to enable ICML to meet social obligations and to manage rising expectations within the affected communities (against the backdrop of delays in resolving the financial uncertainties around the mine), to share the cost burden of road construction and to enhance opportunities for local communities by improving their access to markets, hospitals, schools and electricity. Government authorities were interested in the project as it would enable them to develop infrastructure in the area at a lower cost than would have been the case without private-sector partners.

The key steps taken to develop the partnership were as follows:

- ICML undertook an internal assessment process with its senior managers to agree on the partnership approach and to identify the 'key actors' within ICML to lead the partnership process.

- Following this internal capacity assessment, ICML had bilateral contacts with Burdwan Zilla Parishad (the district self-government) and the Barabani Panchayat Samity (the local government at the block level). Between January and April 2000, a series of informal meetings and workshops were held with the potential partners to explore the potential complementarities (resources and roles) and the potential risks and benefits of adopting a partnership approach to the construction of the link road.

- In parallel with these meetings, discussions were held between the technical specialists of Zilla Parishad and ICML regarding road design issues.

[The contacts with Burdwan Zilla Parishad and Barabani Panchayat Samity] created a comfort zone, where the infrastructure and development plan might be explored without confrontation.

Amit Mukherjee, Integrated Coal Mining Limited

● Discussions were also held with representatives of Barabani Panchayat Samity to explore the possibilities of community involvement in land acquisition and social development activities related to the link road.

● The meetings between ICML, district government representatives and local community representatives created mutual trust among the parties and paved the way for the parties to enter into an agreement (in the form of an MOU) for the construction of the road and associated social development activities. The MOU was signed in July 2000. A copy of the road link MOU is provided in Appendix B.

The partnership was underpinned by an agreed vision statement for the project, as follows: 'This road building partnership will help business and also provide benefits to affected communities in remote areas and have direct impact towards successful development'. Under the terms of the MOU, the costs of constructing the link road were to be shared (in a ratio of 3:1) between ICML and Burdwan Zilla Parishad.

A field committee was formed in August 2000 to supervise and monitor the road link partnership activities and to provide community input to the project. The field committee included representatives from each of the villages along, or affected by, the link road, local political representatives and Burdwan Zilla Parishad officials. The field committee's role included co-ordinating land payments and the compensation process, mobilising community support and design input for the link road, identifying community development activities that could be integrated into the road project, providing information to the road contractors about locally available raw materials, and helping resolve disputes at the local level.

The resources and competences committed by the partners are summarised in Table 4.2.

4.4.1 Outcomes

For all parties, the pooling of competences proved significant benefits for each of the partnership participants. Box 4.2 summarises the added value of the partnership from three perspectives: business benefits, community development and public-sector governance.

4.4.2 Lessons learned

In evaluating the outcomes of the road link partnership, a number of important features need to be recognised. These are (a) the role of local communities in the partnership, (b) the role of the partnership in resolving disputes, (c) the evolution of roles and responsibilities (in particular in relation to the road construction) and (d) the financial contribution of the various parties.

Partner	Roles and responsibilities
Companies: ICML and CESC Limited	• To contribute a share of the capital costs (75%) • To provide project and contract management • To provide technical support • To supervise road construction work and to carry out impact mitigation measures • To carry out road maintenance (for the first four years)
District government: Burdwan Zilla Parishad	• To contribute a share of the capital costs (25%) • To align the project with the government's regional road policy • To provide road design expertise • To carry out road maintenance (from year five onwards) • To contribute to dispute resolution at the district level • To support social development activities in the area (e.g. electricity, health)
Community representatives: Barabani Panchayat Samity	• To ensure local community support for the project • To assist in identifying landowners and in the compensation process • To assist in the identification of mitigation measures • To liaise with affected communities • To contribute to dispute resolution (e.g. with local communities) at the block level • To participate in field committee meetings and related activities

Table 4.2 Division of roles and competences in the link road partnership

Despite the Panchayat Samity being a project partner and despite the establishment of the field committee (including representation from local villages) local communities appear to have been somewhat bypassed in the partnership process. The communities appear to have been first consulted only after the decision had been made to progress with the road link project and, in fact, the field committee was formed only after the signing of the MOU. It is also fair to note that, given the absence of NGOs or strong community-based organisations, the potential contribution of local communities to a road construction project was not obvious. It was, however, clear that the communities had to be involved at the implementation stage to enable the construction to be carried out smoothly with minimal disruption, to agree the necessary impact mitigation measures and to ensure that the land acquisition process was completed on time and within budget. The Panchayat Samity used its convening power to consult the affected communities and to obtain their feedback on the road initiative. However, the main negotiation processes were between ICML and the Burdwan Zilla Parishad. The community consultation on impact mitigation and community development benefits related

Business benefits

- Cost-effectiveness of investment programme:
  - Reduced capital costs for Integrated Coal Mining Limited (ICML): the government has contributed 25% of the capital cost of the road (10 million rupees [US$250,000])
  - Reduced road maintenance costs: after the first four years of operation, the government will take over the maintenance of the road, thereby providing ICML with an estimated saving of between 1.0 million rupees and 1.2 million rupees (approximately US$25,000) per annum
  - Time savings: the time required for the acquisition of land was reduced from two years to four months and there were also significant reductions in the time required to obtain relevant government permits and clearances
- Corporate reputation:
  - Improved support: the partnership provided ICML with stronger community and political support than would otherwise have been the case
- Management of community expectations:
  - Delineation of responsibilities: the link road memorandum of understanding has been used to clearly define the boundaries of ICML's contribution to community development in relation to the road

Community development impact

- Improved infrastructure:
  - Improved access for the community: the partnership has led to the design of a rural road that takes into consideration the need for better community access to markets, the local hospital, schools and business areas
  - Improved impact mitigation measures: more appropriate environmental impact mitigation measures have been identified and implemented, with greater buy-in from communities
  - Improved infrastructure: the development package around the road includes the provision of (a) two new classrooms for the local school and (b) a new building for the local hospital
- Local economic development:
  - Improved access to markets and business areas
- Community capacity-building:
  - Increased capacity: the field committee established for the construction period is likely to evolve into a community-based organisation, with skills and experience in negotiating with the company and local government

Public-sector governance

- Cost-effectiveness of government expenditure:
  - Reduced capital costs for the government: ICML has contributed 75% (30 million rupees) of the capital cost of the road, representing a capital cost saving for government of US$750,000

Box 4.2 **Added value of the link road partnership** (continued opposite)

- Reduced road maintenance costs: ICML is to maintain the road for first four years, providing the district authorities with estimated savings of between 1.0 million rupees and 1.2 million rupees (approximately US$25,000) per annum
- Increased revenue: ICML is to provide the district authorities with a new revenue stream of the order of 0.3 million rupees to 0.5 million rupees per annum for four years as a flat rate licence for road use, thereafter shifting to a toll per vehicle at the standard business rate

● Accountability:
- Provision of a forum for the local communities: field committee meetings provide a forum for local communities to discuss issues with government representatives.

Box 4.2 (continued)

to three specific issues: namely, the provision of a noise barrier and two new classrooms for the Jamgram School, the construction of a new building for the Kelejora Hospital and the construction of a bypass road for Punchra and access roads for two other nearby villages. Local communities were also consulted on relatively minor issues such as the location of ponds (that result from the digging of dirt for use in road construction). ICML provided a sports field as a result of these contacts.

The relative lack of involvement of local communities in the project raises two important issues. The first is that the road is seen by the community as an ICML project (i.e. the primary reason for the road construction is to enable coal to be transported from the mine). The role of the government or the relationship between the link road and the District Road Development Plan does not appear to be widely recognised in the community. The consequence is that government may not receive its share of the credit (e.g. for delivering on promises and strategic plans and for providing infrastructure in a cost-effective manner) for the construction of the link road. The second is that, although the community has been advised regarding the number of trucks that will be using the road (expected to be 25 vehicles per hour between 6 am and 6 pm), some of the impacts (i.e. noise, dust, vehicle movements) may not be fully understood by the community until the mine starts operating. The relative lack of community ownership of the link road project may heighten complaints regarding these adverse impacts.

The partnership has enabled ICML to manage the risks of disruption of the road link project. The most important example was the protests by villagers from Natundih (adjacent to the link road) and Kharbar (2 km from the link road), neither of whom were represented on the field committee. These villagers blocked the road and threatened to disrupt construction until their villages were provided with electricity. Their discontent was exacerbated by the fact that smaller villages in the area are already electrified. The link road MOU stated that electricity would be provided up to the entrance of the village of Natundih. However, ICML did not have the financial resources to extend the line into the two villages (estimated to cost between two and three million rupees). ICML engaged with Burdwan Zilla Parishad to explore options for funding the electrification of the villages. The Panchayat Samities were interested in responding to the villages' requests but did not have sufficient funds to undertake this work. After further discussions, Burdwan Zilla Parishad succeeded in obtaining funds from their development fund for the electrification of the villages. Anecdotally, ICML was able to use its relationships with the West Bengal State Electricity Board to facilitate the process. This example illustrates the broader benefits of the partnership approach to the road link project as it enabled the project partners to address community concerns (even those not directly related to the road construction or involving parties outside the partnership) in a peaceful manner and with minimal disruption to the road project.

It was agreed in the MOU that Burdwan Zilla Parishad would construct the link road from ground level up to sub-base level, with ICML then constructing the remainder of the road (base level, bituminous level, Premex carpet, and seal coat and cross-drainage). However, as a consequences of the financial uncertainties around ICML and the reality that dividing the responsibility for road construction would have created problems (in terms of project management, the allocation of responsibility in the event of faults in the construction, and the timing priorities of the parties), the contract between ICML and Burdwan Zilla Parishad proposed a different model for the relationship between the parties. Under the terms of the contract, ICML took responsibility for the road construction process (contractor management, scheduling, etc.), with ICML paying the contractors and other costs and Burdwan Zilla Parishad then reimbursing ICML for 25% of these costs. That is, the effect was to spread Burdwan Zilla Parishad's contribution over the entire link road project, thereby minimising its exposure (e.g. in the event that ICML was unable to complete the road construction or delays were incurred in the project). Despite these changes, the MOU has been retained and all parties are committed to meeting the objectives specified in the MOU. The changes in roles and responsibilities and the retention of the MOU demonstrate the flexibility that can be offered by partnerships where partners are committed to both the spirit and the letter of the partnership.

> •It would not have been possible for Zilla Parishad alone to upgrade and construct the road.•
>
> **Alokesh Prasad Roy, Burdwan Zilla Parishad**

The partnership has provided a significant benefit to government as it has enabled the government to build a road at 25% of the cost of building the road on its own. Although it could be argued that, as ICML needed to build the road anyway, the government probably would not have needed to make such a large contribution, this argument neglects the fact that the road will provide a longer-term income stream for the government (through ICML's licence fee and through the payment of tolls). Furthermore, ICML will maintain the road for the first four years

> •I feel this (road link) will not only be good for the company but also sufficiently benefit the local people. This is why we have taken up this venture.•
>
> **Sri R.K. Bandopadhyay, Burdwan Zilla Parishad**

after the completion of road construction (thereby saving the Zilla Parishad an estimated 1.0 million to 1.2 million rupees per annum).

4.4.3 Key success factors in the link road partnership

The key success factors in the partnership were:

- The clarity of the main objective of the partnership; furthermore, the specificity of the MOU (including the specification of agreed impact mitigation measures) meant that many of the potential areas of contention (e.g. routing, and allocation of resources) were eliminated before the road construction was started

- The clear definition of roles and responsibilities (which minimised disputes)

- The clear business and government drivers for the project (i.e. for the business, the link road is an integral part of the mine operation; for government, it has allowed leveraging of private-sector investment, enabling government policy to be implemented)

- The effective harnessing of core complementary competences:
  - ICML brought to the partnership its negotiating and partnership establishment ability (some elements of which were established during the LATM partnership process), technical skills (for the road design and construction) and project management skills (e.g. project supervision and financial management)
  - Burdwan Zilla Parishad provided technical expertise (in particular, in road design) as well as its ability to integrate the project into the local District Road Development Plan (i.e. to ensure that the project provided community development benefits and was aligned with government policy initiatives)
  - The Samities provided their convening power (in particular, their dispute-resolution ability), their ability to mobilise participation in the field committee and their local knowledge (e.g. regarding local landowners and the payment of compensation)

> *The coal evacuation link road will be built through a partnership with Zilla Parishad (District government). This is a unique situation . . . in West Bengal.*
>
> **Kallol Basu, President, Integrated Coal Mining Limited**

4.5 Healthcare partnership

The LATM study identified healthcare as one of the main priorities of communities in the mine impact area. The idea of working in partnership around the issue of healthcare was viewed by the principal NGO, ASHA, as a natural development of the earlier, small-scale, but highly successful, health camps held to build trust between the company and local communities at a time of project uncertainty. ASHA, with its core strengths in healthcare, elected to champion the partnering process. Initial consultations were held with the Asansol Mines Board, the District Health Department, the Panchayat Samities and ICML to identify potential complementarities in health and related services. The key stages in the partnership exploration process were as follows:

- In December 2000 ASHA conducted initial field visits to understand the local health situation and to meet with key government officials, community representatives and ICML extension staff.

- In January 2001 an exploratory workshop was held with government officials, community representatives and ICML to identify and agree on health needs, issues and strategies and to explore possible partnership options. The conclusions of the workshop were shared with the local communities.

- In March 2001 a second workshop was held with the potential project partners to clarify roles, activities and resources and to obtain resource commitments. A draft MOU was prepared and circulated to the project partners for review.

- In April 2001 a revised MOU was circulated for signature. All partners signed the agreement, with the exception of ICML. ICML indicated that it would not sign the MOU until the mining project had financial clearance.

The vision for the health partnership, as stated in the MOU, was to promote 'healthy communities, free from infectious diseases, malnutrition and addiction, provided with basic healthcare services through the pooling of resources from all the partners'. The scope of the intended programme included activities such as increasing the availability of safe drinking water for communities around the mine site, improving sanitation conditions in the operational area, improving the primary immunisation coverage of children (in particular, for measles), controlling communicable diseases (tuberculosis, leprosy and malaria), enhancing the acceptance of family planning measures, promoting the safe delivery of babies and improving the nutritional status of women and children.

4.5.1 Outcomes

At the time of writing, implementation of the healthcare partnership has not commenced. ICML indicated that it would contribute funding only after the mine project received financial approval. Despite this delay, the partnering process to date has succeeded in building consensus around the health priorities of the area and clarifying roles in preparation for when funding becomes available.

4.5.2 Lessons learned

Despite the contributions of ASHA, the critical partner was ICML as, without ICML's financial support, the health partnership project could not proceed. Although the main reason for ICML's reluctance to provide financial support related to the financial uncertainty around the Sarshatali coal mine, it is also important to recognise that even though health is clearly an important issue for the local community, health was not perceived by ICML as a core business activity or as a necessary part of the mine's social licence to operate (in contrast to its views on the income-restoration projects). The consequence was that ICML's commitment to the project was, inevitably, less than that for other partnerships (such as those for LATM and the link road). ICML was also concerned that, by focusing on health issues, there was the risk that ICML would be seen as avoiding the key community development issue, namely that of income restoration.

The second issue relates to the process of partnership development. Given the limitations in ICML's capacity to support the project, it could be argued that a more appropriate approach would have been to exclude ICML from the partnership (or for ICML to have a less critical role). In particular, when one considers the core competences of the project partners, it is clear that ICML's contribution was primarily seen in financial terms. That is, the assumption underpinning the partnership exploration process was that ICML would fund most of the activities (a traditional conception of the role of the private sector in development). This represented a fundamental weakness of the partnership process. From discussions with ASHA it appears that limited consideration was given to the potential contribution (financial or in-kind support) of other partners (e.g. other corporations, NGOs or donors). It could also be argued that ASHA failed to fully recognise its own core competences (i.e. its presence in the local community and its contacts with government health authorities, NGOs and donor agencies) that could have been brought to the partnership process.

The third issue relates to the roles of the project partners. From the outcomes to date it could be argued that ASHA paid insufficient attention to the partnership theme (i.e. whether it was ICML's core business) or to the identification of the project partners (i.e. whether the project could have gone ahead without ICML's support). These limitations meant that ICML did not 'buy in' to the partnership. It is, however, also pertinent to note that ICML had been an active party in the partnership exploration process and there are questions regarding how clear ICML made the potential barriers to its participation in the partnership. In some ways, it could be argued that ICML has created a liability for itself by raising expectations that it would participate in the health partnership. It is also important to recognise that ICML appears to be committed to the partnership and has indicated that the necessary funding will be made available once the mine starts production.

4.6 Other partnerships

There are signs that the experience with the LATM and road link partnerships has led to government agencies investigating other possible partnership projects. A summary of these is provided in Table 4.3.

4.7 Conclusions

The link road partnership has been extremely successful (in terms of cost sharing, risk management, infrastructure development) but the health partnership MOU has yet to be signed, and ICML has yet to make significant progress on implementing the income-restoration programme identified in the initial LATM partnership. The common factor influencing all the partnership arrangements has been the financial uncertainty surrounding mine development. For the mine link road this has been deployed as a business driver, providing an incentive for the company to share the cost burden of mine infrastructure with the district authorities and to reduce the long-term liabilities associated with road maintenance. For the more 'peripheral' activities of healthcare and income restoration, the financial uncertainty has reduced the enthusiasm of ICML for the partnership approach, not least because the company sees its role (and is also seen by others) as providing much of the funding for implementing the partnership activities.

Where the parties might look for a way ahead is to revisit the competences that each already has. Instead of looking at the company simply for funds, government agencies and NGOs (as well as the company itself) need to think more deeply about which of the existing resources and capabilities of the company might be relevant to the community development issues in the mine impact area, be that income restoration, afforestation or healthcare. This might include project or contact management, logistical and vehicle support, operational infrastructure and the resources available for occupational health and safety management. Through focusing on existing competences, the incremental costs for the company are likely be much less (as only the variable costs of the company will be affected) and, therefore, the costs are more likely to be affordable at times of financial uncertainty.

One of the key tests for the sustainability of any new development concept is whether the parties involved succeed in replicating the approach without external intervention. Evidence is accumulating that IMCL, local NGOs and the district authorities are beginning to internalise the concept and benefits of tri-sector partnerships and have now developed the necessary skills to explore and negotiate complex partnership arrangements in a variety of settings without external assistance.

> **'A new era has dawned when companies are getting to see the value of NGOs and government programmes.'**
>
> **Rajat Das, Association for Social and Health Advancement**

Topic	Initiating party	Description
Afforestation	ICML and CESC Limited	ICML is presently exploring the possibility of collaborating with the District Forestry Authority and local communities. The aim is to use the obligations placed on the company to afforest areas as compensation for forest loss, as the basis of a broader, joint forestry management programme to provide tree cover, timber, fruits and other non-timber forest products that benefit local communities.
Hospital management	Hindusthan Copper Mines, Ghatshila, Jharkhand State	ASHA has been invited by Hindusthan Copper Mines to assess the possibility of partnering on the management of a 300-bed hospital
Capacity-building	National Bank for Agriculture and Rural Development	An MOU has been negotiated between the Social Welfare Department of the District Authority, the National Bank for Agriculture and Rural Development and ASHA to provide capacity-building in social welfare programming for district-level extension officers and NGOs
Various social partnerships with the mining industry in Chattisgarh State, Central India	Local NGOs	ASHA has been invited to advise local NGOs in Chattisgarh State (part of Mahdya Pradesh) on how to explore the tri-sector partnership approach with local mining operations and with district and state governments
Training and capacity-building for local communities	ICML, and District Scientific Adviser, Burdwan Zilla Parishad	ICML is presently discussing with the District Scientific Adviser, Burdwan Zilla Parishad, the feasibility of implementing training programmes around the mine area. The aim is to use the government's resources, through local technical and training institutes, to provide hands-on training to the local community on farming- and non-farming-related activities

ASHA = Association for Social and Health Advancement
ICML = Integrated Coal Mining Limited (established by CESC Limited)
MOU = memorandum of understanding

Table 4.3 Other partnership projects

5

Placer Dome and Corporación Venezolana de Guayana
(Minera Las Cristinas CA, Venezuela)
Healthcare partnership

James Tull, Edgardo Garcia Larralde,
Alex Mansutti and Santiago Porto,
with Nicola Acutt, Ralph Hamann and Michael Warner

This case study examines the multi-sectoral partnership arrangements developed to improve health services in proximity to the proposed Las Cristinas Gold Mine in Bolivar State, Venezuela. In a highly uncertain investment climate and potentially hostile socio-economic circumstances, the partnership between the mining company (Minera Las Cristinas CA, a joint-venture company formed by Placer Dome and Corporación Venezolana de Guayana), local communities, government agencies and an international health-related non-governmental organisation leveraged nearly US$2.5 million to construct and operate a fully equipped community health centre.

Over and above access to improved essential healthcare for 12,000 people, the benefits to communities of the partnership included improved channels for negotiating with government, reduced tensions between the Creole and indigenous communities and a new regional community institution, registered and able to attract its own funding. From the business perspective, the partnership contributed to the cost-effective maintenance of its social licence to operate at a time of project delays and low cash reserves as well as reducing its future cost and reputation liabilities from community over-dependence on the company in the event that Placer Dome withdrew from the venture (which it subsequently did).

In 1991 Placer Dome Venezuela, a wholly owned subsidiary of the Canadian-based international mining company Placer Dome Inc., entered into a joint-venture agreement with the Corporación Venezolana de Guayana (CVG), a state-owned enterprise body with responsibility for regional development in the Guayana region of Venezuela. The objective of the joint venture was the systematic exploration and, if feasible, large-scale commercial development of the Las Cristinas gold deposits (estimated to be at up to 11 million ounces of gold), located in Bolivar State in south-eastern Venezuela. The joint venture company, Minera Las Cristinas CA (MINCA), was 70% owned by Placer Dome Venezuela and 30% by CVG. However, the commencement of mining was repeatedly postponed as a consequence of low gold prices. In June 2000, the project was placed on a 'care-and-maintenance' footing and the expected capital expenditure of about US$500 million (to establish the mine) was postponed. In July 2001, Placer Dome sold all its shares in MINCA to a subsidiary of Vanessa Ventures of Vancouver, Canada. It was expected that Vanessa would concentrate on a smaller-scale operation, focused on the mining of higher-grade near-surface materials.

5.1 Social context

From the very beginning, social issues played a crucial role in the involvement of Minera Las Cristinas CA (MINCA) in the Las Cristinas area, both in terms of creating and maintaining a safe and secure operating environment and in terms of maintaining the formal licence to operate from the state. Of particular importance was the issue of small-scale (artisan) miners, who had been operating in the concession area for a long time and who were displaced by the mining concession. Indeed, in parallel to partnership efforts to improve healthcare in the region (the subject of this chapter), a collaborative approach was implemented for the purpose of improving the situation of the small-scale miners.

In the 1990s the rural region of Las Claritas (with a population of approximately 12,000 people) was characterised by a contradictory regulatory framework for artisan mining (the dominant local industry) and growing social tensions between community groups and mining investors. Many community members felt they were being sidelined in the state's support for large-scale mining. This resentment was offset by the expectation that the forthcoming Las Cristinas gold mine would bring well-paid and secure jobs and an overall improvement in the area's social infrastructure. As argued by a representative of the Sifontes Municipality:

> Because Sifontes is a mining zone [for large-scale commercial mines], it is a low priority on the national level. The assumption is that there is plenty of money available locally; however, we have seen very little revenue in taxes and almost no employment. Unemployment is very high—35% in Sifontes compared to less than 14% nationally—we were counting on MINCA to help us with that.

Following a fall in gold prices and MINCA's decision to suspend operations in 1999, local frustrations returned, increasing the risk of invasions of the concession area by local artisan miners.

At this time, the overall level of healthcare was low. Two doctors and four nurses worked across the three public healthcare units serving the local population. They used basic medical kits and outdated furnishings and equipment. None of the three health units in the area had facilities for laboratory analyses, X-rays, major surgery or complicated cases. Outreach medical services to indigenous communities were limited to one private doctor and one volunteer working with the Catholic church. These limitations, when combined with low income, poor nutrition, poor-quality water and the prevalence of malaria and other parasitic and water-borne diseases, meant that the health infrastructure was able to do little to alleviate the widespread health problems.

5.2 Business context

In the early 1990s a formal project evaluation and feasibility study was initiated, including social and economic baseline studies and a social and political risk assessment. Between 1994 and 1999 MINCA undertook additional socioeconomic studies (e.g. livelihood impact studies) and implemented a small socioeconomic improvement programme in an effort to compensate for pre-construction disturbance and to provide support for basic infrastructure and public services. In anticipation of construction start-up in early 1999, this programme was re-focused, re-organised and expanded. An implementing department was established inside MINCA to ensure that the potential social and economic benefits of project construction would be maximised. Las Cristinas was formally inaugurated in May 1999, following several legal and permitting delays. However, six weeks later, in the face of a rapidly deteriorating international gold market, Placer Dome decided to suspend construction pending market and price stabilisation. By this time, Placer Dome had already invested over US$100 million in the overall Las Cristinas project. A potentially adverse impact of the suspension decision on company–community relations was apparent, not least because many people in the local communities (in particular, the displaced artisan miners) had been expecting job opportunities in the Las Cristinas mine. In response, MINCA shifted the emphasis of its social development programme to strengthening existing efforts to build the leadership and management skills of local communities and to expanding future opportunities for legally organised small-scale mining activities.

By September 1999 it had become increasingly clear that failure to address local peoples' livelihood concerns would probably lead to confrontation and conflict, the possible invasion of the concession area and a return to chaotic, unregulated, small-scale mining. Hence, MINCA intensified its efforts to work with small-scale miners to gain access to mining areas. By the beginning of 2000, over and above its engagement with the small-scale miners, MINCA's principal community development effort was directed towards a new healthcare partnership.

The initial proposal regarding health provision was to expand the company's healthcare facilities within the concession compound to serve the needs of future workers and their families. However, as the results of subsequent community participatory planning activities emerged, MINCA modified this proposal and began considering whether to invest in a healthcare facility outside the mine site that would serve not only its own workers but also the general community. Placer Dome's commitment to continued community investment, despite the decision to suspend construction, coupled with the uncertainty of the project's future and hence limited financial resources for social investment, acted as incentives to the company's desire to explore the partnership model. Furthermore, MINCA recognised that, regardless of whether or not the project proceeded, local communities and local government agencies needed to be directly involved in any programme of social investment in order to ensure the local relevance and long-term sustainability of the development interventions.

5.3 The partnering process

Exploration and consultation on partnering options was initiated by MINCA in 1999. This quickly led to a focus on healthcare as the social investment 'theme' that most lent itself to a partnership model of delivery. Interested parties were contacted, including the US-based non-governmental organisation (NGO) Humanitarian Medical Relief Foundation (HMRF), government health agencies at the national, regional and local levels and community leaders. The process of building agreement and assigning roles between the parties got under way in March 2000 with a series of facilitated workshops. These provided training to the parties in consensus-building skills and led to a common vision and set of activities captured in a memorandum of understanding (MOU). The MOU was signed by the parties on 26 March 2000.

In the MOU, 18 different stakeholder groups committed themselves to providing skills or resources to construct a community health centre, to the expansion of potable water supplies and to provide health training. Within two and a half months of signing the MOU, 70% of the health centre construction phase was complete. While equipment installation and training in management skills continued, the health centre was formally inaugurated in February 2001. As part of these ceremonies the partners negotiated a second MOU to enable the transition from the construction phase to the centre's full-time operation. Although most of this second MOU reiterates the importance of compliance with past commitments, it is interesting to note that various sectors of government either re-emphasised or increased the level of their commitment to the project at this point. For example, both the governor's office and the mayor's office recommitted themselves publicly to paving sections of access routes to the health centre. This increased government commitment is an important illustration of the momentum generated by the partnership, as it was apparent that government representatives wanted to be seen to be 'visibly' contributing to the initiative.

5.4 Vision and activities

The goal of improved healthcare was expressed in the first MOU in the form of a vision statement, expressing the desire for:

> Healthy communities, free of infection, malnutrition and addiction, provided with high-quality health services that are accessible to all, with a culture that promotes health and education, in an environment free of contamination.

It is possible to read into the vision many of the negative experiences the community had with healthcare in the past. Although the health facilities at that time were adequate for the most basic assistance, they were not capable of leading the community toward 'improved' health, with an emphasis on local accessibility and quality.

The vision was subsequently developed into a set of activities and an accompanying joint work-plan. The key activities of the partnership were to:

- Establish a health centre that focuses on promoting awareness of health issues among the communities and provides the following services: orthopaedic, dental and general surgery; gynaecology; laboratory services; X-rays; ophthalmology; paediatric services; family medicine; hospitalisation; treatment for malaria; and mental health services

- Educate and train local villagers in health issues

- Train users and the community in general in the maintenance, care and administration of the health centre

- Train community members in the promotion of health and the conservation of the environment

- Establish a potable water system for each community

- Establish adequate drainage and sewage control systems in each community

- Set up an efficient waste-collection system for all communities

5.5 Division of roles

During the formulation of the partnership it was agreed, *inter alia*, that MINCA would provide some of the funding for construction, along with project management skills and a 'clerk of works'; the regional government would refurbish the existing public health facility as a residence for medical workers; the Ministry of Health would sponsor training for local residents to act as malaria workers; Corporación Venezolana de Guayana (CVG, the regional government joint-venture partner in MINCA) would improve water supply to the community; and the NGO

HMRF would supply medical equipment for the centre. All parties shared in the provision of labour to varying degrees. The full set of resources and competences committed by the partners is captured in Table 5.1.

Partner	Role and competences
Corporate operation:	
MINCA	• Co-ordination of construction phase (project management) and secondment of a civil engineer (clerk of works) • Contributions to physical construction, including equipment (building, furnishings, air conditioning, generator), materials and labour • Arrangement of import permits • Transportation for medical equipment
Civil society:	
Communities	• Participation in weekly committee meetings (totalling 4,000 hours of contributed time) • Voluntary work for the construction (totalling 30,000 hours)
HMRF (international NGO)	Equipment and technical assistance for the design of the centre
ABB (local power-line contractor)	Provision of trucks and an electrical engineer
Edelca (a state-owned energy company)	Provision of a professional engineer, two technicians and workers for air-conditioning installation
Government:	
Local municipality (mayor's office)	• Transfer of ownership of land for construction and the structure of the existing Phase II Rural Health Centre • Wages for an architect, two specialist bricklayers and construction workers • Equipment loans and construction materials
The Instituto de Salud Publica (government health institute)	• Provision of medicines and malaria treatments • Advice on the design of the health centre • Provision of civil engineering services • Provision of electrical expertise • Provision of microscope training

HMRF = Humanitarian Medical Relief Foundation
MINCA = Minera Las Cristinas CA

Table 5.1 **Division of roles and competences in the health centre partnership**
(continued over)

Partner	Role and competences
Government (continued):	
Ministry of Health (central government)	Provision of medicines and relevant permits
Tumeremo Hospital (regional health authority)	Provision of medicines and training of volunteers
Regional government (Bolivar State)	A commitment to pave the access road to the new community health centre and to refurbish the old public health facility as a residence for medical workers
Military (local army division)	Volunteer work

Table 5.1 (continued)

5.6 Outcomes

For all parties, the pooling of competences proved highly cost-effective, enabling a significant degree of resource leverage from each other. For the most part, each party contributed resources within its normal range of activities, thus affecting only its variable costs rather than introducing new fixed costs. Box 5.1 summarises the added value of the healthcare partnership from three perspectives: business benefits, community development impact and good public-sector governance.

5.7 Cost-effectiveness of public spending

The partnership approach has provided significant benefits in terms of the cost-effectiveness of public spending. It is useful to look at some of these benefits more closely.

5.7.1 Resource sharing

The involvement of non-governmental actors in local health-service delivery in the Las Cristinas area went further than participation in decision-making. It resulted in the leveraging of significant additional resources, materials and labour, both in the construction of the health centre and in its future administration. The disaggregated contribution of resources (totalling US$2,090,910) from sources other that traditional government healthcare providers is summarised in Table 5.2.

Business benefits

- Cost-effectiveness of social investment:
  - Leverage of social investment resources over and above company contributions of US$526,430 during a two-year period to US$2,079,000 (a leverage ratio of approximately 1:4)
  - Reduced cost to company of providing of on-site healthcare to future (community-based) employees (although this benefit has not been realised because of the suspension of construction)
- Security costs:
  - The health centre partnership, when combined with the positive impact of the company-led programme with artisan miners, led to an estimated annual saving of US$700,000 on-site security costs (a 75% saving per year)
- Corporate reputation and risk management:
  - Channels of communication and trust between Minera Las Cristinas CA (MINCA) and local community and government stakeholders improved significantly throughout the construction phase of the health centre
  - Reduced future cost and reputation liabilities from community dependence on the company
- Competitive advantage:
  - Success of the health centre partnership may have contributed to the extension to MINCA's existing concession agreement for the Las Cristinas mine during the 1999 period and may have enhanced a recent bid for a new mining concession in the Dominican Republic

Community development impact

- Access to health services:
  - Access to high-quality healthcare for 12,000 people
  - Anticipated improvements in livelihood productivity as a result of (a) a lower prevalence of preventable diseases and (b) reduced opportunity costs of travelling to a regional centre for medical treatment
- Time to benefit:
  - The health centre was fully constructed and functioning in 11 months
- Sustainability of healthcare provision:
  - Improved community organisational and leadership capacity to sustain health centre management in long-term without the presence of MINCA
  - Long-term operational budget guaranteed from government as a result of an upgrade in the designation of the centre from Rural II to Urban I
  - Improvements in the organisational capabilities of communities, enabling them to register as official community-based organisations (CBOs) and therefore to access dedicated CBO funding
- Infrastructure:
  - Improvements in the reliability of potable water supplies to local communities

Box 5.1 **Added value of healthcare partnership** (continued over)

- Capacity-building and community participation:
  - The sense of community empowerment has been considerably enhanced not only for managing the health centre but also for initiating and securing funding for other community development projects

Public-sector governance

- Cost-effectiveness of public spending:
  - Leverage of healthcare resources over and above contributions from traditional government providers of US$417,200 during a two-year period to US$2,079,538 (a leverage ratio of approximately 1:5)
  - Anticipated 30% reduction in malaria (at a cost-saving to the government health department of US$42,300)
- Visibility of public authorities discharging their civic duties:
  - Improved reputation of government agencies with local communities, in partic- ular for the local municipality (mayor's office), the Instituto de Salud Publica (a government health institute), the Ministry of Health and Tumeremo Hospital
- Responsiveness of government to local need:
  - Creation of a permanent forum (the community executive committee) for ongoing exchanges and negotiation between government health agencies and community groups
- Agency interaction:
  - Collaboration between previously unco-ordinated government agencies to provide more effective rural health services
- Security costs:
  - The health centre partnership, when combined with the positive impact of the company-led programme with artisan miners, led to an estimated annual reduction in the cost of troop assignments of the National Guard in the Las Cristinas area of US$290,000 (a 75% saving per year)

Box 5.1 (continued)

5.7.2 Preventative medicine

Because the community health centre will serve about a quarter of the Sifontes residents, if it is effective, our work at the hospital in Tumeremo will drop significantly. If they develop an effective preventative medicine programme, our work will drop even more. Half of all our cases are preventable diseases.

Pedro Cardoza, Tumeremo Hospital

In the long term, preventative medicine is cheaper to the state. The health centre, through its outreach training programmes for community health workers, will make a significant contribution to preventative disease treatment. It is estimated that preventative medicine can reduce the medical expenses for treating malaria by 30–50%. In the absence of the health partnership, it is reasonable to assume that the government would have had to

Contributions to health centre construction	Dollar equivalent (US$)
From non-traditional government healthcare providers:	
Core to the MOU:	
MINCA: construction and project management	428,572
Mayor's office: including non-traditional salaries	125,400
Community: volunteer construction-hours	77,138
HMRF: medical equipment, training and technical assistance	1,428,500
Sub-total	2,059,610
Non-signatories to the MOU	
ABB: trucks, engineering and supplies	8,200
Edelca: engineering services	14,200
BDC: construction labour	4,000
Others: machinery, suppliers and donations	4,900
Sub-total	31,300
Total	2,090,910
From traditional government healthcare providers:	
Ministry of Health and Social Development, DS and Tumeremo Hospital: medicines, materials, salaries and training staff	9,200
Instituto de Salud Publica: medicines, materials, training and salaries	397,500
CVG: water services	10,500
Total	417,200
Total leverage	**2,508,110**

CVG = Corporación Venezolana de Guayana
HMRF = Humanitarian Medical Relief Foundation
MINCA = Minera Las Cristinas CA
MOU = memorandum of understanding

Table 5.2 Total investment leveraged into the construction of the community health centre

continue with the same level of expenditure on clinical treatment of preventative diseases, at least in the short to medium term. Even with conservative assumptions, the incremental contribution of the health centre partnership is a cost saving of at least US$42,300 per year through preventative measures against malaria.

5.7.3 Institutional learning

The partnership arrangement in Las Cristinas appears to have triggered a learning process among some key senior government officials. Ways are now being explored to reapply the approach to similar situations in other parts of the country: for example, through the Ministry of Environment and Natural Resources to address environmental issues in the Canaima National Park, Gran Sabana and through the World Bank de Venezuela with other companies and national government agencies involved in the extractive industries sector.

5.7.4 Provision of water services

The commitments made in the health partnership MOU not only indirectly led to improved provision of water services for communities but also to the associated benefits for CVG of lower maintenance costs because of the greater community participation and sense of collective responsibility. Although it is difficult to assess the direct impact of the community health centre partnership on water provision to local communities, CVG has reported savings in its maintenance costs and a decreased need for maintenance visits in the Las Claritas community. According to its regional director, Adalberto Mendoza, CVG now spends less time and energy inspecting the water tubes in the area around Las Cristinas than any other area. Inspectors are generally called out to other communities twice as often and spend more time on each visit. He credits the community organisation and contribution-oriented spirit with this difference. He identifies the direct benefits as including:

> *The influence of the partnership model was very positive. The interest in building partnerships for potable water projects was prompted by the experience of creating a partnership between MINCA and CVG. After that, there was direct pressure on me from the President of CVG to use this approach to resolve the potable water project.*
>
> **Adalberto Mendoza, CVG**

- Fewer people breaking into the water pipes.

- A greater community willingness to report problems quickly and to assist in repairing pipes

- Less waste of potable water by artisanal miners

- Better community relationships

> *My inspectors make fewer trips to the region because the trips are more effective with the help of the community. There are 136 water projects and only 8 inspectors—so I don't save money but we are more effective. Most communities don't pay their water bill because they feel the service is over-priced. In Las Claritas, they understand the importance of paying the bills and they get a better service because of it.*
>
> **Adalberto Mendoza, CVG**

5.7.5 Security costs

A more tangible benefit for government is related to the decreased security spending required in Las Cristinas. This has been primarily attributable to the relatively good relations built between the artisan miners, MINCA and the relevant government agencies. The National Guard estimates that they are using roughly 25% of their normal troop assignment for such an area (18 rather than the typical 72). This reduced number of troops translates into a saving of around US$290,000 (based on an expenditure of US$5,142 per year per guard). It is difficult to determine how much of this is attributable to the health centre partnership and how much to MINCA's earlier, unilateral, efforts to build relationships with the miners. However, at present, the partnership ethos is commonly referred to when security issues are raised.

> •The people of Las Claritas are characterised by voluntarism, trust and security. We invest a lot of money in security in most parts of Guyana. If there had been no partnership, we would have to spend far more in Las Claritas.•
>
> **Lieutenant Colonel Pablo Martinez, Commander, National Guard in Guyana**

> •I believe the biggest indicator of success is that there are no conflicts. In other areas of the country there are loads of conflicts with mining companies.•
>
> **Alex Mansutti, UNEG University**

5.8 Development of social capital and human resources

The health partnership has provided an important impetus towards local democracy. It has shown that a process of dialogue and consensual negotiation between cross-sectoral parties can be an effective tool for building consensus around development issues of common concern and that this, in turn, can pave the way for joint action.

The partnership-building process, including training in negotiation and consensus-building, has contributed to the accumulation of human and social capital locally, as newly trained participants take on new roles and responsibilities within their organisations and as community groups develop new motivation, leadership skills and relationships. A key

> •Now that we have contact with the community and they are organised, we could continue the projects even if Placer Dome goes away.•
>
> **Adalberto Mendoza, CVG**

> •Before, the indigenous people did not even want to talk to us. Now we are more unified. The talks between MINCA and the local government always started with "yes, but you guys did this . . ." or "why didn't you do this?" Now they are working with us and agreeing to things more quickly.•
>
> **Creole community representative**

> •The real value of the tri-sector model is that it helps to organise the community.•
>
> **Simon Moya, President, ISP, Ministry of Health**

'There is a big difference as a result of the tri-sector partnership. The community takes more responsibility for their own issues. The workers are re-invigorated. In the past . . . the company would offer to help on projects but it was never clear. They would always end up taking on a supervisory role instead of really being integrated. There is a danger to the project if one party dominates. [In a tri-sector partnership arrangement] each player therefore has the responsibility to help the other two partners.'

CVG representative

expression of this process is a noticeable increase in self-confidence among local stakeholders. This is especially evident in the improved capacity of community-based organisations and their leaders to engage in constructive negotiations with government authorities with whom they had little or no previous contact.

At the community level, the consensus-building model introduced by the health partnership has resulted in indigenous and non-indigenous groups working together for the first time, following a long period of distrust. Inter-community meetings now tend to involve collaborative, rather than confrontational, interactions.

5.9 Key success factors

Overall, the partnership was developed and structured in an efficient manner, as evident from the speed with which the first project sponsored by the partnership—the health centre—was constructed (11 months). Some of the key success factors include:

- There was a high level of participation by all signatories to the March 2000 MOU.

- During the main part of the construction phase, weekly meetings were held between all partners (including high levels of attendance from communities), leading to mutual accountability and delivery on commitments.

- The construction of the health centre occurred with fast, visible progress, forcing all partners to move concurrently in order not to lose face.

- The project was characterised by high-quality project management skills, led by MINCA, and an intimate link between the funds provided for the main construction works (by those in the construction subcommittee) and the project management function.

- Communities had a strong and immediate voice in decision-making through their representation on a dedicated community executive committee.

5.10 Conclusions

The Las Cristinas health partnership played a crucial role in leveraging investment for health-service provision in the region (with a total of nearly US$2.5 million), most notably from government agencies and HMRF. For MINCA, the partnership also helped avoid the potential 'trap' of escalating community dependence on the company for local development at a time of uncertainty over the viability of the mining project.

The principle of 'pooled resources' that underpins the concept of partnering required the wholehearted participation of local communities and hence achieved many of the benefits associated with state-of-the-art, participatory, self-motivated development. Specifically, these consisted of project implementation sensitive to the local context, skills and capacity-building in terms of improved negotiation with the company and government agencies and a capability to fund and manage the administration of the heath centre into the future.

The ability to accommodate 'change' is an important element in the management of any partnership (e.g. changes in key activities or types of partner). The health partnership has to date succeeded in managing these events. However, a more difficult challenge now awaits with the switch from Placer Dome to Vanessa Ventures (the new joint-venture partner in MINCA).

6

Transredes, Bolivia
Managing oil-spill compensation

Vicky Copeman and Enrique Rivas

This chapter examines the first year of activities of a partnership established in response to the need to compensate local people affected by a pipeline oil spill. To plan and implement the compensation programme, the international non-governmental development organisation CARE Bolivia agreed to work with Transredes SA, a Bolivian/Shell/Enron-owned oil and gas transportation company. The shared vision for the partnership has been to transform the act of compensation into a process of sustainable community development. One year on, 122 community projects are under way and others are planned.

If CARE had not been involved, the compensation programme would have been undertaken by the company's staff and consultants. With CARE bringing expertise in household livelihoods and local ownership, the resulting community projects are more likely to be sustainable in the long term. Beyond the compensation programme, CARE has become involved in activities in the wider region, bringing new resources to one of the country's poorest departments. Through the partnership the company saved an estimated US$500,000 (40%) in implementation costs of the compensation programme. More significantly, the company has been able to withdraw from direct involvement in compensation activities, thereby avoiding the liability of long-term community dependence on the company in an area where it has no facilities. With regard to security risks, the shifting of the compensation programme towards community development has reduced many of the tensions surrounding the oil spill and has enhanced the reputations of both parties.

The willingness of CARE to enter into a working relationship with Transredes was underpinned by a partnership framework agreement, negotiated and signed in advance of the separate operational agreement for managing the Rio Desaguadero compensation programme. The framework agreement sets out principles for joint activities involving CARE and Transredes in implementing social projects across the Transredes pipeline network. This wider programme has been slower to materialise. Progress will require senior managers and operational staff to dedicate time to clarifying the priorities and objectives of the partnership and to identifying complementary activities and responsibilities.

6.1 Social context

Despite significant economic and social progress in recent years, Bolivia continues to face daunting challenges. There has been a prolonged period of social unrest associated with indigenous and campesino rights, and distrust of the government and private sector remains high.

This volatile social situation has direct implications for oil and gas companies. In the absence of clear rules and regulations for compensation for the adverse effects of construction projects (e.g. the loss of hunting areas and other rights), some communities have adopted a strategy of blocking construction activities in order to maximise compensation from companies. In addition, the theft of oil by tapping into pipelines is common, despite this being a high-risk activity that endangers nearby communities and the wider environment.

On 30 January 2000 the Transredes-owned OSSA II pipeline, which runs from Cochabamba on the eastern side of the Andes, across the Altiplano, to Arica on the Pacific coast of Chile, was punctured. An estimated 29,000 barrels of mixed crude oil and condensate was released. The spill affected a high-altitude (4,000 m), largely flat, desert area. The oil was transported down the flooding river for approximately 250 km downstream, affecting over 500 km² of the watershed and, directly or indirectly, impacted on land used by over 7,000 families across 400 villages and hamlets. The inhabitants of the affected area are mainly indigenous Aymaran, Quechuan and Uru Muratan people who depend for their livelihoods on subsistence cultivation and livestock production.

6.2 Business context

Transredes SA was created in May 1997 under the Bolivian Capitalisation Programme to own and manage the nation's oil and gas pipeline system. A Shell/Enron consortium was awarded 50% of the company as well as overall management control; 34% of the company is held by Bolivian pension funds, and 16% is held by employees and other private investors. The Superintendent of Hydrocarbons has granted Transredes a 40-year concession for the transport of petroleum liquids and natural gas to national and international markets. The company's oil and gas pipeline network (some 3,000 km for gas, and 2,500 km for liquids) spans the entire southern two-thirds of the country. It currently moves most of the gas and liquid volumes for the domestic and export markets. Transredes also has access to the Argentine market through the southern gas line. For Bolivia, Transredes represents a central element of infrastructure linking the gas reserves of Bolivia to the huge potential market of Brazil. The continued development of the Transredes network is seen as contributing to making the country the hub of the fast-emerging, integrated energy market in the southern cone of Latin America (a stated government policy).

Since capitalisation, Transredes has made significant investments to modernise and expand the infrastructure it inherited. This has included programmes to reach international standards of health, safety and environment. Within a general context of increasing global scrutiny of the social impacts of business, operational risks from community blockades and pipeline 'tapping', and a specific need to secure international financing, Transredes increasingly began to focus on its social performance. As a result, towards the end of 1999 Transredes commenced preliminary discussions with a wide range of national and international stakeholders on the components of a social investment strategy to be implemented in the vicinity of its facilities. This consultation was temporarily suspended after the oil spill into the river Río Desaguadero.

6.3 The Río Desaguadero oil spill

Although the Río Desaguadero had long been contaminated by mining activities, the visible contamination caused by the oil spill was new, sudden and of extreme concern to the local people. During the first few days after the spill, many community representatives travelled to Oruro and La Paz to find company representatives. The tense nature of the situation was illustrated by marches and demonstrations by local communities that, at times, threatened the personnel and equipment of the company.

Transredes quickly initiated a socioeconomic programme and, within a week, teams of community liaison officers, doctors and nurses, veterinary staff and agronomists were travelling to the communities. Their immediate challenge was to identify and contact all the affected communities to provide information, to respond to emergency needs and to minimise any further impacts that could be caused through the clean-up activities. The objective of the social programme was to minimise the socioeconomic impacts caused by the spill and to take advantage of opportunities to create benefits (e.g. through paid work and training). The programme was also designed to assist affected people to secure compensation for loss of natural pastures as a result of clean-up activities, direct damage caused by the oil to pastures and crops, and indirect damages such as forage losses from water shortages induced by canal closures and diminished livestock market prices.

Under Bolivian law, compensation is defined by an environmental audit. However, it soon became clear that the results of this audit would not be available until 12 months after the spill. Such a delay was unacceptable to the communities and would have resulted in civil unrest that would have prevented clean-up activities. Transredes therefore decided to work directly with the communities to take forward a compensation process in advance of the results of the audit. The process was stipulated in a legally binding document (a Convenio Marco) which was signed by the company and the communities. Communities signed in 40 convenio areas, set up by the communities to carry out this process. Transredes committed to compensate individuals and communities affected by the oil spill in Oruro through community projects or in-kind compensation, with the objective of ensuring that community livelihoods were restored or enhanced. For such compensation actions to be successful Transredes recognised that communities would need to be supported in the selection, planning and implementation of appropriate measures.

There were a number of options for providing this support (e.g. through building in-house capacity, by hiring consultants or by forming an alliance with other organisations). Transredes favoured forming an alliance as it was felt that this could deliver additional benefits such as allowing the closure of the Oruro office set up to deal with the spill, lowering the risk to the company that compensation would not be effective and improving the chances of reputation benefits (or at least lowering further reputational risks). Transredes also recognised that implementing long-term community development projects definitely lay outside the core competences of the company. Consultation with national stakeholders was therefore restarted with added urgency with a clear objective of finding partners willing to assist in delivering the company's vision for the compensation programme.

6.4 CARE Bolivia

CARE first began working in Bolivia in 1976, building rural water systems. Over the years, CARE Bolivia expanded its activities to include projects in agriculture and natural resource management, primary healthcare, reproductive health, girls' education, food security and municipal strengthening as well as urban and rural water and sanitation.

In the development of its Long Range Strategic Plan for 2000–2005, CARE Bolivia undertook the development of a strategic framework that would give coherence to its programme decisions. It has adopted as its strategic objective a contribution to the Bolivian government's goal of a 33% reduction in poverty by the year 2015. CARE Bolivia defined four strategic roles on which it will base its interventions: namely, to influence policies and public attitudes, to participate proactively in social and economic processes, to strengthen the capabilities of local actors and to establish a culture of learning. In its strategic plan, CARE Bolivia acknowledged that in order to optimise development goals it would need to partner with other social actors, including the private sector, in order to create synergies from actors with diverse capacities.

6.5 The partnering process

CARE Bolivia and Transredes quickly established a working relationship. CARE Bolivia was willing and equipped to participate in the delivery of the compensation programme but made its participation contingent on negotiating a broader arrangement to work together on social investment activities with communities living in the vicinity of the Transredes pipeline network. In June 2000, less than one month after the first meeting of the senior managers of both organisations, a strategic framework agreement was signed. The subsequent operational agreement for implementing the Río Desaguadero compensation programme took a further month and a half to finalise.

Transredes was under substantial pressure to initiate compensation activities quickly. This limited the time available for meetings between the senior managers of the two organisations. Consequently, the partners agreed to postpone more detailed negotiation on objectives, roles and responsibilities under the framework agreement and to concentrate efforts instead on the compensation programme.

6.6 The framework and Río Desaguadero agreements

The goals of the partnership were expressed in the framework agreement as follows:

> CARE and Transredes commit to develop together a strategic alliance, based on respect and mutual benefit, with the objective of improving the livelihoods of communities, indigenous peoples and municipalities that live in the areas where Transredes carries out its activities.

This vision was further developed to guide the activities under the subsequent Río Desaguadero operational agreement for the compensation programme. Given the potentially controversial nature of an international non-governmental organisations (NGO) becoming involved in compensation for an oil spill, the concept of transforming a process of compensation into a process of sustainable community development was of great importance to both parties. The vision was developed into a work-plan, with the key activities being to:

- Teach communities about participative management for project identification and development

- Rehabilitate and/or improve the productive base of the communities affected by the spill

- Share the experience of the partnership between CARE Bolivia and Transredes in order to develop norms, regulations and procedures for future compensation processes

- Facilitate and strengthen the bonds among different parties to promote development in the wider region

Although most activities in the plan were directed at developing and implementing compensation projects, some were aimed at promoting development in the wider region. The work-plan emphasised the actions to be taken by CARE Bolivia, although some activities were envisaged as being undertaken jointly with Transredes.

6.7 Division of roles

Under the Río Desaguadero operational agreement there is a clear division of roles. Once CARE Bolivia began work, the role of Transredes was reduced to providing funds and undertaking monitoring and evaluation. As such, the relationship is in many respects more a client–contractor than a power-sharing relationship. However, this does not necessarily mean that it is not a partnership. The client–contractor relationship can be a valid partnership model if, for example, it is characterised by shared responsibility for success, shared risks, the 'pooling' of competences, transparency and open communication. Although many of these characteristics are in place, ongoing tensions surrounding the overheads paid by Transredes to CARE Bolivia, and other administrative issues, are indicative of the importance of maintaining partnership principles over time (in particular, the importance of maintaining open communication).

With regard to 'pooling' competences, in the framework agreement it was recognised that both parties would contribute funds, skills and resources. For example, Transredes undertakes to be involved in the planning and execution of social investment projects at the strategic and local level, and CARE Bolivia is committed to contributing 50% of the finance or funding for community development activities. As described in Section 6.8, on outcomes, these activities have yet to be realised. To date, government involvement has been limited to the participation of local authorities in the development and implementation of some of the Río Desaguadero compensation projects (see Table 6.1).

Given the wide geographical area of potential partnership activities under the framework agreement (as the Transredes network spans much of Bolivia), it is likely that central government ministries will need to be involved at some point, at least at a strategic level. However, owing to the perceived conflict of interest that might result from partnering with those responsible for regulating the clean-up operation, the involvement of central government is currently considered inappropriate. As the framework agreement becomes operational it is expected that opportunities will emerge for central government to play a role in knowledge-sharing, funding and in improving linkages with regional development plans.

6.8 Outcomes

One year into the compensation programme, CARE Bolivia and Transredes have substantial achievements to report. Some 122 community development projects are under way in the area of Río Desaguadero, under the direction of 109 community-based administrative committees. Although the full impact of the projects is yet to be felt, early indications suggest that the programme is on track to achieve its objective of transforming a process of 'compensation' into a process of 'development'. Box 6.1 summarises the added value of the compensation programme over and above that which would have been achieved if the programme had been

Partner	Role
Corporate operation:	
Transredes	• To establish compensation processes and evaluate damages
	• To provide compensation funds and finance for implementation
	• To communicate with internal and external stakeholders
	• To monitor and evaluate the process
Civil society:	
CARE Bolivia	• To carry out community training on project development processes
	• To perform participatory needs assessments
	• To implement the project
	• To communicate with outside stakeholders
Local non-governmental organisations	• To provide project implementation assistance
Communities	• To participate in the compensation process
	• To participate in diagnostic and project planning
	• To assist in project implementation through participating in administrative committees
	• To carry out voluntary work during project implementation
Government:	
Local municipal government	• To assist in project design and implementation
	• To provide additional funding from annual budgets
	• To be involved in project monitoring and evaluation
Central government	• To ensure regulatory requirements are met
	• To evaluate the process

Table 6.1 Division of roles and responsibilities in the Río Desaguadero compensation programme

implemented by consultants alone. Three perspectives are given: business benefits, community development impact and good governance.

Although progress with social investment activities in the vicinity of the Transredes pipeline network (as envisaged under the framework agreement) is anticipated, the overall objective of the programme and the roles and responsibilities of each partner remain to be determined. Both parties recognise the need to invest time in negotiating the details of the programme if it is to go forward.

Business benefits

- Cost-effectiveness and efficiency of the compensation programme:
  - Cost savings: using the CARE Bolivia team rather than a consultancy team provided savings of US$486,000, a 35% saving
  - Reduced supervision and support time needed for in-house Transredes staff: provided a saving of US$60,000 over two years
  - Leverage of an additional US$100,000 for compensation projects from other sources (municipalities, local non-governmental organisations [NGOs] and other CARE projects)
- Security costs and risk management:
  - Less unrest and a lower profile: the reduced levels of social unrest during the compensation programme, combined with a lower company profile in the spill-affected area, allowed Transredes to reduce its security personnel, providing a saving of US$100,000 over two years (a 90% saving)
  - Reduction of disputes: in contrast to the period prior to CARE's involvement, over the past two years there have been no disputes with communities that have required the suspension of compensation activity, providing a saving in the cost of stoppages of approximately US$40,000
  - Support on social aspects: CARE Bolivia has provided assistance to Transredes to assist in managing the social aspects of two subsequent contingencies
- Corporate reputation:
  - Increased international reputation: the consultants of an international finance institution highlighted the compensation programme as an example of the social management capability of the company, improving the prospects of Transredes securing US$600 million in project finance

Development impact

- Quality and sustainability of compensation projects:
  - The creation of more and better projects: some 122 community development projects have been, or are being, implemented in the Río Desaguadero area; these projects are receiving inputs from CARE Bolivia of a type unlikely to have been provided by consultants (e.g. it is involved in providing 40 courses in community participatory assessment and project identification methods and in the establishment of and capacity-building for 109 administrative committees responsible for the transparent use of compensation funds)
  - Increased empowerment: with the support of CARE Bolivia the affected communities have been empowered not only to develop community projects as part of the compensation programme but also to initiate and secure funding for a wider range of community projects; for example, in the past year, community groups have developed proposals for six new projects (totalling US$150,000), with 40% of the funding already secured from local municipalities
- Increased resources for development of the wider region:
  - Increased presence of development NGOs and increased access to funds: the compensation programme acted as a catalyst for CARE Bolivia to establish an office in a previously untargeted department of Bolivia; as a result of CARE's presence, an additional US$339,000 of development funds has been brought to

Box 6.1 **Added value of the partnership approach to the Río Desaguadero compensation programme** (continued over) the wider department (US$239,000 from the Department for International Development's Poverty Alleviation Fund and US$100,000 from CARE central funds for flood inundation relief)

Good governance

- Reduced social tensions:
    - Faster normalisation of a situation of high social tension following the oil spill, as indicated by indigenous leaders dropping their demand that government oversee the compensation process
- Responsiveness of government to local need:
    - Creation of six new community projects, designed with use of participatory techniques, to be co-financed by local municipalities
    - Establishment of 109 administration committees to oversee compensation projects
- Transparent administration of funds:
    - The ability of communities and local government to comment proactively on the transparency of CARE's administration of the funds
- Improvements to regulations:
    - The prospect that management of the Río Desaguadero compensation programme might lead to improvements in compensation regulations

Box 6.1 (continued)

6.9 Conclusions

6.9.1 The partnership between Transredes and CARE Bolivia

The delivery of compensation programmes (e.g. for land acquisition, loss of community assets and the effects of accidents) is a common function of a natural resource company. However, in many countries the rules governing compensation are not well developed. Furthermore, such companies often operate in areas where communities have a largely subsistence lifestyle such that the payment of 'cash' compensation is unlikely to restore livelihood security and may even result in further damage. Transredes found itself confronted by exactly these circumstances after the oil spill into the Río Desaguadero.

Through its partnership with CARE Bolivia, Transredes has honoured its commitment to the affected population to implement a compensation programme that promotes long-term community development. The partnership has also allowed Transredes staff to withdraw from an affected area where it has no facilities. This has helped to reduce the risk of escalating community expectations over what the company could deliver—expectations that began to build during the earlier clean-up and damage-evaluation activities. Together, these outcomes have contributed to a lowering of tensions in the area of the spill and a reduction in risk for all parties—for CARE Bolivia, Transredes and the municipal authorities. There is no doubt, however, that the pressurised circumstances under which the partnership for compensation was formed has slowed the progress in implementing the wider framework agreement.

6.9.2 Contingency planning and partnership

Reflecting on the experiences of the partnership between Transredes and CARE Bolivia, it would seem that, where contingency plans require consideration of social issues, the implementation of the resulting response plan is likely to require skills and resources that lie outside the core competence of the company. These include, *inter alia*, participatory community project planning, local institution building and medical and veterinary assistance. Therefore, the processes of developing such plans should include the identification of what competences will be needed and where they might be found.

It may also be possible to develop relationships with potential partners and, where appropriate, to develop prior agreements for how the parties will work together. This type of partnership is likely to be far easier to establish in 'times of peace'. Under such less inflamed circumstances, the prospects of adherence to the principles of successful partnering when work begins will be improved, as will the prospects of maintaining those principles over time.

In the context of the specific partners that should be considered, it is relevant to note that the partnership that has been the focus of this case study has involved government only at the operational level. Given the wide geographical boundaries of the partnership, only central government could be engaged within the overall partnership agreement. Although this was considered to be inappropriate by the government and the partners, the absence of central government does weaken the partnership in a number of ways. For example, complementary competences and resources that the government sector might bring include the political mandate to formulate national and regional development policies, the strategic co-ordination of different sectors through development plans, the allocation of budgets for the provision of public services and a role as a broker or capacity-builder. It may be that government could be included as a consultative and knowledge-sharing partner, thereby providing the partners with benefits such as access to the government, a greater degree of legitimacy, access to joint funding and improved linkages with existing development plans.

7

BP and others, Azerbaijan

Conflict prevention

Nick Killick

Azerbaijan is poised to enter a new era of growth, spurred on by an estimated US$10 billion of investment over the next few years, much of it in the oil and gas industry. Although this investment has the potential to stimulate economic and social development in both Azerbaijan and neighbouring Georgia, it carries with it the danger of deepening inequalities and corruption, which has the potential to fuel conflict both internally and with Armenia.

International Alert, a London-based not-for-profit organisation, began an initiative in late 1999 to engage multinational oil companies investing in Azerbaijan in a multi-stakeholder dialogue. The process was designed to find ways of preventing oil investment from acting as a trigger for conflict. The approach aims to generate dialogue and, where practicable, to build partnerships, within and between different sectors in society.

Six themes were identified as critical to the peaceful development of Azerbaijan in the context of the exploitation of its oil reserves: namely, supporting the development of local business in order to diversify the economy, meeting the needs of internally displaced people and refugees, the strengthening of civil society, democratic reform and development, regional political stability and oil industry co-operation. The most progressed theme, to date, is business diversification. A new multi-sectoral body has been established to manage the evolving programme—the Business Development Alliance (BDA)—with a Steering Committee comprising BP, Citizens' Democracy Corps, Azerbaijan Entrepreneurs' Confederation, the Eurasia Foundation, Kosia-Smeda (a local NGO) and the American Chamber of Commerce.

7.1 Social context

Although a cease-fire has been in place since 1994, Azerbaijan remains officially at war with Armenia over the disputed territory of Nagorno-Karabakh. The conflict, the result of a complex and long-standing historical struggle, reached its height in the early 1990s. In total, approximately 15,000 people have been killed and one million displaced. Many thousands more have been seriously injured, and the damage to physical infrastructure has been severe. In territorial terms, Azerbaijan emerged the loser, ceding de facto control not only of Nagorno-Karabakh itself but also of some 20% of its sovereign, undisputed territory.

The resulting displacement of large sections of the population constitutes the most serious social problem facing the country. Internally displaced persons (IDPs) and refugees constitute some 10% of the country's population, the vast majority of whom have languished in temporary camps or have occupied abandoned buildings. Finding sustainable solutions to this crisis in Azerbaijan remains a distant prospect, despite a massive, albeit diminishing, humanitarian intervention on the part of the international community over the past few years.

Adding to the tensions, growing social and economic inequality in the country has precipitated numerous demonstrations and protests in recent years. The country is controlled by its authoritarian president, Heydar Aliyev (who, during Soviet times, led Azerbaijan for almost 30 years, and returned to power in 1993 following a five-year interregnum caused by the collapse of the Soviet Union), and true democracy is, at best, fragile. The situation is complicated by the fact that Aliyev is now 78 years old and in poor health. Considerable uncertainty surrounds the identity of his likely successor and few expect a smooth transition to the post-Aliyev era. Some minor improvements in democratisation and human rights legislation have been seen more recently under pressure from the Council of Europe.

7.2 Business context

7.2.1 The wider economy

The end of the Soviet Union, exposure to market forces and an economy built on decades of failed communist policies precipitated a collapse in domestic industries in Azerbaijan. In the early 1990s the country suffered one of the worst recessions in all of the former Soviet Union, with real gross domestic product (GDP) more than halving between 1992 and 1995. Since then, significant foreign investment in the oil sector and related industries, such as construction and communications, has reversed this decline and contributed to strong economic growth. This investment has simultaneously created difficulties of its own, with export revenues now highly dependent on oil and oil products (84% in 2000), the remainder of the economy struggling, unemployment at 20% and GDP at $600 per capita. Over the next few years investment in the oil and gas industry and associated infrastructure is set to increase substantially, potentially exacerbating these imbalances. The danger is that the prospect of large inward flows of foreign investment and guaranteed revenues from oil will provide a false sense of security, masking the urgent need for profound and far-reaching reform of the country's democratic and economic base.

7.2.2 Business drivers

The Azerbaijan multi-stakeholder dialogue was conceived in the belief that that the companies investing in Azerbaijan could be engaged not only in the socially responsible management of their own operations but also in tackling some of the underlying, structural causes of conflict in the region. The rationale for engagement from the companies' perspective is that reputations and profits suffer when violent conflict breaks out, regardless of the causes. Preventing conflict, therefore, becomes a business interest and necessitates involvement in issues that may lie outside the company's core operations. This is true of the private sector as a whole, but particularly so in the case of the oil industry.

7.3 The partnering process

'Conflict prevention' is a broad term encompassing a multitude of approaches and interventions to prevent and manage conflict situations, ranging from community development to high-level political negotiations. Many of the approaches draw on a cross-section of society. Governments, multilateral institutions, non-governmental organisations (NGOs), community and religious organisations and the media are all recognised as having potential roles to play. Increasingly, so too is the private sector.

The approach to the multi-stakeholder dialogue adopted by International Alert followed a framework comprising five interdependent principles, as follows:

- Strategic commitment, consisting of a willingness to engage in and recognise the value of partnerships

- Shared analysis, including a joint understanding of common issues as well as of the different standpoints, interests, agendas and concerns

- Dialogue and consultation, identifying common ground and building strong relationships

- Partnership and collective action, cementing trust and confidence through shared activities; in conflict prevention terms, a primary objective is to achieve the trust and understanding implicit in the word 'partnership' rather than necessarily a tangible output

- Sustainability, in the medium to long term

During the first few months the work focused on gaining an understanding of the conflict and of the political and economic situation in Azerbaijan. The second priority was to identify representatives from the various stakeholder groups who have (or could develop) a commitment to engage in dialogue to bring about change. The participating organisations were: Socar (the state-owned oil company), BP, Statoil, Exxon (as an observer), the Azerbaijan Entrepreneurs' Association, the Association of Farmers, the Institute for Peace and Democracy, the Association for the Protection of Women's Rights, the Human Rights Centre Azerbaijan, the FAR Centre, the British Embassy and the Norwegian Embassy.

Initially the concept of a multi-stakeholder dialogue was viewed with a mixture of suspicion and confusion. The confusion was partly because the concept itself was something of a novelty in Azerbaijan; the suspicion arose because any multi-stakeholder dialogue presents risks and threats to its participating organisations. Furthermore, the outcomes were uncertain and the benefits unproven.

In a broad-based initiative such as this, with an overall goal as complex and as intangible as 'conflict prevention', the approach was not so much about creating partnerships as about creating mutual understanding and a platform for joint analysis of what might be achieved together. Six themes were agreed by the participants as being critical to the peaceful development of Azerbaijan in the context of the exploitation of its oil reserves: namely, (a) supporting the development of local business in order to diversify the economy, (b) meeting the needs of internally displaced people and refugees, (c) the strengthening of civil society, (d) democratic reform and development, (e) regional political stability and (f) oil industry co-operation.

> •This is the reality of trying to pursue a multi-stakeholder approach to conflict prevention. There is no single process, but rather a collection of processes which may have no direct links other than the role of the facilitating organisation, in this case International Alert.•
>
> **Nick Killick, International Alert**

With differing degrees of success, the dialogue developed programmes to address these challenges. Although the ideal would have been to maintain the original participants as the focus for designing and implementing these programmes, the breadth and variety of the themes identified meant that very different approaches were developed for each programme, involving different combinations of the participants at different times. The original goal of 'conflict prevention' is retained and can be considered as the combined objective and effect of the portfolio of programmes.

Fundamental to the success of the overall work has been a core group, including 'champions' from each sector, who are aware and supportive of the programmatic work on the individual themes. The two key companies in this regard have been BP and Statoil.

> •It is crucial to have leaders from different sectors driving the process forward. Those who can bring others along and sustain the momentum in difficult times.•
>
> **Nick Killick, International Alert**

7.4 The Business Development Alliance

Given the diversity of themes it was recognised that some areas would progress faster than others. The most advanced is the work on supporting business diversification, through a body known as the Business Development Alliance (BDA). The rationale for the BDA is that if Azerbaijan is to reap the full social and economic benefits of its oil and gas wealth, it will need to invest heavily in strengthening and broadening its economic base. The BDA is not a traditional business or trade organisation; it is a network of international and local companies and business associations, government, international and local NGOs and international development agencies. The founding principles of the group are that partnership and co-ordination are the most effective means of achieving the goal of local business development. The agreed objectives of the BDA are to:

- Promote the growth of the Azeri private sector

- Provide a unique multi-sectoral forum for information-sharing, consultation and advice on issues related to private-sector development in Azerbaijan

- Enhance co-ordination and coherence among different economic development initiatives (e.g. government, multilateral organisations, private companies, international NGOs, donors and international financial institutions)

- Identify gaps in and obstacles to economic development in Azerbaijan and develop strategies and recommendations to address them

- Define and recommend policy and legislative changes that will enhance private-sector growth

- Collectively, and through individual members, implement initiatives drawing on members' core competences and constituencies

- Provide a comprehensive information resource for local and international businesses on investment opportunities, on potential business alliance partners, on financing, on the capacity-building services and programmes available and so on

The BDA is an entirely voluntary organisation. However, in order to develop, expand and sustain its work, the BDA (which is presently supported by BP and some of BP's partners) will be establishing a permanent secretariat and setting up an office within a local enterprise centre. The role of the secretariat will be to drive the BDA's work-plan (in particular, to identify broad topics requiring support, to map existing initiatives in these topic areas, to undertake research to remove obstacles and to develop recommendations), provide essential support to various working groups, facilitate dialogue between local and international businesses and other stakeholders, ensure the effective targeting of the resources of the alliance members and improve co-ordination on economic development initiatives.

To date, the BDA has established five working groups focused on issues identified as having joint priority and that match the expertise and capacity of its current members. These are: the creation of a supplier database, the provision of training, the assessment of oil industry needs, policy development, and the provision of credit and finance. The goals, deliverables and benefits to the various participants in each of the working groups are summarised in Table 7.1.

Working-group focus	Goals	Deliverables	Anticipated benefits
Supplier database	• To achieve an instant connection between buyers and sellers • To be 'the' database for supplier capability in Azerbaijan	• A web-enabled database recording supplier capability in Azerbaijan • Staff dedicated to maintaining and updating the database • 250 suppliers listed on the database by the end of 2002 • Detailed supplier capability	• Easy access to information about supplier availability and capacity • Increased use of partnerships between international and local businesses
Training	• To increase the amount and quality of business management and vocational training available to SMEs	• The development of criteria for a 'quality training provider' • A feasibility study and draft project document for a new training project for SMEs in health, safety and environment and in quality assurance • Encouragement of international training providers to take a 'train the trainers' approach • Co-ordination of major training efforts	• Increased number of competent local companies that will be suppliers or contractors to the oil and gas sector • Increased number of alliance relationships with international partners that are able to find more trained, competent local partners

Table 7.1 Working groups of the business development alliance [continued over]

Working-group focus	Goals	Deliverables	Anticipated benefits
Oil industry needs	• To actively encourage, develop and engage Azeri companies to supply goods and services in the expansion of the Azerbaijan economy	• An assessment of oil industry needs and demands in relation to new expansion and pipeline projects • A feasibility study of five new Azeri companies to cover the supply or services of key sectors within the supply chain • Implementation of a system to manage supplier performance • The creation of a model of the future development of Azeri companies	• A co-ordinated programme matching capacity with needs • The focused development of local businesses • Enhanced capacity of local businesses to act as suppliers to the international oil industry
Policy	• To develop recommendations to enable the government of Azerbaijan and established businesses to assist and encourage local entrepreneurship • To develop a system of actions that fosters growth and stability among local businesses	• Seminars for local companies on the rights and responsibilities of companies in Azerbaijan • Conveying and advocating lessons learned from transition • Good governance programmes for local businesses • Recommendations for international businesses on increasing the local content of their operations	• A greater understanding of credit and financing options • Improved conditions for accessing credit • Growth in the quantity of SMEs

Table 7.1 (from previous page; continued opposite)

Working-group focus	Goals	Deliverables	Anticipated benefits
Credit and finance	• To increase awareness and availability of credit to deserving Azerbaijani SMEs • To encourage the creation of new institutions (e.g. the creation of a micro-credit bank), credit lines and programmes to increase the availability of credit • To develop recommendations for the government and donors on how to implement and co-ordinate SME credit programmes efficiently	• A published brochure on financing for SMEs • Concrete proposals to address the impediments in lending and finance in general • Report to the Government and IFI community outlining the importance of enforcing anti-monopoly and bankruptcy law • A roundtable on credit and regulatory issues	• Positive changes in the business environment • Definition, prioritisation and implementation of policy proposals for government and for international and local businesses

IFI = international financial institution   SMEs = small and medium-sized enterprises

Table 7.1   (continued)

7.5 Roles and responsibilities within the Business Development Alliance

The steering group of the BDA comprises BP, the Citizens' Democracy Corps, the Azerbaijan Entrepreneurs' Confederation, the Eurasia Foundation, Kosia-Smeda (a local NGO) and the American Chamber of Commerce. Table 7.2 captures the main roles of the Steering Committee, the Secretariat, the working groups and the members.

•Third parties are an important component of the process. They can create the conditions in which constructive dialogue is possible and can ensure follow-up. Without them, trust is much harder to build and the process much more demanding for the participants.•

Nick Killick, International Alert

Partner	Roles and responsibilities
Steering Committee	• To shape the strategic direction of the BDA • To monitor and advise on the progress of the working groups • To represent the BDA in discussions with government and other sectors • To encourage wider support for and participation in the BDA • To take responsibility for the finances of the BDA
Secretariat	• To draw up a charter for registration • To work with the Steering Committee to develop a long-term strategic plan • To manage the expenditure and budget of the BDA • To give practical support to the working groups • To develop and maintain strong relations with government and local business • To co-ordinate meetings • To ensure cohesion with other business development initiatives • To create and maintain a website • To conduct research • To raise funds (nationally and internationally) • To seek new members
Working groups	• To take responsibility for implementing the activities outlines in the working-group plan • To make regular reports to the Steering Committee, the Secretariat and members on progress
Members	• To commit themselves publicly to the BDA • To discuss and approve or amend recommendations made by the Steering Committee and the working groups • To participate in BDA projects according to their skills, resources and expertise

Table 7.2 Division of roles and responsibilities within the Business Development Alliance

7.6 Lesson learned

In general, multi-stakeholder dialogues and partnerships involving the extractive industries are a 'means to an end'. A 'conflict prevention' approach is somewhat different, as the process is also an 'end in itself'. In conflict situations, trust is deficient and the risks of miscommunication are high. In this context, the goal of dialogue and partnership is as much about undertaking a shared analysis of the situation, of understanding one another's underlying interests and of establishing channels of communication between non-traditional parties as it is about the outcomes of some physical activity based on collaborative working. This conclusion has an important implication: given that multi-stakeholder dialogue takes time to develop, the desire to see concrete results should not detract from the importance of building strong relationships.

7.7 Web address

International Alert: www.international-alert.org

8

Kahama Mining
Corporation Limited, Tanzania
Social development programme

Rory Sullivan and Aida Kiangi

This chapter examines the partnership approach underpinning the social development programme of Kahama Mining Corporation Limited (KMCL), the developers of the Bulyanhulu gold and copper mine in the Shinyanga Region of Tanzania. The mine started production in April 2001.

In recent years, the Tanzanian government has opened its mining industry to the private sector. This process has been accompanied by public expectations that the granting of mining concessions will lead to local community benefits beyond employment. Another important element of government policy is for political and administrative decentralisation, although this process has been impeded by the limited financial resources available to local government. For example, although Kahama District Council has committed 25% of its locally derived income to implement a district development plan, this represents just 2% of the overall anticipated expenditure. With central government likely to contribute only a further 12%, the District Council is looking to non-governmental organisations (NGOs), donors and, in particular, KMCL to fill the void.

To generate community benefits in this complex working environment, KMCL instigated a social development programme (SDP) centred around the provision of infrastructure for water supply, healthcare and primary education. The primary business drivers were the broader need to ensure the acceptability of the mining industry and the specific KMCL objective of reducing its expatriate workforce by 70% over five years, requiring that KMCL needs to construct housing and related infrastructure of a quality sufficient to attract Tanzanian managers to the region. This infrastructure will be extended to the local community, thereby improving local infrastructure and the level of delivery of basic services, as well as enabling the development of other businesses in the area.

A number of multi-party steering committees have been formed to co-ordinate the programme design and resource inputs from KMCL, communities, the District Council, NGOs and donors. The SDP has been closely aligned with the Kahama District Development Plan, thereby meeting local infrastructure priorities and the government's policy for a 'bottom-up' approach to community planning. KMCL provided most of the investment capital and has used its competence in contract and project management to oversee contractors. The steering committees have now shifted their emphasis towards building the capacity of local government, communities and NGOs to take over the long-term management and maintenance of the infrastructure facilities. With many of the facilities to be managed on a 'user-fee' basis, and with the anticipated improvements in the capacity of the district government to manage public services, there is every prospect that KMCL will be able to stand back from the leadership role it has taken to date and to contribute to local society on a more equal and sustainable footing with its government and civil society partners.

8.1 History of the Bulyanhulu mine project

The Bulyanhulu gold mine is located approximately 45 km south of Lake Victoria in the Kahama District in North Central Tanzania. Artisan gold mining started in the Bulyanhulu area in the 1970s, although the number of individuals involved in mining was small. The acquisition of the mine property in 1989 by Placer Dome and the subsequent discovery of gold deposits led to a 'gold rush' in the area. It is estimated that between 30,000 and 40,000 people migrated to the area between 1989 and 1995. At this time, a new settlement was established in Kakola (near to the present mine site and located on the official mine property).

Placer Dome relinquished its exploration rights to the property in 1992. In 1994, a prospecting licence was granted to Kahama Mining Corporation Limited (KMCL), a subsidiary of Sutton Resources. Barrick Gold Corporation subsequently acquired Sutton Resources in 1999, with KMCL then becoming a completely owned subsidiary of Barrick Gold.

When, in 1994, KMCL first became active at Bulyanhulu the government informed the artisan miners that they would have to leave the mine area. In July 1995 the government decreed that the artisan miners must leave by August 1995. The artisan miners did not respond and in April 1996 the Shinyanga Regional Commissioner ordered the immediate departure of the illegal artisan miners. These miners dispersed widely to other areas of the country. There have been allegations that some people were unlawfully killed as part of the process of removing the artisan miners from the mine lease area. Formal investigations have been conducted by the Tanzanian government, but none of these has provided evidence that has supported the allegations. However, the Tanzanian media and national and international non-governmental organisations (NGOs) have continued to raise concerns about the issue.

The mine started production in April 2001. Approximately 2,500 tonnes per day of ore are processed, and the mine is expected to produce approximately 13 tonnes of gold and 2,600 tonnes of copper concentrate per annum. The mine lifetime was originally expected to be ten years, but the discovery of additional reserves on the mine lease area means that the mine is likely to continue operating until at least 2016. KMCL directly employs approximately 1,200 people, of whom approximately 160 are expatriates. There are several contractors on-site employing a further 260 people.

8.2 Social context

Despite the relatively low population density in the area, and despite access to moderate to good agricultural soils, the quality of life of local communities is poor, as a consequence of poverty, low levels of education and skills, and chronic ill health. The majority of households in the area are involved in subsistence crop farming (mainly in the production of cassava, maize, beans and sweet potatoes). In addition, a variety of fruit trees (including banana, mango and paw-paw) are grown. Animal husbandry forms an important part of household survival strategies, with approximately 65% of households owning cattle and many also owning goats, sheep and poultry. Despite the different potential sources of food, food shortages are common, in particular during the early part of the wet season, before crops are ready for harvesting.

A national report for the period 1990–2000 noted that, although Tanzania has a strong commitment to ensuring the realisation of education for all, the primary school net enrolment rate dropped from 69.7% in 1990 to 56.7% in 1998, and the national literacy rate dropped from almost 90% in 1986 to 84% in 1992 and has continued to decline since that time. The decline has been attributed to a range of factors, the most significant of which are inadequate funding by government and donors, low-quality teacher training, wide gaps between government and district co-ordination, lack of community involvement, especially in rural areas, lack of textbooks and a lack of spaces in form 1 (i.e. secondary school) to absorb all children leaving standard VII (primary school).

There is a general scarcity of water in the area of the mine. The common sources of water for domestic use are open traditional wells and a few wells fitted with hand pumps. Most of the wells are considered 'unsafe' and have very low yields, especially during the dry season. There is a prevalence of water-borne disease in the area because of the lack of improved water points and poor environmental sanitation. Many households do not have latrines or other sanitation structures and there are significant limitations to the community's knowledge regarding water, water management and sanitation.

The key medical issues in the region are the high incidence of diseases such as diarrhoea, pneumonia, anaemia, malaria, and HIV and AIDS. The health infrastructure in the region is in an extremely poor state, with shortages of medical staff and equipment.

8.3 Business context

The Tanzanian government has recently amended its legislation to promote Tanzania as an attractive investment location for the global mining industry. Barrick Gold hopes to establish a regional mining zone in Tanzania, and the Bulyanhulu mine is viewed as the first in a series of such operations. The increasing involvement of the private sector in industrial development has led to political and public concerns regarding the role and activities of the private sector. Local and national governments as well as various interest groups are taking a keen interest in whether greater economic prosperity will result from large 'Western' commercial mining ventures. Concerns have been expressed in the Tanzanian media that, in some cases, communities have been impoverished rather than developed by the granting of mining concessions. The consequence has been that, while Tanzania is offering favourable investment terms for the mining industry, companies are expected to provide community development benefits as a part of their 'licence to operate' (even if such requirements are not explicitly specified in licence conditions). KMCL recognised that it needed to provide development benefits, yet it was also concerned that expectations be managed so that the cost to KMCL is sustainable, that KMCL did not create longer-term liabilities for itself and that social development expenditures were cost-effective. KMCL also recognised that it was important that community development expenditures be sustainable, by providing long-term benefits to the community as a whole, by enabling the community and government to maintain the infrastructure and assets provided and by ensuring that the community can continue to function effectively (i.e. provide for itself, generate its own income and wealth) even if KMCL is no longer there.

> ⁹Mining companies have traditionally assumed that providing jobs alone would be enough but it is increasingly clear that the industry needs to do much more on community development.⁹
>
> **Roy Meade, Kahama Mining Corporation Limited**

One of KMCL's objectives is to reduce the number of expatriates at the mine by 70% within five years. KMCL's experience has been that Tanzanian managers will be unwilling to move their families to such a region unless infrastructure such as schools, health and housing matches that available elsewhere in Tanzania.

Finally, KMCL is aware that its reputation as a 'socially responsible mining company' depends on it effectively managing, among the whole range of business issues, social issues. KMCL has recognised that corporate reputation is difficult to measure or describe in strictly objective terms but sees its reputation in terms of the quality of the company's relationships with the local community, various levels of government and NGOs. In this context, KMCL has recognised that it can control the quality and quantity of its community development activities, its own delivery on promises or commitments and its openness and transparency in dealings with government, communities and NGOs.

KMCL chose to adopt a multi-sector partnership approach, involving not only different parties but also the pooling of their resources and competences. The partnership approach was adopted for a number of reasons:

- To enable KMCL to focus its efforts on those areas where social needs were greatest and where KMCL could provide maximum value to community development

- To enable KMCL to work with potential partners and, through this, to develop trust and understanding and a more secure social licence to operate

The approach adopted by KMCL aims to bridge the gap by addressing areas where there is a real need and where KMCL can make a real difference. The ultimate aim is for government, communities and NGOs to take over. However, to get things started, KMCL has had to adopt a role that is closer to that of an NGO.

Aida Kiangi, Kahama Mining Corporation Limited

- To manage community expectations of KMCL for local development, through clearly defined and agreed goals and work-plans that engage all sectors of local society in taking action and assuming responsibility

- To enable KMCL to 'hand over' the long-term management and maintenance of infrastructure and other projects to communities and government

8.4 Governance context

The aim of the Tanzanian local government reform agenda is to enable local government authorities to be more autonomous. Kahama District Council (KDC) issued its first district development plan in 2001. The aim of the plan is to improve the welfare of the population by enhancing food security and rural income and by improving social services in the district. The participation of local communities in both planning and implementation of the plan is seen as essential to strengthen the responsibility and capacity of communities to solve their own development problems. This approach reflects the 'bottom-up' focus of the local government reform agenda, where there is an emphasis on the delegation of authority and responsibility to the lowest practicable level of governance. At the time of writing, the processes of planning and implementing the district development plan were still relatively new, and there were significant limitations to the resources available to communities and government to effectively implement the plan.

8.5 The partnering process

In 2000 KMCL commissioned Planning Alliance, a Canadian consulting company, to assist in the development of KMCL's housing scheme, as part of the social development programme (SDP). The SDP focused on the development of a housing scheme for mine employees and the manner in which KMCL could assist the communities surrounding the mine in the areas of health, education, water supply and micro-enterprise development. The SDP preparation process involved extensive consultation and negotiation with KMCL management, existing residents, government agencies and mine-workers. A specific aim of the consultation process was to ensure that the SDP reflected the priorities in the district development plan.

The SDP was seen as enabling KMCL to gain a strategic position within the communities through proactively engaging with community concerns and through establishing effective programmes. Apart from aligning the SDP with the outcomes of the bottom-up planning process, KMCL, through discussions with KDC and with the village councils, identified the areas where there was a need to bridge the gap between the delivery of development programmes and the needs of local communities. Wherever possible, KMCL has encouraged the community to mobilise their own resources. Where resources are not available, KMCL has assisted in various ways, such as providing technical know-how, financial support, capacity-building and so on. The objective underpinning the SDP was to ensure that communities were not dependent on the mine for development but rather were empowered to be independent and to realise avenues of assistance for development purposes.

Instead of establishing a development foundation to implement the SDP, KMCL decided to adopt a company-managed approach, as this would enable KMCL to:

- Form community development partnerships across its business units: that is, KMCL recognised that community development projects would require skills and resources from the company in addition to those in its Community Development Unit, including equipment and materials, and contract management skills

- Investigate possible partnerships between departments or contractors that could enhance the programme benefits (e.g. procurement from small enterprises, facilitation of dialogue between companies in the region and vendors)

- Transfer responsibility for community development to the community and to government rather than having the responsibility remain with a development foundation; this approach was also seen as allowing KMCL to avoid the potential longer-term liabilities associated with funding a development foundation

- Avoid the transaction costs that would be associated with the operation of a development foundation

- Enable KMCL to be a partner in development rather than simply a source of funds

KMCL created a Community Development Unit to implement the company's development plan in collaboration with the community and other development stakeholders. The programme is supported and monitored by steering committees (or by equivalent structures) for each programme. The steering committees include relevant stakeholders (e.g. district and government representatives, NGOs, KMCL, community representatives).

8.6 Partnership activities

At the time of developing the SDP, community and government capacity and resources were extremely limited, not least in the techniques of community participatory planning. There was also a general lack of understanding of the role that could be played by the private sector in community development. Although KMCL's original intention was that the SDP implementation would be based on principles of equal contributions and responsibilities, the practical limitations meant that, although the direction of each of the projects was defined by all partners, KMCL was compelled to take a leadership role by providing the bulk of the funding as well as contributing contract and project management skills. Despite this, the partnership principles of joint design and decision-making, shared risks and responsibilities and a pooling of resources and competences were adhered to through the establishment of a series of multi-party committees for each of the main programme components. Each steering committee comprised representatives from local and district government, NGOs, KMCL and the affected local communities. The committees provided a means for ensuring that KMCL focused its resources on those areas where there is a need to bridge resource gaps (i.e. on specific activities or projects that could not be implemented by others because of a lack of resources or capacity). Where these resources already existed, KMCL encouraged the relevant communities, NGOs or government agencies to mobilise themselves. In practice, this meant that KMCL assisted principally with technical know-how, financial support and capacity-building in infrastructure management and maintenance.

The KMCL SDP provided the broad framework and starting point (e.g. initial budgets, initial dialogue with communities and government, a broad outline of the aims and intent of the project, and allocation of KMCL roles and responsibilities) for each of the partnership projects being implemented. The partnership projects that have been established to date have included a worker housing scheme, a community health programme, a community education programme and the provision of water to local communities (for an overview of the SDP, see Box 8.1).

8.6.1 Community health programme

We will describe the community health programme in more detail than the other programmes as many of the issues in partnership establishment and implementation are common to all the partnerships that have been established by KMCL.

The African Medical and Research Foundation (AMREF, an African NGO with its headquarters in Nairobi, Kenya) had been working in the Great Lakes area, in conjunction with the London School of Hygiene and Tropical Medicine and the

- Housing scheme:
  - To develop a housing scheme (consisting of a total of 600 houses) for mine employees and their families
  - To enable local communities to benefit from the infrastructure (roads and community services) associated with the housing scheme
- Community education programme:
  - To improve the quality of the educational infrastructure (buildings and facilities)
  - To improve the quality of primary education in the area (covering approximately 3,000 children)
  - To provide access to basic adult education
- Community health programme:
  - To ensure that there is a basic health system available to all communities in the vicinity of the mine operations
  - To educate communities and workers on diseases and health issues such as HIV, AIDS and malaria
- Water programme
  - To provide safe, reliable and affordable water supply to local communities
- Other programmes:
  - To promote local enterprise development
  - To develop better housing infrastructure

Box 8.1 Scope of the social development programme of Kahama Mining Corporation Limited

Tanzanian National Institute of Medical Research, on various research-based projects around HIV and sexually transmitted infections (STIs). The researchers began to see an increased level of exploration and mining activity in this region and were concerned about the impact of these developments on populations in the Great Lakes area. AMREF held a number of awareness workshops for people involved in mining, but there was limited interest from the mining industry in this work. This changed, however, following a meeting between Barrick Gold and AMREF Canada and a subsequent meeting between AMREF staff based in the Great Lakes area and KMCL management.

❝While the initial discussions centred around conventional ideas such as the construction of medical facilities, the proposed programme then evolved into something more substantial . . . AMREF was impressed with the way in which KMCL accepted AMREF's arguments regarding the importance of HIV to the company and how, in some ways, KMCL could be seen as the cause of the problem.❞

Simon Clift, African Medical and Research Foundation

Following these discussions, and building on earlier discussions between KMCL and local communities regarding health needs and expectations, AMREF submitted a concept paper for the development and implementation of a community health programme. Based on the concept paper, KMCL signed a contract with AMREF in

2000 to implement an initial two-year health programme valued at US$300,000. Since signing the contract, AMREF has worked closely with the District Health Management Team (DHMT) to develop and implement a programme of health promotion, disease prevention and improved treatment for mine-workers and communities surrounding the mine, with a particular focus on HIV and AIDS, other STIs, tuberculosis and malaria. A baseline health survey was completed in November 2000. Since that time, the project team has implemented a comprehensive package of measures, including the establishment of a peer health educator scheme, the social marketing of health products (e.g. insecticide-treated bed nets to guard against malaria; and condoms to guard against HIV and other STIs), focused interventions for women at high risk of infection with HIV and STIs (specifically, commercial sex workers and their clients) and the operation of a voluntary counselling and HIV testing centre. The key objectives of the community health programme are presented in Box 8.2.

- To assist in building the capacity of the recently refurbished Bugarama Dispensary in conjunction with the District Health Management Team (DHMT), along with other specified health facilities accessed by mine-workers, their dependants and individuals from the communities surrounding the mine, in light of the expected increase in demand for quality services and in light of the local epidemic of HIV and sexually transmitted infections (STIs); this will involve the supervision of the equipping and running of these health units and the recruitment and training of staff

- To ensure high-quality care and management of common conditions, including malaria, tuberculosis and STIs among residents of communities around Bulyanhulu Mine and among mine-workers and their dependants

- To ensure the participatory involvement of the DHMT, local communities and health workers in the implementation of a community-based programme focusing on reproductive health and malaria control in the communities around Bulyanhulu Mine

- To design and implement interventions to control the spread of malaria, HIV and STIs in the mining workforce and surrounding communities

- To assist in enhancing specific services at Kahama District Hospital to improve the quality of care, with logistical support from Kahama Mining Corporation Limited and International SOS

- To organise and run HIV, tuberculosis, STI and malaria awareness workshops and a peer educator scheme for mine staff

- To measure the impact and assess the effectiveness of the community health programme in the communities around the mine and among the mine-workers themselves

Box 8.2 **Key objectives of the Bulyanhulu Mine health project**

The DHMT facilitates and co-ordinates the programme and ensures that the activities are consistent with national and district health policies. In addition, the DHMT has specific responsibilities, such as ensuring that the dispensary is staffed and adequately resourced with medicines and equipment. Each of the villages has a village health committee, and these committees ensure that the specific needs and expectations of the village are highlighted in their development plans. These committees also obtain feedback from the district medical officer (DMO) on the community health programme. The village health committees have assisted in identifying and supporting the work of the community peer educators. Box 8.3 provides a summary of the current status of implementation of the programme.

The African Medical and Research Foundation (AMREF):

- Has participated in supervising the rehabilitation of selected health units and assisted in ordering supplementary drugs and consumables for the selected health units
- Conducts monthly supportive supervision and monitoring visits to the selected health units as well as carrying out other community services
- Attends monthly meetings with the District Health Management Team (DHMT), conducts quarterly supportive supervisions of health units and community structures with members of the DHMT, holds monthly support meetings for community peer educators and provides ongoing peer educator training and supervision
- Is in the process of designing and implementing interventions to control the spread of malaria, HIV and sexually transmitted infections (STIs) in the mining workforce and surrounding communities; it has:
    - Held sensitisation meetings with the owners of food and recreational facilities and with commercial sex workers (CSWs)
    - Provided a baseline supply of condoms, insect nets and insecticide tablets in order to establish a revolving fund mechanism
    - Provided support and supervision for schoolteachers
    - Produced and distributed health learning materials
    - Has recently established in Kakola, in partnership with Kahama Mining Corporation Limited (KMCL), a community-based voluntary service providing counselling and HIV testing
- Has provided in-service training for laboratory personnel at Kahama District Hospital and has assisted the hospital in procuring laboratory equipment, and surgical and maternity ward furniture and equipment
- Has organised and run initial and follow-up HIV, STI, tuberculosis and malaria awareness workshops for mine staff
- Provides monthly progress reports to KMCL, detailing the action completed and outcomes achieved

---

Box 8.3 Current status of the implementation of the community health programme

KMCL has built a privately run clinic on the mine site that is accessible to mine employees and surrounding communities. The clinic is intended primarily to serve the mine-workers and to address health issues associated with mine operations, although the clinic is also accessible to local communities (the cost to the community of attending the clinic being subsidised by the slightly higher charges paid by KMCL employees). Apart from the mine clinic, KMCL has decided that it will not build private medical facilities. Rather, KMCL has decided to support community health programmes and to ensure that government-provided services and facilities meet the community's requirements. Therefore, as part of the community health programme, KMCL has assisted in the refurbishment of the Bugarama Dispensary, including the construction of a new wing, the provision of furniture and equipment and the building of staff houses. In addition, KMCL will, during the period 2002–2003, provide assistance in the rehabilitation of the Lunguya Health Centre and the Kahama District Hospital. KMCL's overall aim is to ensure that there is a consistently high standard of healthcare available at all levels, from government facilities, the dispensary, through to the health centre and the district hospital. This maximises the likelihood that the facilities will be maintained and operated even after the mine closes. This approach should also mean that KMCL will not be required to provide longer-term support to such facilities. A further advantage is that KDC has the responsibility for providing staff for the dispensary and for the other health facilities. KDC has welcomed KMCL's focus on public health services, as this approach provides the district with resources and capacity that are not presently available while also ensuring that KMCL's interventions in health services are sustainable and provide a longer-term resource for the local community. KDC has approached the Tanzanian Ministry of Health to increase the number of health workers in the area and has transferred four staff to operate and manage the dispensary.

Whereas the funding for the community health programme is provided by KMCL, the implementation of the programme is guided by the district and the villages. A steering committee has been established to oversee and facilitate the community health programme. The steering committee includes representatives from International SOS (which manages the clinic at the mine site), KMCL the DMO, the London School of Hygiene and Tropical Medicine and AMREF. The steering committee meets on an as-needed basis, and a subcommittee (comprising the DMO, KMCL's Medical Director and AMREF) meets every month. The minutes of subcommittee meetings are provided to all members of the steering committee.

8.7 Division of roles

The resources and competences committed by the partners are summarised in Table 8.1. Although KMCL has played a lead role in specifying tasks and activities and defining schedules, the roles and resources are not as clear-cut as those of a project manager specifying tasks and activities, with contractors then implementing those tasks. The process, in fact, involves multiple actors contributing to the process. The use of contracts and KMCL's project management resources provides the means whereby the various projects are implemented, with the other project partners contributing resources and expertise in line with their core competences and resources. In fact, on the health and education programmes, even though KMCL provides the financial resources the projects are led by the NGOs in close collaboration with KDC and the local communities, KMCL having a relatively minor role to play in implementation.

Partner	Partnership focus			
	Education	Health	Housing	Water
Business:				
KMCL	• Project management • Financial resources • Construction of classrooms	• Project management • Financial resources • Refurbishment of dispensary	• Project management • Financial resources • Facilitation of employment creation in the local community	• Project management • Financial resources for construction and community education
NGOs:				
	CARE Tanzania • Project management • Produce training manuals • Train and mentor teachers • Community mobilisation	*AMREF* • Training of health workers • Supervision of dispensary • Production of health-promotion materials • Liaising with government and local communities		*WEDECO* • System operation and maintenance • Community mobilisation • Community education
Government:				
KDC	• Recruitment of teachers • Supervision of schools • Provision of learning materials • Provision of construction materials for school buildings • Logistical support for the programme	• Recruitment and training of dispensary staff • Supervision of the dispensary • Procurement of drugs and other materials • Logistical support for programme	• Preparation of land-use plans • Assistance to KMCL in land acquisition and negotiations	• Contributing to the design of the water system

AMREF = African Medical and Research Foundation
KDC = Kahama District Council
KMCL = Kahama Mining Corporation Limited

Table 8.1 **Division of roles and competences in the social development programme**
(continued over)

Partner	Partnership focus			
	Education	Health	Housing	Water
Government (cont.):				
Village government and local communities	• Contribution to labour and land for construction work • Exploration of the community's potential financial contribution to education • Mobilisation of the community to participate in adult education • Provision of feedback on the education programme	• Facilitation of the identification of peer educators • Assisting peer educators with awareness campaigns • Provision of feedback on the health programme	• Assisting KMCL in the payment of compensation • Preparation of land-use plans • Provision of advice on the required social facilities • Mobilisation of the communities to assist in building facilities	• Contribution to the identification of water points • The building of water points • Participation in water user groups • The taking of long-term responsibility for the operation and management of the water system

KMCL = Kahama Mining Corporation Limited

Table 8.1 (continued)

‛At this stage, it is probably fair to say that our community development programme is not a 'perfect tri-sector partnership'. However, we are moving in that direction and expect that future projects and programmes will be much closer to the partnership model. The reasons are that we are now seeing capacity being developed from the community development projects to date, the community-based organisations that are being established and the evolving experience with the bottom-up planning process.‛

Aida Kiangi, Kahama Mining Corporation Limited

It could be argued that the projects examined here are not really partnership projects (given that KMCL provides the bulk of the resources), but it is important to recognise the relative shortage of resources available to the communities concerned. For example, even though KDC has committed 25% of its locally derived income to implement the district development plan, this represents just 2% of the overall anticipated expenditure on the development plan. In this context, the resource contribution of KMCL has helped to overcome the key barrier to development (i.e. the limited financial resources that are available for development, in particular for infrastructure); also, through identifying potential revenue streams (e.g. water charges), KMCL has helped to ensure the longer-term financial sustainability of the various projects. At the start of the SDP process, community and government capacity was extremely limited, the bottom-up planning process was a new initiative (i.e. the community had to develop the capacity to define its own priorities), there were extremely low levels of education and skills in the local communities and there was a general lack of understanding of the role that can be played by the private sector (in particular, by large international corporations) in

> •KMCL is trying to get communities to contribute to their own development, and a key part of KMCL's activities is to give local communities the skills and information so that they can effectively lobby government, donor agencies and NGOs by themselves.•
>
> **Tony Meade, Kahama Mining Corporation Limited**

community development. Although KMCL's original intention was that the projects would be more equal partnerships, the lack of capacity in the community and in government and the absence of NGOs and community-based organisations in the local area meant that KMCL had to adopt a more 'hands-on' approach to the implementation of the SDP. KMCL has tried to structure the implementation of the SDP to ensure that community and government capacity and expertise are being developed as an integral part of the programme.

8.8 Outcomes

For all parties, the pooling of competences and sharing of responsibilities has provided measurable benefits. Box 8.4 summarises the added value of the partnership from the perspectives of business, community development impact and public-sector governance.

8.8.1 Business benefits

Even though the SDP has only been in place for approximately 18 months there are signs that the partnership approach adopted by KMCL is providing significant business benefits. In terms of the broader questions around the longer-term future of mining in Tanzania and the reputations of KMCL and Barrick Gold, the outcomes to date have been overwhelmingly positive. Although many of the debates around the future of mining in Tanzania are outside the direct influence of KMCL, it is clear that the SDP has enabled KMCL to provide real development benefits to local communities and to the region and to have these benefits recognised by local communities and local government. Furthermore, the SDP has enabled KMCL to demonstrate its openness, its commitment to community development and its willingness to be accountable to local communities.

At the operational level, it appears that the partnership process will enable KMCL to meet its own business objectives. The employee housing scheme is nearing completion and, based on the evidence that is available to date, it looks like the health, education and water programmes will help create a location where mine employees are happy to live and to bring their families. This should, in turn, enable

Business benefits

- Access to new mineral resources in Tanzania:
  - Enabled Kahama Mining Corporation Limited (KMCL) to demonstrate its commitment to community development as an integral part of mine operations
  - Enhanced community and political support (as evidenced by strong public statements of support for KMCL and the active involvement of community and government in the implementation of the SDP (social development programme).
- Recruiting and retaining high-quality employees:
  - Expedited land acquisition and minimised delays to the construction of the housing scheme
  - Increased the likelihood of the successful integration of mine-workers into the local community as a consequence of the good relationship between KMCL and the local community
- Management of community expectations and reduced community dependence:
  - The SDP is understood by all parties to define the scope of KMCL's community development activities, thereby enabling KMCL to manage community expectations
- Cost-effectiveness of community development expenditure:
  - Leverage of contributions (labour and materials) from local government and communities for the construction of school classrooms and other buildings
  - Transfer of the longer-term responsibility for infrastructure management and maintenance to communities and local government
  - Ensured that local government is committed to staffing schools and health facilities adequately (with these costs to be met from the District Council's budgets)
- Corporate reputation:
  - Communities, non-governmental organisations and government see KMCL as trustworthy and committed to community development

Community development impact

- Improved infrastructure:
  - Access to a reliable water supply for the 5,000 residents of Bugarama and Ilogi villages and the 30,000 people that live along or in proximity to the Lake Victoria pipeline
  - Improved local infrastructure (e.g. shops, community centre and school buildings), designed in accordance with the community's needs
  - Development of community capacity (e.g. management skills and implementation of revenue-earning systems) to effectively manage the provided infrastructure
- Educational security:
  - Increased rates of enrolment in primary schools (in Standard I, the enrolment and attendance rates are close to 100%, compared with historic levels of 60–80%)

Box 8.4 **Added value of partnership process** (continued opposite)

- Health security:
  - Increased community knowledge of HIV, AIDS and malaria and the adoption of improved health practices to prevent the spread of these diseases
- Local economic development:
  - Increased employment opportunities for local people in the construction of the housing scheme
- Community capacity:
  - Improved community capacity to manage infrastructure
  - Improved capacity to make decisions on community development (e.g. through project steering committees) and to lobby government

Public-sector governance

- Effectiveness of social programmes (health and education):
  - The SDP has enabled Kahama District Council to implement most of its development plans for the Bugarama area, despite the limited budgets available to the council
  - The development of community capacity to manage infrastructure projects (e.g. regarding water supply and school buildings) means that a longer-term liability for the district council is not being created
  - The SDP is assisting the district council in ways that benefit the entire Kahama District (e.g. through the refurbishment of the Kahama District Hospital)
- Accountability and transparency:
  - Increased accountability of district council to local communities (as a consequence of increased community knowledge of their rights)

Box 8.4 (continued)

KMCL to meet its targets for reducing the number of expatriate employees. It is too early to say how effective the community health education programme will be but it appears that the integration of mine-workers into the local community (into stable social and community structures) and the provision of a comprehensive community health system will help minimise the problems with HIV, AIDS, STIs and malaria in the workforce.

The partnership approach has also been cost-effective. The relationships with local government and local communities have reduced the time required to implement various initiatives (e.g. expediting the land-acquisition processes for the housing scheme). Through the processes of discussing, communicating and implementing the SDP, KMCL has created an understanding in the community and in government of the role to be played by KMCL in community development, thereby helping KMCL to manage community expectations. The high degree of community and government involvement in the various programmes is also likely to reduce longer-term dependence on KMCL. There are signs that the community is increasingly capable of managing its own infrastructure, and the community and government support for the health and education programmes increases the likelihood that these initiatives will provide sustainable, longer-term benefits. That

'The credibility we have gained through the SDP has enabled us to develop good relationships with all communities in the region. For example, our ongoing exploration programme has impacted on some individuals in the community, necessitating the payment of compensation for land disturbance. Rather than these becoming disputes, communities see that they can approach us directly and we will help them solve the problem, quickly and fairly.'

Aida Kiangi, Kahama Mining Corporation Limited

is, although KMCL has provided much of the initial (capital) investment, the majority of the operational costs (e.g. the salaries of teachers and health professionals and the cost of infrastructure maintenance) will be borne by local government or by local communities. It also appears that, through ensuring that community development initiatives are focused on activities that are sustainable in the longer term, KMCL has helped to significantly reduce its longer-term liabilities (e.g. when looking at mine closure and decommissioning). However, it is too early to draw firm conclusions on this issue.

A number of risks still remain. The first is the reality that the mine is by far the largest investment in the area, with the likelihood that local and regional economic development will rely on the presence of the mine. The consequence is that there may be significant economic dislocation when the mine is finally closed, and this may create a pressure for compensation or for post-closure community development activities. The second is that there is a question regarding whether or not community development activities (e.g. health, education and infrastructure) will lead to additional business development or donor or NGO activity in the area. To date, much of the community development activity has proceeded on the assumption that these additional benefits will follow as infrastructure and local education levels improve. It is not possible, at this stage, to draw a firm conclusion on the accuracy of this assumption.

'Many NGOs still seem to be sitting on the fence and watching how projects proceed before deciding to enter into partnerships.'

Aida Kiangi, Kahama Mining Corporation Limited

8.8.2 Community development and public-sector governance impacts

The implementation of the SDP has provided direct benefits to the local communities in terms of infrastructure, health and educational outcomes and in terms of community capacity. The infrastructure benefits (in particular, water supply, educational and community infrastructure) are the most tangible outcomes. In all of these areas, KMCL worked with the local communities and with the village governments to identify needs and to agree priorities. The infrastructure is, progressively, being handed over to the community for management and maintenance. Significant time and effort has been invested to make sure that the community is in a position to ensure the long-term sustainability of the infrastructure. This has included making the community aware of its responsibilities for infrastructure management and maintenance, mobilising the community to be involved in the provision of the infrastructure (e.g. construction) and providing the community with the skills necessary to manage and maintain the infrastructure.

The aims of the education programme are to improve the quality of teaching in the schools, strengthen school committees, provide access to basic adult education and assist the communities in improving the physical infrastructure (e.g. classrooms and teachers' housing). On health, the intention is to implement a programme of health promotion, disease prevention and improved treatment for mine-workers and communities surrounding the mine, with a particular focus on HIV and AIDs, STIs, tuberculosis and malaria. Although it is too early to say what the outcomes of the health and education programmes will be, there is a consensus that government and community support maximise the likelihood that both programmes will achieve their specified outcomes and provide long-term sustainable health and educational benefits to the community.

Community capacity-building has been an integral part of the various partnership projects. The community has been extensively consulted on the SDP and has played an active role in the various projects and programmes. Significant improvements in community capacity (e.g. ability to contribute to decisions, and willingness and ability to take responsibility for infrastructure maintenance) have been reported.

From a public-sector governance perspective, the primary outcome has been that the SDP has enabled KDC to progress the implementation of the policy goals specified in the district development plan. This, by extension, has enabled the village and ward governments to achieve the outcomes defined in the community bottom-up planning process. The other important outcome has been that the implementation of the SDP has reinforced the importance of government to the local communities.

8.9 Conclusions

Two factors were central to the effectiveness of the partnership arrangements. The first was that the partnership process actively sought contributions from a range of stakeholders (from different levels of government, from local communities and from NGOs). This created collective ownership of the projects and ensured that different resources and capacities were brought to the implementation of the SDP. The second was that KMCL's core competences (in particular, its contract management, quality control and project management skills) were brought into the SDP. KMCL is now using the SDP to develop these and other competences in its partner organisations.

Through the SDP, KMCL has acted as a catalyst for community development in the vicinity of the mine by overcoming a major barrier to providing basic infrastructure (i.e. a lack of financial capacity) and by developing community and government capacity to take over responsibility for infrastructure management in the long term.

The situation faced by KMCL (i.e. pressure to provide additional social benefits, combined with limited financial and management capacity in local government) is common in the global mining industry. KMCL's approach to community development (i.e. convening multi-sector steering committees and focusing on community infrastructure that draws on the core competences of the business and contributes to the business case for staff recruitment) perhaps offers a framework by which others can think through how social issues might best be managed in the vicinity of mining operations.

As a consequence of KMCL's SDP, there is increased interest in Tanzania both in partnership processes and in the potential contribution of the private sector to development outcomes. Although some government officials continue to see the debate in terms of the private sector's financial contribution, there appears to be a growing recognition that the partnership model, where resources are pooled and where capacity-building (e.g. through the integration of community training into infrastructure development projects) is an integral part of the project, offers the potential for real development benefits. The NGOs involved with KMCL have indicated that they strongly support the concept of partnering with the private sector and that they see the partnership with KMCL as a model for future development projects. However, other NGOs in Tanzania remain unconvinced, and although some have asked CARE Tanzania and AMREF about the manner in which the partnership process works and the advantages and disadvantages of partnering, it appears that many are adopting a 'wait and see' approach to see how the current partnership projects evolve over time.

Perhaps the most interesting perspective has been the way in which the community has responded. At the start of the SDP process, KMCL's experience was that community members either had no understanding of what KMCL could offer or expected KMCL to do 'everything'. Since then, KMCL has noted a significant change in the community, not only as a result of the capacity-building and education processes but also from the actual implementation of projects. KMCL has indicated that the requests for assistance from the local community have reduced in number and, more significantly, the requests for assistance are becoming more specific and are for assistance where the community has exhausted other avenues for addressing the problem. That is, there are growing signs that the local community is increasingly willing and able to take responsibility for its own long-term development.

9
Konkola Copper
Mines plc, Zambia
Local business development and partnerships

Rory Sullivan and Michael Warner, with Theo Hacking

This chapter examines the partnership approach that has underpinned the efforts of Konkola Copper Mines plc (KCM) to (a) develop local businesses and contribute to poverty alleviation in the short term and (b) diversify the economy of the Zambian Copperbelt in the longer term. Zambia, in common with many countries, has privatised its mining industry in an effort to revitalise loss-making mines that were threatened with closure. The privatisation process has been accompanied by a significant downsizing of the labour force as older mines have been worked out and because of the need to restore the international competitiveness of the remaining mines. Local business development is seen as critical to reducing the effects of retrenchments on the Copperbelt. The privatisation process has been complicated by the historical role of the state-owned mining industry as the dominant development agent, providing virtually all social services to the communities in which it sourced its labour. With the significant economic and other challenges faced by the newly privatised industry it has become clear that the industry is not in a position to alleviate poverty or diversify the local economy on its own and needs to work in partnership with government and civil society to achieve these aims.

The approach adopted by KCM involved a detailed stakeholder mapping exercise to identify potential partners, their underlying interests, their core competences and their willingness to enter into partnership projects relating to local business development. This process led to four themes for local business development being identified: namely, the establishment of a venture capital facility for small and medium-sized enterprises (SMEs), the mapping of SME facilitation and capacity-building services, the preparation of a feasibility study to look at the constraints and opportunities for micro-enterprise development in the agricultural sector and the securing of a 'champion' within central government to further the 'enabling environment' for effective SME development. The stakeholders identified objectives for each of these themes and the possible contributions that each could make to enable these objectives to be met. These were carried through into the social management plan (SMP) prepared by KCM, which, among other community development initiatives, detailed the contribution that would be made by KCM to local business development.

Since the completion of the SMP there has been considerable uncertainty around the future of KCM. This has delayed the implementation of certain components of the SMP, in particular those relating to local business development. However, it is expected that, once implemented, the SMP will provide a significant boost to efforts to alleviate poverty and diversify the local economy, through enhancing the institutional structure for SME development.

9.1 Social context

The Copperbelt of Zambia and the Democratic republic of Congo contain approximately 10% of the world's copper reserves. The Zambian mining industry was nationalised in 1970, and the industry was subsequently consolidated under the centralised management of Zambia Consolidated Copper Mines Ltd (ZCCM). Historically, copper mining has contributed over 85% of Zambia's foreign exchange earnings and, in some years, as much as 20% of gross domestic product (GDP). However, by the end of the 1990s this contribution had dropped to between 8% and 10% of GDP.

In the mid-1990s the Zambian government moved to privatise the mining industry in an effort to revitalise the industry and attract investment. This process was accompanied by retrenchments (see Table 9.1) and the withdrawal of the mining industry from the provision of many services (physical infrastructure, housing, healthcare, education and food) that it previously provided to communities in the vicinity of the mines.

Mine	July 1998	End 2000
Konkola	4,637	2,972
Nchanga	8,578	6,490
Nampundwe	384	293

Table 9.1 Changes in employment in ZCCM's Copperbelt mines

In the past, retrenched or retired employees tended to return to their home districts. More recently, the trend has been for former employees to remain on the Copperbelt. There has also been an influx of people into the Copperbelt from elsewhere in Zambia where economic circumstances are even more severe. The consequence has been that the effects of the retrenchment programmes have become more localised, with greater impacts on the communities in the immediate vicinity of the mining operations. Although the formula used by ZCCM to calculate retrenchment benefits was considered generous by international standards, it has been common for individuals to quickly exhaust their retrenchment package and, with few alternative sources of employment, to become dependent on family support and subsistence farming to survive. The effects have been further exacerbated by the high dependence of communities on the revenue and employment generated by the mining industry.

9.2 Business context

In the privatisation of Zambian Consolidated Copper Mines (ZCCM), Konkola Copper Mines plc (KCM) acquired the assets of the Konkola Division, the Nchanga Division and the Nampundwe pyrite mine and an option to acquire the smelting and refining divisions of the Nkana division. KCM's shareholders were Zambian Copper Investments (ZCI), ZCCM Investment Holdings, International Finance Corporation (IFC) and CDC Group (formerly the Commonwealth Development Corporation). Anglo American plc owned 51% of ZCI, giving it an effective shareholding in KCM of approximately 33%. As part of the privatisation process, KCM undertook to investigate the development of the Konkola Deep Mine Project, which would have become the world's largest underground copper mine. However, it was not possible to raise the financing that would have enabled the deep mine project to proceed. In August 2002, Anglo American announced that agreement had been reached with the government of Zambia and with the other investors for Anglo American, IFC and CDC Group to withdraw as direct or indirect shareholders of KCM. The key elements of the agreement are that (a) Anglo American will contribute a further US$30 million in cash and lend up to US$26.5 million on favourable terms to KCM in order to keep the mines operating, (b) KCM will be restructured so that the new shareholders of KCM will be ZCI (58%) and ZCCM (42%), (c) Anglo American will establish an independent foundation to invest in projects aimed at diversifying the economy of the Copperbelt and (d) Anglo American will transfer a 41.4% shareholding in ZCI to the foundation.

9.3 The partnering process

As part of its shareholder agreements, KCM was required to develop a social management plan (SMP) covering all the company's operations. The SMP development process was highly participatory, involving engagement with society and stakeholders and with KCM management and staff. The engagement process was intended to (a) improve the relevance of the SMP to local community needs, (b) create ownership among stakeholders, (c) foster ownership of the SMP within KCM, (d) build the capacity of KCM management and staff to implement the plans developed and (e) create a process of active dialogue between KCM and society that would continue beyond the SMP preparation process.

The SMP preparation process involved a participatory sustainable livelihood analysis to determine the key development issues and an assessment of KCM's potential to contribute to community development. This ensured that the proposed development strategy was aligned with KCM's core business strategies and hence able to add value across a number of fronts. Box 9.1 summarises the commitments made in the SMP to local business development.

KCM recognised that it could not address local employment needs on its own and that political and community support and involvement were necessary for its initiatives to be effective. In July 2000 KCM invited Business Partners for Development (BPD) to facilitate a process of dialogue and partnership-building with civil society and government, with the aim of finding the most efficient use of available resources, expertise, leadership and opportunities in the vicinity of KCM mines in order to promote local business development.

An initial scoping workshop was held in October 2000 to explore future directions for a partnership approach to sustainable local business development in the vicinity of KCM's facilities and operations. The participants included representatives from KCM, municipal councils, small business advisors, social development consultants, community-based non-governmental organisations (NGOs), govern-

---

In its social management plan, KCM committed itself to:

- Design and implement a retrenchment training plan for its workers from 2001 until the closure of the various facilities and mines

- Implement multi-skilling and training programmes, focusing on life skills, agriculture, manufacturing, information technology and business management

- Design and implement local employment enhancement strategies, focusing on the employment of local residents (e.g. during the construction and operational phases of the Konkola Deep Mine Project)

- Investigate the provision of micro-business development training

- Investigate opportunities and design a plan for employing more women in the company

- Design and implement an 'expatriate replacement strategy' to ensure that over a feasible period of time expatriate employees will be replaced by local expertise where possible

- Implement a procurement strategy that supports local economic development, including publishing and distributing information and material about how to do business with KCM and assisting with the development of mechanisms for joint ventures and other partnerships between suppliers

- Establish a fund to promote the development of the agriculture and medium-scale manufacturing sector

---

Box 9.1 Konkola Copper Mine (KCM)'s local business development commitments

ment development programmes and vocational training organisations. As an outcome from the workshop, a consultant was commissioned to consult with stakeholders, to undertake a 'situation analysis' of the options and needs for long-term sustainable local business development and to identify the resources and services that organisations might be willing to commit and under what conditions.

In February 2001 partnering workshops were held with the aim of reaching consensus on the vision and objectives of the partnership (see Box 9.2), allocating roles and responsibilities and preparing a work-plan. From the workshops, organisations identified the resources they could contribute to promote local business and/or the resources or roles needed to overcome key local business constraints.

Four 'themes' to promote local business development in the Copperbelt were agreed:

- The development of a KCM-funded venture capital facility to finance small and medium-sized enterprises (SMEs)

- The mapping of SME facilitation and capacity-building services

- The preparation of a feasibility study looking at the constraints and opportunities for micro-enterprise development in the agricultural sector

- The need to secure a 'champion' within central government to further the 'enabling environment' for effective SME development

Financing for small and medium-sized enterprises

•Empower Zambian citizens to become key players in the economic activity of the Copperbelt.•

Creating an enabling environment

•Ensure the implementation of policies, laws and systems that actively promote local business development, and are easy to understand and operate.•

Support for micro-enterprises

•Improve the livelihood of vulnerable groups, which includes: retrenchees, un- and under-employed and orphans, single/female-headed households, the elderly and pensioners, in selected areas through the promotion of largely agro-based micro-enterprises.•

Facilitation and capacity-building for small and medium-sized enterprises

A series of objectives were identified, covering activities such as training, technical assistance, facilitation of business linkages, capacity-building and business plan development.

Box 9.2 Vision statements for partnership themes

Source: partnering workshop, February 2001

9.3.1 Implementation of the SMP

Due to the uncertainties surrounding KCM's future, there has been limited progress on the four partnership themes identified at the February 2001 workshop. The one exception has been the further investigation of the structure and operation of the SME Venture Capital Facility. It was agreed that, given the capacity and expertise available within KCM and its shareholders, this initiative could be fast-tracked, without (at least in the initial stages) the involvement of the other organisations that attended the February 2001 workshop. This approach offered the potential for a more rapid implementation of the SME Venture Capital Facility than would have otherwise been the case.

Consultants were commissioned to prepare a report to assess the possible forms that the SME Venture Capital Facility could take and the manner in which the fund could be capitalised. Following this initial investigation, the IFC commissioned an independent consultant to conduct a more detailed investigation of the scope of such a facility. The IFC report proposed that the SME fund would be US$3.6 million, which would be used for equity, quasi-equity and loan financing. It was envisaged that the facility would be 100% owned by KCM, with KCM meeting all set-up and operating costs of the facility. The initial investors were expected to be KCM, ZCI, IFC and CDC Group. The IFC report was presented to KCM's board at the end of 2001 and the board agreed, in principle, to take the idea forward once KCM had attained profitability. However, since that decision, the uncertainties around KCM's future have meant that the company has not been in a position to provide the initial funding (capital or establishment and administration costs) required to establish the Venture Capital Facility.

At the time of writing (September 2002), KCM has adopted, and started to implement, the final SMP. The Copperbelt Development Foundation, once established, is likely to take on the functions that were originally envisaged for the SME Venture Capital Facility. It is likely that, once funds are available, the initiation of these functions will be reasonably quick, given the time and effort that has been invested in developing the conceptual design for the SME Venture Capital Facility. In the interim, the KCM Small Business Development Unit (SBDU) has continued to promote the local SME sector. Since vesting, contracts worth over K1.7 billion (approximately US$390,000) have been awarded to local small businesses through the SBDU and, in total, KCM has awarded contracts worth approximately US$226 million to local suppliers (some 68% of the total value of contracts awarded).

There is also evidence that KCM is starting to internalise the concepts of partnership and apply these concepts in other areas, as illustrated by the examples in Box 9.3.

- KCM has instituted a malaria control programme (in partnership with district councils) addressing all of the houses within the mine site and municipal areas around Konkola, Nchanga and Nampundwe. Over 32,000 housing units have been sprayed, resulting in a reduction of 58% in the incidence of malaria. In Kitwe, Smelterco is one of the partners (along with the government, other businesses and NGOs) in a malaria control programme. KCM's malaria control programmes have been recognised as a model for the Zambian government's 'Roll Back Malaria' Campaign.

- In 2001, in conjunction with the Mine Workers Union of Zambia (MUZ), KCM launched the first HIV prevalence survey to be undertaken in the Zambian mining industry. Over 9,000 employees participated in a confidential survey to enable KCM to determine the nature of the HIV/AIDS problem and to identify appropriate interventions. The survey was supported by a voluntary counselling and testing scheme to enable KCM employees and their dependents to know more about HIV/AIDS and to find out their HIV status.

Box 9.3 Emerging partnerships

9.4 Division of roles

The resources and competences that could be contributed to a partnership by various parties were identified during the partnering workshops. The proposed commitments are summarised in Table 9.2.

9.5 Outcomes

Box 9.4 summarises the added value expected from the partnership approach adopted for local economic development. Added value is considered from three perspectives: business benefits, community development impact and good public-sector governance.

9.6 Conclusions

The business context on the Copperbelt is extremely complex, with KCM having to address issues as disparate as a loss-making business, the need to reduce employee numbers, community dependence on ZCCM, capacity and resource deficits in government, and the uncertainties resulting from Anglo American's withdrawal from its investment in KCM. The partnership approach to local business develop-

Partner	Partnership			
	SME financing	**Enabling environment**	**Support for micro-enterprises**	**Facilitation and capacity-building**
KCM	• Capital • Co-ordination	• Identifying of government sponsors • Contributing to dialogue	• Approaching ZCCM regarding the availability of land for agriculture	• Retrenchee counselling and training
BBZ and INVEST	• Leasing, banking and insurance services	N.A.	N.A.	N.A.
World Bank	N.A.	• Identifying government sponsors • Contributing to dialogue	N.A.	N.A.
DFID and USAID	N.A.	• Contributing to dialogue	N.A.	N.A.
Town clerk (Nchanga)	N.A.	• Contributing to dialogue	N.A.	N.A.
CARE Zambia, ZAMTIE and EU	N.A.	N.A.	• Gathering and sharing information	N.A.
APDF, IESC and CBE	N.A.	N.A.	N.A.	• Training • Provision of technical assistance

N.A. = not applicable   APDF = African Project Development Facility   BBZ = Barclays Bank Zambia
CBE = Citizens for a Better Environment   DFID = Department for International Development
IESC = International Executives Service Corps   INVEST = Invest Trust   KCM = Konkola Copper Mines plc
PSDP = Private Sector Development Programme (EU)   SMEs = small and medium-sized enterprises
USAID = US Agency for International Development   ZAMTIE = Zambian Trade and Environment Enterprise
ZCCM = Zambian Consolidated Copper Mines   ZCSMBA = Zambian Chamber of Small and Medium Business
Associations

Table 9.2 Division of roles and competences

Business benefits

- Managing community expectations during a period of business uncertainty:
  - Achievement of political and community consensus around the contribution of Konkola Copper Mines plc (KCM) to local business development and employment
  - Ability of KCM to budget accurately for local business development initiatives and to contain this expenditure within agreed limits
- Reduced dependence on KCM over time:
  - Greater resources and a broader set of competences and skills brought to local business development programmes
  - Government and communities take responsibility for the overall implementation and success of the programme, thereby reducing community expectations of, and dependence on, KCM
- Quality of local business development initiatives:
  - Greater likelihood that local business development initiatives will be successful (e.g. through the development of an enabling environment, through the provision of support and resources for local businesses, through focusing on areas of greatest opportunities and through creating a culture where mining is not seen as the only source of income or employment)
- Cost-effectiveness of business development expenditure:
  - Clear definition of the financial contributions of KCM to (a) retrenchment payments and associated training and counselling services, (b) initial funding for the development fund (which will be run on a commercial basis) and (c) some co-ordination, facilitation, support, capacity and skills provision
  - Commitment of other parties to contribute resources and competences to the local business development programme
- Corporate reputation:
  - Enables KCM to demonstrate its commitment to community development
  - Enables KCM to develop good working relationships with key stakeholders (government, donor agencies and local communities)

Community development impact

- Local economic diversification (i.e. to be less dependent on mining):
  - Leverage of resources and competences into a structured programme for local economic development, with a focus on economic diversification and market development, both within and beyond the mining industry
- Creation of enabling environment for local business development:
  - Active government support for local business development initiatives
- Broadening of the sources of finance for small and medium-sized enterprises (SMEs):
  - Provision of a source of funds for SMEs established by retrenched miners and facilitation of market access for these SMEs

Box 9.4 **Expected added value of the partnership process** (continued over)

- Community capacity:
  - Development of management skills and knowledge of partnership processes for local business development
  - Improved understanding of the potential of other actors (e.g. KCM, other companies, government and donor agencies) to contribute to local business development

Public-sector governance

- Leverage of resources from other parties:
  - Receipt of additional resources from partners
  - The creation of a more strategic local economic development strategy that harnesses the contributions of different parties to multiply the economic benefits of local business development initiatives
- Government capacity:
  - Enhanced capacity of government to contribute to partnerships for local economic development

Box 9.4 (continued)

ment consequently offered a range of business benefits to KCM. These included a much more co-ordinated approach to local business development, reduced dependence on ZCCM over time and reduced expenditures on local business development activities.

Although there have been delays in establishing the partnerships projects, KCM's own local business development initiatives (through, in particular, its Small Business Development Unit) have provided benefits for the partnership process, including (a) the development of some momentum for the four partnership themes, (b) the provision of a forum for updating the partners on KCM's situation, (c) enabling the partners to identify alternatives (e.g. lower-cost options and different lead agencies) to the partnership themes, (d) maintaining and developing relationships between the project partners, (e) developing trust and mutual understanding between the partners and (f) developing the capacity required to undertake more ambitious projects. It is interesting to see that KCM is beginning to internalise the concept and benefits of tri-sector partnerships (as evidenced by the partnership initiatives in relation to employee and public health) and appears to have developed the necessary skills to explore and negotiate complex partnership arrangements without external assistance.

The process followed by KCM to map and engage stakeholders, to establish competences and to determine how these competences may be combined led to four potentially effective partnership themes being identified. However, the uncertainty around KCM's future is a common feature of many mining projects. In the broader context of the mining industry, KCM's experience indicates that capacity-building needs to be explicitly considered at the start of the partnership-building process in order to reduce dependence on the company as soon as possible, thereby increasing the likelihood of the partnership continuing to function even if circumstances force the company to relinquish its leadership role. Although there is a risk that such capacity-building may be perceived as the company replacing government, the critical issue is that building the capacity of communities (e.g. to manage their own development and to establish and grow their own businesses) is essential to ensure that communities are not dependent on the company in the longer term.

10
Kelian Equatorial Mining, Indonesia
Mine closure

Ralph Hamann

It is becoming increasingly important for mining companies to manage social issues resulting from mining activity and to demonstrate maximum development benefit. This is especially pertinent to the closure phase of mine operations, particularly in rural areas where communities are dependent on the socioeconomic benefits of the mine. This chapter describes and analyses the tri-sector partnership approach applied to the management of environmental and social issues related to the closure of the Kelian Equatorial Mining (KEM) project. In the context of a highly dynamic and difficult operating environment, this partnership achieves positive outcomes and promises further benefits for all participant stakeholders, and it is likely that its overall objective— 'responsible mine closure'—will be met. These benefits are related primarily to the ability of the partnership to establish the buy-in of all relevant stakeholders and to create an accountable and transparent framework for making consensus-based decisions, which allow for the collective ownership of decisions and actions taken. This case study, therefore, shows that tri-sector partnerships can be successfully implemented in a highly dynamic and even conflict-prone institutional context, but that this requires far-reaching commitment from all participants—from the company in particular.

10.1 Context

Kelian Equatorial Mining (KEM) operates a large open-cut gold mine in a remote area 200 km north-west of Balikpapan in East Kalimantan. The mine has had significant impacts on the rural economy and local communities over the past decade. It is owned 90% by Rio Tinto plc and 10% by PT Harita Jayaraya, an Indonesian partner. The mine began commercial operations in 1992, after a contract of work was signed with the Indonesian government in 1985, and produces an average of 400,000 ounces of gold a year. The mine is scheduled to close in 2004. Since the fall of President Suharto in 1998, the importance of local government and the need for local people to participate in and benefit from decision-making have increased significantly. These national developments have implications at the local level at Kelian and impact on the way KEM is perceived.

The mine was established in 1985 under the Suharto regime, when most benefits of large industries went to central government, with little concern for local communities. So, although KEM did, in fact, demonstrate some measure of social responsibility towards local communities (as is evident from the provision of infrastructure in a number of local villages, as well as other social services), more recently KEM has been confronted with perceptions that local communities have not benefited enough from mining. These perceptions were further strengthened because local people were concerned that benefits or compensation needed to be guaranteed before the closure of the mine. These institutional changes have contributed to a large degree of uncertainty at the local level. In the period 1999–2000 there was a period of troubled relations between KEM and local communities (culminating in a 40-day shutdown of operations). This conflict revolved around a number of issues, the most important of which were that:

- Most significantly, local community members felt that they had received no or insufficient compensation for the land that was used by the mine (either in the lease area or areas needed for mine-related infrastructure, such as the access road)

- There were allegations of human rights abuses by KEM staff, involving allegations of sexual misconduct

- Local communities felt that promises made by KEM regarding community development projects had not been met

- KEM employees were concerned that retrenchment packages were inadequate

These tensions were particularly problematic because the successful management of closure-related issues, such as the loss of local livelihoods, dam safety and environmental concerns, required the involvement of local communities and government. For the company, improved relationships with local stakeholders and a responsible mine closure planning process were vital both for continued operation until closure and for reputation assurance after closure.

10.2 Partnership process and structure

Early attempts to initiate a partnership for mine closure were hampered by the troubled relationship between KEM and local stakeholders, which concerned mainly grievances related to compensation for land. It was therefore necessary to first implement a dedicated and mutually agreed grievance-resolution process. The dispute did not need to be resolved entirely, but what was required was the initiation of a sincere and respected process that all parties believed would eventually lead to the resolution of all grievances. This allowed all stakeholders to come together to explore and design the partnership structure.

The Mine Closure Steering Committee (MCSC) was established in late 2000. Its first few meetings were dedicated to defining the objectives of the MCSC, its decision-making mechanisms and the roles and responsibilities of the representatives. It was also decided that there would be four working groups to research, explore and propose options as directed by the MCSC and take responsibility for consulting with constituents:

- Working Group 1: Dams

- Working Group 2: Environment

- Working Group 3: Site Uses and Assets

- Working Group 4: Community Development and District Planning

These decisions were formalised in the MCSC charter (see Appendix C), which provided a vital guide and point of reference for the ongoing process, allowing the partnership to adapt to changing circumstances or objectives.

Eligibility for MCSC membership is defined in the charter as those 'who are affected by, or who can affect, the closure of Kelian Mine' (see item 2.1 in Appendix C). This includes representatives from the company (at operational and corporate level), local, provincial and national government and local community groups. Although the MCSC consists of high-level representatives (it is co-chaired by the head of the district government and by the managing director of the mine), the working groups generally comprise more technically oriented representatives. Table 10.1 summarises the partnership development process.

The MCSC charter stipulates a clear focus for the partnership, mutually agreed criteria for membership, roles and responsibilities of members, consensus-based decision-making principles and dispute-resolution mechanisms. A list of criteria to be used in devising and deciding among options was also established, thereby providing for an objective framework for decision-making. These far-reaching measures to increase accountability and transparency, the company's commitment to a consensus-based decision-making process, the MCSC Secretariat's proactive communication strategy, the separation of the political and technical aspects of decision-making and effective third-party facilitation may be seen as key success factors for the partnership's success.

Local context	Partnership-related activity	Outcome

Mid-1999 to late 2000: partnership exploration

Local context	Partnership-related activity	Outcome
• Community and employee protests occur related, *inter alia*, to grievances about land compensation • Local community institutions are fragmented and conflicting and there are no rules of engagement or dispute resolution between stakeholders • Concerted dispute-resolution efforts in mid-2000 generate a principle-based framework for resolving the dispute, with an agreement on compensation payments in September 2000 • This agreement provides for better relationships between key stakeholders and a growing awareness about the need to work together	• KEM seeks to implement a closure statement, including a village baseline survey and setting up a consultative steering committee, but this is hampered by local community resistance, premised on the need to address the land compensation dispute • KEM and BPD–NRC explore the partnership opportunities, including a definition of key company objectives and process requirements • Persons within KEM who will take the partnership forward are identified	• KEM gained a heightened awareness of the need for an integrated and committed approach to building better stakeholder relationships and planning for mine closure • The land-compensation dispute-resolution process improved relationships between KEM and local stakeholders and demonstrated the benefits of facilitated negotiation rather than protest action by local communities

Late 2000 to mid-2001: partnership building

Local context	Partnership-related activity	Outcome
• Implementation of the land-compensation process is ongoing • Relationships are improved between KEM and local stakeholders (based also on improved communications after two communication offices were opened in the villages and one employee office opened on-site)	• In October 2000 local parties are convened by BPD–NRC and agree on a definition of joint work plans on mine-closure issues: this is the basis of the MCSC • The first three meetings of the MCSC are dedicated to reaching agreement on process issues, resulting in the MCSC charter • Communication activities are implemented, including communiqués after MCSC meetings, and a dedicated website is established	• The MCSC is set up as a structure for joint engagement, including initial agreement on its purpose, roles and responsibilities, its composition and its decision-making modalities • The MCSC charter provides a crucial guideline and point of reference for the partnership process

BPD = Business Partners for Development   KEM = Kelian Equatorial Mining
MCSC = Mine Closure Steering Committee   NRC = Natural Resources Cluster

Table 10.1 **Summary of the partnership development process** (continued over)

Local context	Partnership-related activity	Outcome

Mid-2001 to present: partnership maintenance

Local context	Partnership-related activity	Outcome
• Land compensation process nears completion • Relationships between KEM and local stakeholders improve on the basis of the MCSC and its initial tangible outcomes	• Quarterly meetings of the MCSC are held, convened by independent facilitators (in May, September and November 2001, and in February and March 2002) • Concomitant quarterly meetings are held of the four working groups (on dams, environment, site uses and assets, and community development and district planning) • There is increased deliberation and agreement on modalities and key indicators and objectives of the partnership	• Continual improvement of partnership structure to suit stakeholder requirements (e.g. in the selection of meetings locations) • Achievement of a tangible sense of progress and higher levels of buy-in from most stakeholders (although challenges related to representation and accountability remain) • Initial agreements reached on key closure issues (e.g. standards for dam safety) and responsibilities for implementation

KEM = Kelian Equatorial Mining   MCSC = Mine Closure Steering Committee

Table 10.1 (continued)

10.2.1 Decision-making processes

The MCSC and the working groups essentially constitute a participatory, deliberative decision-making forum. The implementation of decisions is not an explicit objective of the partnership, although the forum assigns roles and responsibilities for such implementation. However, there are a number of project-based or issue-based partnerships, particularly with respect to community development projects, that have varying degrees of interrelationship with the MCSC process. The most notable example is the school dormitory, which is a direct result of MCSC discussions and is currently being established with the active participation and contributions from the company, district government and local communities.

Whereas the partnership-building phase was characterised by negotiations on the process and decision-making procedures, a vital element of this phase of the partnership was the identification of substantive objectives and targets. In the February 2001 meeting of the MCSC, a set of questions were defined for each of the four working groups (see Box 10.1). These questions and the process of answering them were important in enabling the MCSC to achieve agreement on a number of substantive issues in May 2001. During the latter half of 2001, as the content issues became more familiar to all participants, it became clear that many of these issues were related to each other through a complex web of interdependences. It was therefore important to consider options for closure-related actions in an integrated

Working Group 1: Dams

- What engineered water-holding structures and associated facilities on-site will need to be maintained after closure?
- How do we know that they will be safe from earthquakes and floods (natural events) post-closure?
- How will the dams be protected from logging, mining and other human activities post-closure? Is liaison with the Working Group 3 required for this solution?
- To what standards (international and/or local) are the dams engineered?
- Who will take over responsibility for the dams and when?

Working Group 2: Environment

- What will be the quality of water bodies on the site and of water exiting the site post-closure?
- What environmental regulations are relevant post-closure?
- What will be the environmental monitoring programme post-closure, including water quality and rehabilitation?

Working Group 3: Site Uses and Assets

- What is the current and proposed status of the site (production forest or protected forest)?
- What can the site facilities and surrounding areas be used for?

A range of questions are to be considered for each option; for example, concerning whether the option is feasible, legal or beneficial to all stakeholders.

Working Group 4: Community Development and District Planning

- What are the community development programmes in the areas impacted by KEM?
- What are the completion dates, end-point criteria and transition plans for the community development programmes?
- How will the government and KEM progressively move responsibility for infrastructure and facilities to government, community and/or other parties?
- What needs to be done to attract developmental partners to the area?
- How can the district government, non-governmental organisations and other community groups be increasingly involved in the community development programmes?
- How will the community development programmes be aligned with the district development plan?

Box 10.1 Selected questions issued to the working groups by the Mine Closure Steering Committee in February 2001

fashion. The issue of the post-closure use of the site and assets (e.g. the mine camp) on the banks of Kelian River illustrates the complexity of the issues faced. Early agreements made by the MCSC specified that the water quality of drainage into the Kelian River must be of a high standard. This would require the establishment of wetlands in the area presently occupied by the mine camp, which would therefore have to be dismantled. However, dismantling the camp is contrary to the wishes of some local communities, who would like to see some of these buildings used for their benefit. A further complication is that the wetlands and their water-cleaning function would be jeopardised by alluvial mining in the area. Hence, a transparent and collective identification of priorities and commitments needs to take place by a range of different stakeholders in order to guarantee a sustainable, holistic and mutually beneficial solution.

10.2.2 Accountability and communication

The accountability measures and commitments contained in the MCSC charter are implemented and strengthened by a consistent and rigorous communication strategy employed by the Secretariat. So, for example, each working-group meeting, including extraordinary meetings, is documented so as to provide a clear 'decision-making trail' for how options to be recommended to the Steering Committee were arrived at. Most importantly, decisions made during MCSC meetings are summarised in a succinct communiqué and signed off by all members before the close of the meeting. This communiqué provides the basis for communication between the MCSC and the broader public (an easy-to-read version is prepared by the Secretariat), and is distributed in local communities and on the dedicated website (www.kelianmineclosure.org). Other channels of communication, such as radio broadcasts, are also used by the Secretariat. Over and above providing for public accountability of the process, this signed-off and broadly distributed communiqué also establishes commitment to decisions that have been taken, thereby preventing (at least to some extent) continuous attempts to re-open completed discussion topics. The incentive for expediency is, of course, particularly pertinent given the short time-frame before closure of the mine.

There are two further challenges related to this process. First, it gives MCSC and working-group members relatively little time to communicate with their constituents. So, for example, in June 2001 it was noted that: 'There was little evidence that representatives from working groups had spent time socialising information with their people, nor with respective members on the MCSC.' The second is that time constraints make it particularly challenging to involve people with limited technical training or education, especially considering the necessity of continuous translation. One way in which the process attempted to deal with these challenges was to hold extraordinary meetings of the working groups, which apparently contributed to the fact that 'by November 2001 communication within and between groups had improved considerably—resulting in a number of important agreements at that meeting'.

10.2.3 The relationship of the Mine Closure Steering Committee with project-based or issue-based partnerships

The MCSC has spawned or benefited a number of project-level and issue-based partnerships. Although it is difficult to summarise the way in which the MCSC has interacted with or benefited these various initiatives, it is apparent that the improved relationships and regular forums for both formal and informal communication established between key stakeholders during the MCSC process are likely to have benefited many of these project-level partnerships. In a number of instances, however, the contributions of the MCSC went much further, in that various partners contributed not just information and buy-in—important as these aspects are—but also more tangible assets, such as land or finances. The most illustrative example of this is the *asrama*, or school dormitory, which will be constructed in the village of Linggang Bigung, as a direct result of deliberations in the MCSC and its working groups. These deliberations initially revolved around the post-closure sustainability of the school bus service, which KEM has been providing to villages in the area around the mine. Through communication with relevant government departments it became clear that government could not maintain this service. The alternative identified by members of the Working Group on Community Development and District Planning was to construct a dormitory next to the school. This Working Group, through community representatives, then initiated a survey of students and parents, in which 67% of respondents supported the dormitory. It was also proposed that the teachers would manage the dormitory, with the guidance of Yayasan Rio Tinto (the Rio Tinto Indonesia Foundation) staff. The district government will provide the land for the dormitory (which will house about 200 students), and construction will be financed and managed by KEM. In addition to the dormitory, KEM and Yayasan Rio Tinto staff will oversee the establishment of a six-hectare farm, which will provide subsistence and cash crops (as well as agricultural training) to the students.

In broad terms, the MCSC has benefited various project-level or issue-specific partnerships in some combination of the following capacities:

- Through improved communication between the various stakeholders and hence through better exchange of information and more effective planning

- Through leverage of crucial resources or competences from the various actors, such as:
    - Human resources (e.g. the provision of agriculture extension officers for agricultural projects), legal licences and land from government
    - Labour, land, buy-in and local knowledge from local communities
    - Finances, expertise and guidance, machinery (e.g. tractors) and project management capacity from KEM

- Through improved governance based on the explicit and public acceptance of certain responsibilities by government during the partnership process, the integration of KEM's community development efforts in

district development planning and improved relationships and communication between government and community institutions

10.3 Outcomes

The evidence that is available at time of writing indicates that the partnership is
'on track' to achieve its overall objective of implementing a 'responsible mine
closure' with sustainable benefits for local communities. Most of the objectives
identified by the various partners as indicators of success in early 2002 have been,
or are likely to be, met by the partnership. Box 10.2 lists some of the key agreements
reached by the MCSC prior to May 2002, as well as some of the community
development initiatives supported.

Although there is a risk that the partnership might yet fail in achieving its
objectives, there is a consensus among the partnership participants that this
would be due to circumstances beyond the control of any one party. Significantly,
there is broad agreement that the partnership approach is the best way of dealing

---

- Agreement on international standards and procedures to guarantee dam safety,
  including an agreed process for the formulation of a risk management plan, agreed
  distribution of responsibilities and the identification of suitable trust-fund options

- Agreement on high water-quality standards for drainage from the post-closure mine
  site, including the identification of resulting implications for post-closure site uses,
  such as the need for wetlands

- Identification of a preferred 'integrated site use'—chosen from a range of options—
  which requires, *inter alia*, the demolition of all site buildings, the use of the building
  materials at a nearby village and the establishment of wetlands for water-quality
  maintenance

- Implementation of a drilling and sampling programme to ascertain the feasibility of
  mining alluvial gold deposits with benefit-sharing among the partners (as a
  prerequisite to establishing the wetlands)

- Agreement on suitable hand-over arrangements (from the company to relevant government institutions) for maintenance and operation of community infrastructure
  established by the company (e.g. roads, schools, clinic, electricity supply)

- Agreement on statutory and contractual requirements for the company with respect
  to mine closure

- Construction of school dormitory as a sustainable solution to the absence of a school
  bus

- Co-ordination of various community development projects, including support for
  agricultural projects, the establishment of self-help groups and the identification of
  suitable trust-fund options for sustainable community development after closure

---

Box 10.2 Agreements reached and initiatives supported, to May 2002

with the considerable challenges faced by mine closure and that alternative approaches would not have had such positive outcomes.

From a business perspective, the benefits of the partnership include a marked decrease in the risk of disruption to mining operations prior to closure, an increased likelihood of effective returns on mine-closure investments, effective legal compliance, effective returns on social investments and reputation assurance at local, national and international levels. The development benefits of the partnership relate to the continued operation of the mine, increased information about the closure, less likelihood of conflict among community groups, more effective community development projects, improved governance and increased human and social capital in local communities. In terms of public-sector governance, the partnership provides an important model for mine closure, by providing procedural and substantive standards for the management of a wide range of mine-closure issues (e.g. dam safety). It also provides a model for participatory decision-making and accountable governance—it is widely seen as a 'pioneer process'—and this is particularly significant in this time of political and institutional change in Indonesia. Box 10.3 summarises the business, developmental and public-sector governance benefits of the partnership.

Business benefits

- Decreased investment risk: mine is likely to operate until closure:
    - Partnership is widely seen as contributing to better relationships and improved planning, preventing possible causes for community protest
- Increased effectiveness of mine-closure investments:
    - The Mine Closure Steering Committee (MCSC) provides a platform for effective closure planning with stakeholder buy-in
- Legal compliance:
    - The MCSC provides a platform for clarifying legal requirements and provides a process for meeting those requirements
- Increased effectiveness of social investments:
    - Most community development projects benefit from the partnership by means of improved communication, leverage of critical resources (e.g. land) and improved governance
- Reputation assurance:
    - Partnership is widely seen as a 'model' process, thereby improving the company's reputation at a variety of levels
    - Better relationships with local stakeholders, leading to improved local reputation
    - Spread of responsibility among partners for decision-making and post-closure management diminishes the likelihood of the company being solely blamed in the event of negative post-closure impacts

Box 10.3 Added value of the partnership process (continued over)

Community development impact

- Maintained socioeconomic benefits from mine operation:
  - Partnership has contributed to continued operation until closure, on the basis of improved planning and relationships
- Improved access to information and less likelihood of conflict:
  - Partnership has provided a forum for proactive supply of information, including also a communication strategy with the wider community
- The creation of development projects that are more effective and sustainable:
  - Partnership has allowed for accountable hand-over arrangements for community development projects from Kelian Equatorial Mining (KEM) and has also contributed to the successful planning and implementation of new projects (e.g. the dormitory)
- Increased human and social capital:
  - Partnership has contributed to the improvement of skills and confidence among local community representatives, improved community representation structures and improved relations between communities and government and among different community groups

Public-sector governance

- A model for mine closure:
  - The MCSC process is recognised as a model for mine closure in Indonesia, indicating the extent to which the process is seen to hold replicable lessons for other mine closures
- A model for participatory and accountable governance:
  - The process has set a high standard for the participation of local communities in decision-making and for transparent and accountable governance
- Improved responsiveness, accountability and visibility:
  - The partnership has provided for improved interactions between government and local communities and has allowed government to make public commitments to respond to community concerns
- Improved cost-effectiveness of social spending, improved regional planning and better co-operative governance:
  - Public spending (e.g. on the dormitory) has increased community benefits as a result of contributions from other partners
  - The partnership has allowed for effective co-ordination between government and company plans and activities as well as between different levels and departments within government
- Development of human capital:
  - The partnership is widely seen to have contributed to increased skills in negotiation and participatory decision-making as well as in technical competences

Box 10.3 (continued)

10.4 Emerging lessons

Many of the lessons of this case study relate to the relationship between tri-sector partnerships and context. At KEM, far-reaching sociopolitical and institutional changes at a national and regional level, and troubled relationships between the company and local stakeholders, provided crucial incentives for the adoption of a partnership approach, as well as significant challenges. The fact that many participants in the process feel that 'there was no alternative' indicates that tri-sector partnership may be particularly apposite in instances where the stakes are high—as in the case of mine closure—and where distrust among stakeholders requires a high degree of commitment to accountable, transparent and consensus-based decision-making. Far-reaching commitment from the company has been an especially important factor, demonstrated by the adherence to consensus-based decision-making rules and the designation of the MCSC as the strategic decision-making body for the company in all matters related to closure. A key lesson, therefore, is that tri-sector partnership may be an effective, even necessary, approach in challenging circumstances, but that such a partnership cannot be implemented half-heartedly.

The case study also shows that a tri-sector partnership cannot be implemented unless a parallel and separate process is initiated in order to deal with unresolved grievances. This process need not be completed prior to partnership-building but needs to have the commitment and buy-in of all relevant stakeholders.

Other success factors of the MCSC process worth considering in difficult circumstances are the following:

- The assistance of external, trusted facilitators

- Dedication early on in the process to negotiating and determining a jointly agreed process and decision-making principles

- Demonstrated commitment from top-level stakeholder representatives

- Persistent dedication to involving local stakeholders and supporting stakeholder representatives in their role as intermediaries with their constituents

The case study demonstrates that tri-sector partnerships can be highly effective in helping companies improve and maintain their reputation. In particular, it suggests that the company can secure itself against reputation damage after closure by implementing and demonstrating commitment to a process that is respected and appreciated by a wide array of key stakeholders. This is especially because the MCSC process spread the responsibility and ownership for decisions taken in mine-closure planning. It also provided all stakeholders with a better understanding of why these decisions were taken. In this way, even when events occur that could harm the international reputation of Rio Tinto such events are less likely to be blamed unfairly on the company, and respected local stakeholders are more likely to defend its reputation.

Finally, the case study has shown how the MCSC, essentially a strategic, deliberative forum, has interacted with, and benefited, implementation partnerships at the project level. The dormitory is the most illustrative example in this regard. This 'nested' complementarity may also apply at higher levels (e.g. regarding industry-level partnerships). There is thus considerable scope for developing a better understanding of the potential for partnerships at different scales and for the development of more explicit linkages among them.

11

BP Exploration Company

Contributing to long-term regional development in Casanare, Colombia

Michael Warner, Edgardo Garcia Larralde and Rory Sullivan

This chapter examines three regional-level tri-sector partnership arrangements, each involving the BP Exploration Company (BPXC) in the Casanare department of Colombia. Although ten years of oil production has improved the average social and economic status of the department as a whole, a number of barriers to the development of the region remain. These include the poor management of public expenditure within departmental and municipal government agencies, the unsustainable dependence for regional development programmes on oil-related tax revenues, and limited trust and collaboration between the three sectors of society, associated in part with the ever-present threat of political violence. Like other businesses within the BP Group, BPXC in Colombia has begun to look again at its policy of localised social investment. Notwithstanding the success of this investment in securing a local social licence in difficult circumstances, the business has turned its attention to the alignment of operations with the long-term, non-oil-dependent, economic development of the wider region.

Oil production in the Casanare region reached its peak in 1999. Since then BPXC has positioned itself as the catalyst for three new strategic partnerships: (a) a multi-sector department-wide forum to foster long-term, participatory, regional economic planning and democratic development, (b) the School for Leadership and Governance programme, which by 2002 had graduated more than 200 candidates from government, business and civil society in skills that include ethics, law, social justice, conflict resolution and community project planning and (c) a joint public–private–community road project providing access to isolated communities and to the oil exploration site of Niscota. It is too early to judge the impact of this more strategic approach to social investment or whether it will afford BPXC the long-term 'right to growth' in Colombia; however, leadership capacity is clearly being strengthened across the department in preparation for the transition to a regional economy without oil.

11.1 Social context

The lowland region of Casanare (estimated population 270,000 people) in north-east Colombia is a little larger than Switzerland. Prior to the 1990s the region was economically predominantly dependent on agriculture and ranch cattle. In 1991 significant crude oil reserves were discovered—one of the largest discoveries in Latin America in the past two decades. The subsequent ten years of oil development and production significantly improved the average standard of living in the region, with many social indicators (e.g. access to healthcare, education, water supplies, electricity and employment) showing an improvement over comparable regions. Improvements have, however, been geographically unequal, and poverty and social deprivation continues in many areas. A recent people's survey revealed the following social and economic regional priorities for the next decade:

- Long-term employment (many of the 12,000 jobs available during the peak construction period of the oil fields have long since gone, leaving local people and recent migrants unemployed)

- Vocational and business management training

- An improvement in access to basic housing and facilities for healthcare, education and water

- A reduction in the threat of violence linked to political instability

11.2 Business context

Since 1987 BP has operated several exploration and production blocks in the Casanare department of Colombia, through its subsidiary BP Exploration Company (BPXC). These include the Cusiana and Cupiagua oil-producing fields, which together account for close to half of the country's total oil production (production reached a peak of 434,000 barrels of oil per day [bopd] annual average in 1999). Until recently, the broad thrust of BPXC's social investment strategy in Casanare has been aimed at securing an informal licence to operate from those local communities most directly affected by operations. This has resulted in a wide range of company-led community projects in areas such as employment creation, training and community infrastructure.

As with many other BP operations in the developing world, there is now an increased emphasis on linking social investment to the corporation's global reputation and international and national competitiveness. For leadership companies such as BP, with a need to satisfy the demands of institutional investors for long-term, high-yield growth, and with BPXC exploring other parts of Casanare and in the Niscota region to the north, there are good reasons for the company to widen its social management strategy from 'localised' community social development to alignment with long-term 'regional' sustainable economic development. With the future life of the Cusiana and Cupiagua oil fields limited by their natural decline, this implies a strategic approach that deploys the current tax and royalty revenues, along with the business resources of BPXC, to establish a regional economy independent of oil.

11.3 Governance context

A total of 20% of the overall production of investing oil companies is paid in royalties. In turn 47.5% of this is transferred to the Casanare departmental government (approximately US$100 million during 2002) and 12.5% to the oil-producing municipalities within the region; the remaining 40% is transferred to central funds. With a sparse population, the development potential of oil royalties in Casanare is substantial. However, the petroleum boom has brought new problems for municipal governments, including elevated operating costs and levels of borrowing and an over-dependence on oil-related royalty revenues for funding infrastructure and services and for servicing debt. Further, the use of royalty revenues is limited by law to social development, education, water and sewage projects and infrastructure purposes.

Equally important, there remains little institutional capacity at the departmental level to transparently plan for sustainable regional development or manage the implementation of such a plan. For example, co-ordination between municipalities is weak, there is a general failure to assign royalties to priority development areas, and accountability in the allocation of resources is lacking. These inefficiencies are complicated by a short, three-year, electoral cycle, corruption and the threat of violence from insurgency and paramilitary activity. The indirect effect of these constraints is to inhibit village associations and other civil-society groups and organisations in exercising a voice in the development of their own region.

11.4 Overview of the partnering process

In 1998 BPXC led efforts towards the formulation of a shared economic vision for Casanare. Although initially supported by the regional governor, this soon waned. A year on and the departmental government, through the formal regional planning process, developed a master plan for the department; but this, as with previous plans, was criticised for its weak stakeholder participation and poor prospects for implementation—the latter a consequence, in part, of the short electoral cycle.

In 1999 BPXC engaged with the Business Partners for Development (BPD) programme and began to promote a tri-sector partnership model centred on long-term regional, non-oil-dependent economic development. The initial challenge was to find an existing, credible multi-sector regional forum that could act as a platform for strengthening the prospects for long-term regional planning. For a while consideration was given to augment the brief of CODEPLA—the official, multi-sector planning body charged with advising the governor on the details of the regional plan. The statutory requirement to advise on the three-year regional planning process, combined with a low level of civil-society representation, suggested a wider search.

By 2000, three different regional-level partnership arrangements were emerging:

- The Grupo Gestor: a multi-sector forum for promoting long-term economic and democratic development across the region

- The School for Leadership and Governance: a programmatic multi-sector partnership to address the institutional and governance weaknesses in the department

- Construction of the Nunchia–Morcote road: a regionally strategic partnership to construct a new transport route through a remote northern region of the department

Milestones in the evolution of these three partnerships are listed in Table 11.1.

11.5 Overview of the three partnerships

The main activities of the three partnerships and the division of roles of the partners are described below.

11.5.1 Grupo Gestor

The founding members of the group include a government-sponsored solidarity network, two regional non-governmental organisations (NGOs) (one independent, and one established by BPXC and its oil-industry partners), BPXC and ECOPETROL. The Diocesan Catholic church of Yopal joined soon after. After more than a year of discussions with the departmental government, and, after a decision to open the forum to others, the governor, the regional chamber of commerce and representatives of the region's cattle ranchers and millers joined existing members and agreed a more formalised structure for the group. As a first step, a regional land-use planning consultative process has been initiated, promoted by the group's new technical secretariat.

11.5.2 School for Leadership and Governance

Early in its deliberations the Grupo Gestor identified three obstacles to improved governance and economic development within the department: (a) a lack of knowledge among civil society about how government works and about how to access resources and implement development projects, (b) a fear of reprisals and

Grupo Gestor	School for Leadership and Governance	Construction of the Nunchia–Morcote road
2000		
• Initial meetings of the 'group of friends' • Grupo Gestor agrees a provisional vision and mission promoting a tri-sector partnership model to achieve sustainable development in Casanare based on an agriculture and livestock economy		• Exploratory discussions with Casanare regional government, the local government of Nunchia and community leaders about the merits of the Nunchia–Morcote road
2001		
• Chamber of Commerce joins the Grupo Gestor at the beginning of 2001 • Casanare departmental government joins Grupo Gestor • Grupo Gestor agrees a more developed vision, mission and route map to promote a tri-sector partnership model to achieve sustainable development in Casanare	• BPXC leads in establishing a School for Leadership and Governance • First leadership course held for more than 200 leaders from government, civil society, BPXC and schools	• Work commences on the Nunchia–Morcote road
2002 to the present		
• Departmental government becomes an active member of Group Gestor, and a new formal governance structure is agreed	• Departmental government provides resources to widen the reach of the School for Leadership and Governance programme, and regional academic institutions begin to participate	• The Nunchia–Morcote road is completed, with no incidents of sabotage to date

BPXC = BP Exploration Company

Table 11.1 **Milestones in the evolution of the Grupo Gestor, in the School for Leadership and Governance and in the construction of the Nunchia–Morcote road**

rejection from holding political views and (c) a lack of general awareness that governance in the region was suboptimal. The design of the programme for the School for Leadership and Governance was borrowed from a similar scheme sponsored by ECOPETROL in another part of the country. Initiated through the Grupo Gestor, the programme leaders soon assumed overall management of the scheme, drawing on financial support from BPXC, local municipalities (the *alcaldías*) and the departmental government and with curriculum input from BPXC, ECOPETROL, the municipalities, community development organisations and the Casanare university Unitrópico.

The first cohort of 220 leadership trainees were drawn from government agencies, civil-society organisations, BPXC and secondary school teachers. For two days a month over eight months the participants were tutored in modules that included: ethics and leadership, instruments of law for public participation, development and investment project models, social justice and conflict resolution, environment and sustainable agriculture projects, and gender. In addition to these, supervised exercises were undertaken enabling the skills to be put into practice.

11.5.3 Construction of the Nunchia–Morcote road

Morcote is a small community, 20 km from Nunchia, north of Yopal, Casanare's capital. The area is mountainous, susceptible to guerrilla activity and en route to the Niscota area being prospected by BPXC. Construction of a road to Morcote had been requested by local communities for decades, and it is unlikely the road would have been built without the specific public–private partnership arrangement between BPXC and the governments of Casanare and the neighbouring Boyaca department. Critically, the involvement of local communities in both the design phase and the long-term maintenance of the road has helped to reduce the effect of opposition from insurgency groups.

11.6 Division of roles

The different roles and responsibilities played by the main actors in the above three partnerships are summarised in Table 11.2.

Partner	Grupo Gestor partnership	School for Leadership and Governance	Nunchia–Morcote road
Business:			
BPXC	• Taking visible leadership of the GGP and providing part of Technical Secretariat	• Providing funding for the scheme • Contributing to academic content of courses	• Principal source of funding to construct the road • Construction management skills • Sharing of cost and responsibility for road maintenance with local authorities • Provision of funding for and supervision of the NGO Minuto de Dios
ECOPETROL	• A member of GGP	• Providing trainers from other similar projects in other parts of the country brought to Casanare • Contributing to academic content of courses	N.A.
Communities:			
Community representatives	N.A.	• Participating in community action boards • Facilitating the involvement of local organisations	• Taking shared responsibility for road maintenance
NGOs:			
Fundación Cemilla	• Promoting the voice of *campesinos* and the poor	N.A.	N.A.
Red de Solidaridad	• Providing links to central government peace-building activities	N.A.	N.A.

N.A. = not applicable   BPXC = BP Exploration Company

Table 11.2 **Division of roles and competences in the Grupo Gestor Partnership (GGP), the School for Leadership and Governance and the construction of the Nunchia–Morcote road** (continued over)

Partner	Grupo Gestor partnership	School for Leadership and Governance	Nunchia–Morcote road
NGOs: (continued)			
Fundación Amanecer	• Providing a bridge between community groups and the oil sector	N.A.	N.A.
Church of Yopal	• Voicing the concerns of communities	N.A.	N.A.
Minuto de Dios	N.A.	N.A.	• Guiding community participation in the design and maintenance of the road • Facilitating relations between communities and other parties
Government:			
Local government and mayoral offices (*alcaldías*)	N.A.	• Contributing resources to scheme • Providing academic content	• The local authorities of Nunchia and Paya share the cost and responsibility for road maintenance with BPXC
Regional government of Casanare	• Membership of the Departmental Planning Council • Proposed formalising the group into a regional development Corporation • Membership of the Technical Secretariat	• Contributing resources to scheme	• Sharing the costs and responsibility for road maintenance

N.A. = not applicable   BPXC = BP Exploration Company

Table 11.2 (from previous page; continued opposite)

Partner	Grupo Gestor partnership	School for Leadership and Governance	Nunchia–Morcote road
Other institutions:			
Casanare Chamber of Commerce	• Supporting the formalisation of the GGP into a regional planning corporation	N.A.	N.A.
Unitrópico (Casanare university)	N.A.	• Contributing new content and instructors	N.A.
Army Engineers Battalion	N.A.	N.A.	• Contributing to the construction phase and to road maintenance
Other private sector:			
Molinos El Yopal	• Representing the milling industry	N.A.	N.A.
Fertiagro Ltd	• Representing agri-business	N.A.	N.A.
Cattle rancher trade associations	• Representing cattle ranchers	N.A.	N.A.

N.A. = not applicable

Table 11.2 (continued)

11.7 Partnership impacts

It is too early to evaluate the final impact of these three strategic partnerships on the prospects for a transition to a regional economy without oil. However, some indication can be given of the current and anticipated benefits. These are captured in Boxes 11.1–11.3.

Business benefits

- Right to growth:
    - Prospect of reduced long-term legacy and liabilities of community dependence on BP Exploration Company (BPXC) and therefore enhanced business development prospects in Colombia
- Security:
    - Loss of legitimacy of violent protest: for political negotiations in the midst of conflict to be successful, violent methods must lose all legitimacy
- Stakeholder relations:
    - Provision of a safe space for BPXC to explore social investment and (future) site transfer options without raising community expectations

Benefits for civil society

- Infrastructure:
    - Prospect of regional infrastructure resourcing suffering less interruption from electoral cycle
- Local economic development:
    - Provision of a safe space for expression of needs and proposals by civil-society organisations
- Community capacities:
    - Increased visibility and legitimacy of participating non-governmental organisations in the eyes of government and BPXC
    - Increased trust: dialogue has helped to overcome mistrust of government by civil society

Public-sector governance

- Cost-effectiveness of government expenditure:
    - Enhanced opportunities for 'synergy' and capital cost savings in implementing regional development objectives
- Discharging civic duties:
    - Provision of a safe 'political' space for more transparent and accountable government
    - Provision of a basis for long-term policy consistency in regional development planning

Box 11.1 **Added value of the Grupo Gestor partnership**

Business Benefits

- Right to growth:
  - Enhanced global and national reputation, in particular the credibility of the recent stance of BP Exploration Company (BPXC) on observance of human rights
- Security:
  - Prospect that enhanced relations with a diversity of future leaders will lead to reduction of security risks
- Stakeholder relations:
  - More favourable relations between BPXC and a wide range of regional communities, non-governmental organisations (NGOs) and local government

Benefits for civil society

- Infrastructure:
  - Creation of a bank of global projects
- Local economic development:
  - Application of new skills to economic projects (e.g. agriculture, livestock and community infrastructure)
- Community capacities:
  - Creation of community and NGO leaders skilled in investment plans, output-driven development projects, gender and equity issues and sustainable agricultural projects

Public-sector governance

- Cost-effectiveness of government expenditure:
  - Legitimate governmental action through citizen participation
- Discharging civic duties:
  - Creation of 'leaders' from government with upgraded skills in ethics, law, social justice, conflict resolution and use of the media

Box 11.2 Added value of School for Leadership and Governance

Business benefits

- Right to growth:
  - More cost-effective access to prospective area (Niscota)
- Security:
  - More secure access to prospective area
  - Reduction of risk of sabotage to the road
- Stakeholder relations:
  - The visible delivery commitments by BP Exploration Company (BPXC) has strengthened its social licence to operate with communities and local government in the vicinity of the prospective area

Benefits for civil society

- Infrastructure:
  - Without the partnership approach the road is highly unlikely to have been constructed
- Local economic development:
  - Over 80% decrease in journey times from Morcote to Nunchia
  - Faster access to markets and to superior health and education services
  - Employment opportunities created from the need for road maintenance
- Community capacities:
  - Improved inter-community relations and collaboration
  - Creation of transferable construction skills

Public-sector governance

- Cost-effectiveness of government expenditure:
  - Increased legitimacy: the multi-stakeholder design process has enhanced the legitimacy of the government's resource allocation processes
  - Road construction is highly unlikely to have occurred without combined public–private funding
- Discharging civic duties:
  - Increased physical presence of government extension officers in region accessed by road

Box 11.3 Added value of Nuchia–Morcote road partnership

11.8 Lessons learned

11.8.1 A novel approach to institutional strengthening

In all three partnerships discussed in this chapter the active involvement of the regional government has been critical, but it is worth recalling that this engagement has not been without difficulty. For much of 2001 the Grupo Gestor concurrently played an 'external' waiting game with the regional government, while holding 'internal' discussions aimed at overcoming opposition to government participation from within the group. In the final analysis, though, all parties recognised that, if public resources were to be allocated through a regional plan with longer time-horizons than the three-year electoral cycle, then it was essential for departmental government to be actively engaged in and supportive of the process. The strategic intervention of the Casanare governor to propose transforming Grupo Gestor into a formal development corporation with a long-term planning and consensus-building mandate was decisive.

Concurrent with this intervention, a parallel regional partnership was under way—the School for Leadership and Governance—providing government institutions, among others, skills relevant to financial management. The combined effect of these two regional-level partnerships is interesting and may carry lessons for other oil operators as they forward-plan for a positive social and economic historic legacy in their regions of operation. The effect of the two partnerships has been to coincide a sense of government ownership for regional development planning with new skills and capacity in revenue management. In essence, the partnerships have put in place two of the principal building blocks of any process of institutional reform: namely, ownership and training.

There is also growing evidence of the cross-fertilisation of ideas and practices between the different partnerships, leading, not least, to a rebuilding of trust (or the gradual overcoming of distrust) between parties that have a long-standing suspicion of each other. In a context of a region characterised by violent conflict and the effects of that conflict, these results should not be underestimated.

11.8.2 Long-term sustainable regional development

As a result of the redistribution of royalty revenues, public investment in the Casanare region is currently greater than that of Cundinamarca, a department with a population nine times that of Casanare. Such a phenomenon is not uncommon in countries where a proportion of revenues return to the region of operations. Even if the allocation of these regional resources is inefficient, it is likely, as has been the case in Casanare, that tangible improvements in a range of public services will result. In such circumstances the key issue is perhaps less about whether resources are allocated efficiently, or even whether these resources 'reach' the poorest communities (important though this is), and more about the long-term sustainability of recently introduced public services in the context of declining oil-related revenues.

A broader lesson from this case study revolves around the extent to which the competences of the production operations of BPXC in Casanare have been able to be aligned with long-term, non-oil-dependent, regional economic development, both directly though community investment and the rolling-out of operational infrastructure and indirectly by acting as a catalyst for regional planning and institutional strengthening.

With regard to operational infrastructure, the strategic deployment of the Nunchia–Morcote road as a means to engage local communities en route to the Niscota area will have a lasting impact for BPXC's business prospects in Colombia and for the welfare and development potential of the wider region.

More important, where BPXC has been particularly creative is in using its convening power both to bring together regional actors to overcome the constraints to long-term regional planning posed by the three-year regional electoral cycle and to initiate and seed-fund a long-term programme of institutional strengthening aimed at improving financial management across government authorities in the region.

The limited time available for this study did not allow a close investigation of the contents of the courses being offered at the School for Leadership and Governance. It is hoped, however, that close attention is being paid to the skills needed within the regional and municipal authorities to stabilise the public accounts such that, as oil revenues reduce, government institutions do not find themselves exposed to unsustainable debt-servicing charges or unmanageable infrastructure maintenance costs.

11.8.3 The long-term right to growth

For BPXC, the transformation of the company's engagement with society in Casanare from an inward-looking strategy of localised community investment to acting as a regional convenor and catalyst for oil-independent sustainable development has been well received, both regionally and internationally. Indeed, BP, at its new LNG (liquefied natural gas) operations in Tangguh, Indonesia, where production is not anticipated until 2008, is already pursuing a diversified growth strategy to guard against unmanageable inward migration and to prepare the way for a legacy of non-gas-dependent regional economic growth across the operating region.

Whether the managers of the BP Tangguh project fully exploit the experience and lessons learned by BPXC in Casanare remains to be seen. For BPXC in Casanare, where oil production has already peaked, the key question is whether this new strategy of working in partnership at the regional level will afford the company the long-term 'right to growth' both in the wider region and in the country as a whole.

Perhaps the last note should be directed at the Grupo Gestor, or, as it may soon be called, the Casanare Development Corporation. To have reached this far, the group has not only had to overcome the inherent lack of trust presented by the current political insecurity in Casanare but also secure buy-in and leadership from the regional governor to evolve what was an informal ad hoc grouping into an increasingly legitimate forum for regional consensus-building and development planning. This is a substantial achievement.

Part 2
Partnership tools

12
Getting started

Michael Warner

This chapter provides guidance on how to develop partnerships to manage social issues in the extractive industries. The partnership model promoted here is based on the pooling of core competences across organisations drawn from the three sectors of society: business, civil society and government.

The partnering process can be divided into the following three phases:

- Partnership exploration
- Partnership building
- Partnership maintenance

Each of the phases is discussed in more detail below. The key tasks and deliverables in the partnering process are shown in Figure 12.1.

12.1 Partnership exploration

The task of exploring the possibilities of collaboration between oil, gas or mining companies, civil-society organisations and government authorities falls into two parts: namely, internal assessment and consultation.

12.1.1 Internal assessment

A common error in trying to build partnerships is for a company to launch into discussions with potential partners before fully understanding its own internal needs and interests. A short (typically between two and five days) office-based assessment should first be conducted. This will include identification of the core

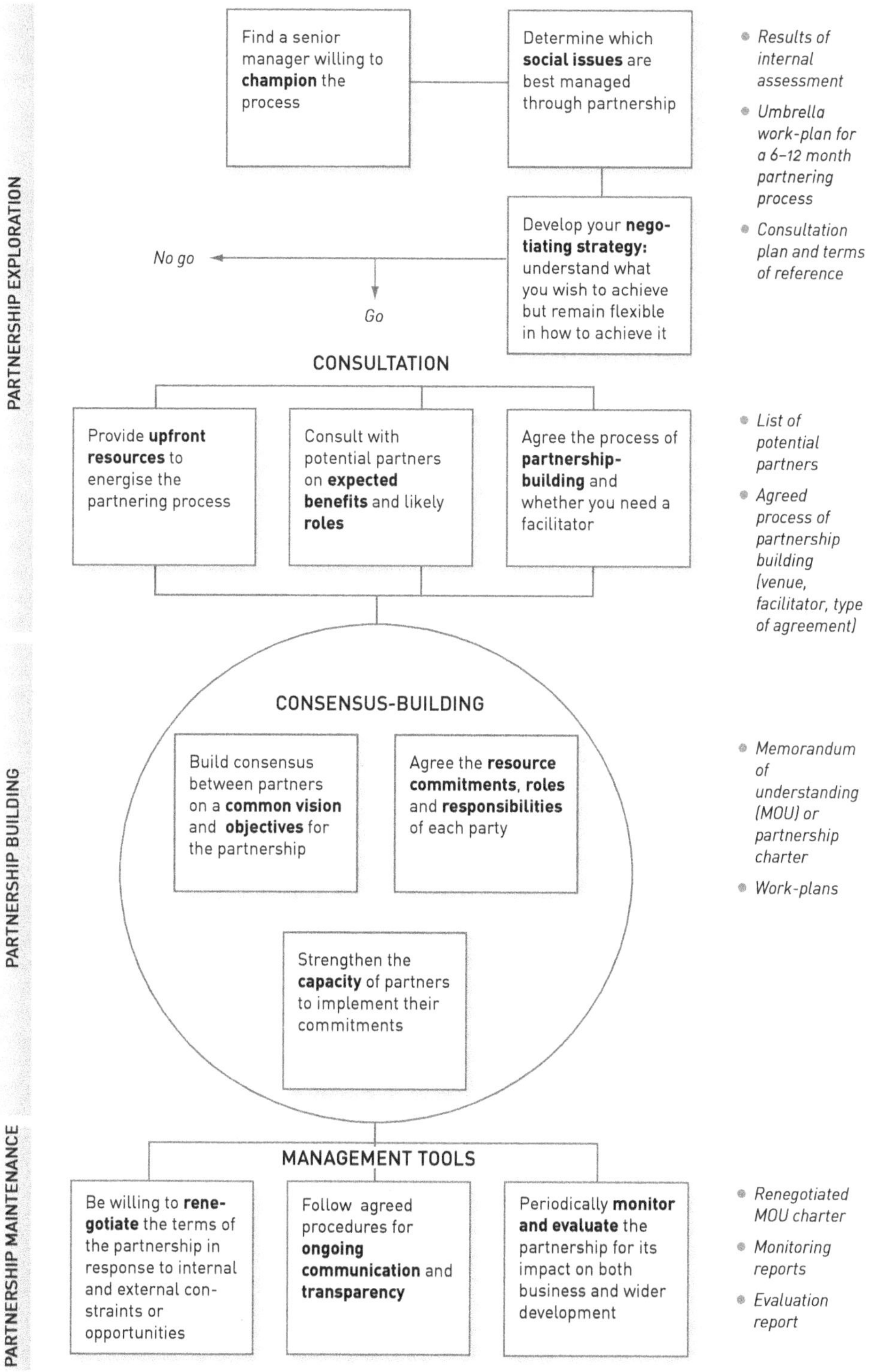
PARTNERSHIP EXPLORATION
Find a senior manager willing to champion the process
Determine which social issues are best managed through partnership
Develop your negotiating strategy: understand what you wish to achieve but remain flexible in how to achieve it
No go
Go
Results of internal assessment
Umbrella work-plan for a 6–12 month partnering process
Consultation plan and terms of reference
CONSULTATION
Provide upfront resources to energise the partnering process
Consult with potential partners on expected benefits and likely roles
Agree the process of partnership-building and whether you need a facilitator
List of potential partners
Agreed process of partnership building (venue, facilitator, type of agreement)
PARTNERSHIP BUILDING
CONSENSUS-BUILDING
Build consensus between partners on a common vision and objectives for the partnership
Agree the resource commitments, roles and responsibilities of each party
Strengthen the capacity of partners to implement their commitments
Memorandum of understanding (MOU) or partnership charter
Work-plans
PARTNERSHIP MAINTENANCE
MANAGEMENT TOOLS
Be willing to renegotiate the terms of the partnership in response to internal and external constraints or opportunities
Follow agreed procedures for ongoing communication and transparency
Periodically monitor and evaluate the partnership for its impact on both business and wider development
Renegotiated MOU charter
Monitoring reports
Evaluation report

Figure 12.1 **Key tasks and deliverables in the partnering process**

business interests to be served by the partnership, identification of the ongoing social management programme or project into which the partnering process will integrate, formulation of the company's negotiating strategy and an assessment of the anticipated benefits of the partnership weighed against the costs and risks. This process will enable the company to judge the merits of trying to develop partnership arrangements with civil-society organisations and government agencies, and, if it is to form such a partnership, around which particular social issue (e.g. employment, the supply chain, resettlement, community development, wealth distribution).

For many natural resource companies, the formation of voluntary partnerships with government and civil-society organisations is a new type of undertaking. Although the benefits for business (in terms of risk management, meeting compliance requirements and enhancing reputation) can be great, the partnering process is not without risk. For example, the company's existing external relationships and its ability to comply with the environmental and social obligations of investors and regulators may be at risk if one of the partners reneges on its commitments.

It is, therefore, critical first to find a senior manager to 'champion' the partnering process. This should be someone capable of viewing the inevitable tensions that will arise from time to time between the partners, as part of a longer-term goal to construct a new capacity within society for the company, government and civil society to work together.

Not all social issues facing natural resource companies lend themselves to management through partnership approaches. Box 12.1 provides a checklist to help managers decide which social issues lend themselves to a partnership approach. The more 'yes' answers able to be given, the greater the probability that a partnership model of social management will be effective.

Above all else, companies fear the loss of control that a voluntary partnership can bring. A common question asked by managers is: 'How can I guarantee that the partnership will deliver the quality and timeliness of social management required by our investors and regulators?' The key is to view the development of a partnership with government and civil society as a process of consensual negotiation. The partnership will not progress unless all parties are able to reach consensus over how their underlying interests will be fulfilled. For the company this may mean seeking assurances from the other partners that its corporate policies, compliance obligations and deadlines will be met. In return, the company will need to help the other partners deliver on their underlying interests, be that alignment with government local development plans or contributing to the national strategies and development programmes of non-governmental organisations (NGOs) or development assistance agencies. What should be avoided is any one partner (including the company) dictating the objectives of the partnership. The company's negotiating strategy should therefore include:

- Firmness about what compliance requirements, deadlines and values need to be met
- Flexibility in how these underlying interests might be delivered

The more 'yes' answers given to the following questions, the greater the probability that a partnership model of social management will be effective.

- Are there clear social or local environmental needs in society (e.g. poverty reduction, employment, basic infrastructure, healthcare) that coincide with aspects of the company's social and environmental management programmes (e.g. corporate sustainability policies, social impact mitigation requirements, social investment and/or community development projects)?

- Is the company is under pressure to deliver community and/or regional benefits that are more properly the responsibility of government?

- Is the company seeking to work in collaboration with local communities but lacking the 'softer' social skills needed to be effective?

- Is the company facing investment uncertainty (e.g. delays, suspension, downsizing)?

- Is the company under pressure from investors, regulators or corporate head-quarters to demonstrate improvements in its social performance (e.g. to improve the 'business return' on community development or social investment expenditure)?

- Does the company have core resources and competences (e.g. heavy equipment, technical skills, project management tools) that would assist government authorities or civil-society organisations in delivering community development?

- As part of its core business activities, is the company providing employment opportunities or constructing physical infrastructure (water, electricity, health facilities, roads, etc.) that would have a greater benefit for local society if government authorities or civil societies were involved in their implementation and/or expansion and 'rolling-out'?

- Would the dialogue between the company and parties opposed to the project benefit from consolidation in the form of more practical joint action?

- Does the company wish to minimise the risks of local hostility towards its operations and/or improve its local reputation?

Box 12.1 **When is it appropriate to adopt a partnership approach to manage social issues?**

- Acceptance that there will be deviations from prescribed detailed social management or community development plans

- Effort spent keeping investors and regulators informed of these changes

Box 12.2 lists the elements that form an internal assessment. A key feature of the assessment will be an in-house exploration of the strengths of the organisation relevant to its contributions to the partnership.

The overall results of the internal assessment will inform the decision whether or not to move forward with developing tri-sector partnership arrangements to manage particular social issues. If the decision is affirmative, the company needs to begin a process of consultation to find suitable partners.

Elements to be considered in an internal assessment of whether to enter into a tri-sector partnership are:

- The urgent social or local environmental needs in the area or region
- The organisation's current social investment strategies and programmes
- The main alternatives to adopting a partnership model (i.e. the most likely approach to be taken in discharging the social strategies, such as use of in-house expertise, outsourcing or local foundations)
- The priority social 'theme' that lends itself to implementation through a tri-sector partnership approach (i.e. through the pooling of core strengths)
- The organisation's underlying interests and motivations that lie behind the priority social theme (e.g. legal or contractual obligations, corporate policy, a 'social licence to operate', risk management, local and global reputation)
- The added value anticipated for the organisation of working in a partnership
- The type or style of partnership to be adopted (e.g. whether it will involve information exchange, dialogue, a shared work-plan, shared responsibilities, etc.)
- The geographical and population reach of the partnership activities
- The financial and human resources, capabilities and expertise available to the organisation to invest in partnerships (i.e. its relevant and affordable core competences)
- The anticipated resources and expertise likely to be brought to the partnership by other parties
- The organisation's available 'room for negotiation' (e.g. its non-negotiable and negotiable, sharable or transferable interests)
- Initial stakeholder mapping to identify potential partners, protagonists and those to be consulted and the underlying interests and potential resource contributions of these stakeholders
- Any immediate obstacles to successfully forming partnerships (e.g. legal, cultural or logistical barriers, difficulties in past relationships, financial obstacles, power imbalances or a lack of a 'champion') and measures to circumvent these
- An estimate of the costs and benefits of the partnership in the short and long term
- The risks involved in working through a partnership, and measures to mitigate these risks

Box 12.2 **Elements of an internal assessment to explore the partnership option**

12.1.2 Consultation

Once this early, internal assessment is complete it is still not certain that a partnership will develop. Before this can happen a degree of 'buy-in' has to be generated within suitable partner organisations. A targeted process of consultation is the best way to secure such buy-in (see Fig. 12.1). Consultation is needed to (a) validate current assumptions about external stakeholders, (b) establish channels of communication with suitable partners, (c) explore possible roles and resource commitments of prospective partners and (d) agree on the process by which the partners will come together and negotiate the terms of the partnership.

Providing adequate resources to consult with prospective partners and formulate tri-sector partnerships is essential. The costs need not be excessive. Most companies already have many of the skills needed to transform external relationships into partnerships. These include skills in risk assessment, public consultation, external communications and public relations (PR), and project management. However, because the prospective partners are likely to be unfamiliar with working so closely together, two other, less common, skill sets are also needed: namely, consensual (interest-based) negotiation and, where needed, third-party facilitation or mediation. These skills can be strengthened in-house through short training courses. Alternatively, the skills can be contracted-in in the form of advisors or brokers. Box 12.3 provides some additional comments on the qualities required for partnership facilitators and on the situations where a third-party facilitator may be helpful.

Table 12.1 summarises the expertise needed to develop tri-sector partnerships, the source of this expertise and the likely time in person-days required to do the job. These 'average' costs (in person-days) are based on the assumptions that key in-house staff will have already received basic training in how to partner and that third-party facilitation skills are available locally.

The following qualities are emerging as minimum standards for those offering to help to design or facilitate partnerships between companies, government and civil society:

- A professional qualification in some form of 'interest-based' negotiation

- Practical experience in designing and facilitating multi-party workshops

- A thorough understanding of the extractive industries and the social issues raised by their operations

Circumstances in which a third-party facilitator may be helpful include:

- Assisting prospective partners to assess the benefits, risks and costs of engaging in partnerships

- Convening a multi-party dialogue that leads to a robust partnership

- Building consensus between prospective partners

It should be noted that third-party facilitation (i.e. external brokering) is not a prerequisite to formulating effective social partnerships in the extractive industries. In many of the societies where hydrocarbon and mining companies operate, local stakeholders would rather see a face that they recognise, trust and respect than a stranger carrying no such authority. Most important, therefore, is not the independence of the facilitator but the degree to which he or she is trusted to behave in a neutral and impartial manner. Alternatively, with the right experience, partners may be entirely capable of negotiating the terms of the relationship without the need for a third party (e.g. see the case involving Integrated Coal Mining Limited and the construction of a link road, discussed in Chapter 4; and the case of the social development programme of Kahama Mining Corporation Limited, discussed in Chapter 8).

Box 12.3 Third-party facilitation and brokering

Expertise required to expedite the partnering process	Cost (in person-days), by source of expertise	
	In-house	Consultant
PHASE 1: PARTNERSHIP EXPLORATION		
Internal assessment:		
Assessment of partnership options, risks, costs and negotiating strategy	3	–
Design and third-party facilitation of exploratory workshops with selective representative from company, civil society and government	–	4
Consultation:		
Finding suitable partners	10	–
Designing a mutually acceptable process of consensus-building and partnership formulation	–	2
PHASE 2: PARTNERSHIP-BUILDING		
Consensus-building:		
Third-party facilitation to build consensus on objectives, roles and resource commitments	–	4
Reaching agreement on detailed work-plans and on monitoring regimes	2	–
PHASE 3: PARTNERSHIP MAINTENANCE		
Management:		
Adapting the partnership to changing circumstances (cost per year)	–	4
Periodic monitoring of outcomes for business development and governance (cost per year)	4	–
TOTAL COST	19	14

Table 12.1 'Resourcing' the partnering process

There is no guarantee that those civil-society organisations or government agencies with which the company wishes to engage in partnership will be willing partners. There is also no certainty that, even if willing, these partners will bring resources, knowledge, skills or leadership that will add value to what the company could achieve alone. For these reasons a prior period of consultation with prospective partners is required. The issues that need to be understood (i.e. the outcomes) from this prior consultation process are described in Box 12.4.

1. Gauge the level of 'buy-in' from key civil-society and government stakeholders, in relation to

   (a) The overall 'theme' that will be the focus of the partnership (e.g. healthcare, education, resettlement, employment, environmental management)

   (b) The belief that a partnership model might improve the way in which this 'theme' is addressed

2. Determine whether in principle those being consulted would be interested in collaborating in such a partnership and, if not, who else they could suggest

3. Identify the resources the prospective partners would bring that would add value to the partnership and determine what roles they anticipate assuming

4. Solicit any conditions or assurances needed for the partner to commit resources

5. Gauge the partners' capacity to implement the roles they are likely to assume

6. Agree an acceptable process of negotiation for developing the objectives and activities of the partnership; for example:

   (a) Whether there should be a single event, or a series of ad hoc meetings

   (b) Whether the process should be facilitated, or not, and, if so, who should be the facilitator

   (c) The venue and duration of the event

   (d) The type of agreement anticipated (e.g. a legal document, a memorandum of understanding, or a charter)

Box 12.4 Key tasks for consultation in the partnering process

12.2 Partnership building

It is still rare for private-sector companies to participate in voluntary partnerships with civil society and government authorities to jointly manage social issues. One reason for this is that each potential partner—be that a local government department, NGO, community leader, church group, union, industry regulator, investor, international development agency or natural resource company—often has distinctly different organisational objectives, staff incentives, methods of working, behaviour and attitudes, institutional culture and perceptions of each other. These are frequently seen as obstacles that 'cannot be overcome'.

The building of successful partnerships requires that all partners be able to adopt a style of negotiation that accommodates these distinct differences and yet still achieves consensus. Conventional 'adversarial' styles of negotiation often lead to 'win–lose' outcomes and are a poor basis for developing tri-sector partnerships. More effective is consensual ('win–win') negotiation, where mutual understanding and a 'celebration of difference' are key features of reaching consensus. The four key principles of consensus-building are summarised in Box 12.5 (see also Fig. 12.1).

- Build trust through mutual understanding and meaningful communication
- Focus on satisfying underlying interests rather than surface positions
- Widen the options through joint problem-solving
- Reach agreement that adds value for all parties

Box 12.5 **Principles of consensus-building**

In negotiating the objectives, roles and resource commitments that will form the basis of the partnership, partners can choose either to negotiate together directly (i.e. face-to-face) or to invite an agreed third-party facilitator to guide the negotiation process. If a third-party facilitator is invited, the factors identified in Box 12.3 (i.e. the training and skills of the facilitator and their knowledge of social issues relevant to the extractive sector) need to be taken into consideration.

The effectiveness with which a partnership functions in practice and delivers its agreed objectives is dependent on how it has been structured. Box 12.6 lists the key elements of agreement required to construct successful partnerships. All parties

Agreement must be reached on each of the following:

- The representatives for each partner organisation
- The geographic boundaries and/or target population of the partnership activities
- A (common) vision statement
- The objectives of the partnership, both shared and individual (including rapid visible benefits)
- Joint work-plan, encompassing activities, schedules and performance indicators, resource commitments, and roles and responsibilities
- Funding arrangements (if applicable)
- Decision-making principles
- A grievance mechanism to resolve differences
- Procedures for transparency and ongoing communications between partners
- Measures to strengthen the capacity of partners to meet their commitments
- Measures to mitigate external risks and threats to the partnership
- A strategy for communicating with constituents and other interested parties
- Procedures for monitoring and measuring the impact of the partnership on business and development
- Procedures for assuming new partners or to cope with partners exiting from the partnership

Box 12.6 **Key elements of agreement in constructing a partnership**

need to reach agreement on all elements. An example of a partnership agreement is presented in Appendix B.

12.2.1 Core complementary competences

Central to successful partnerships are the resource commitments made by each party. These can include funds or finance, staff time, expertise, local knowledge, technical equipment, mediation skills, influence and access to key officials, willingness to adopt a leadership role and capacity to leverage resources from others. The key factor here is the degree of complementarity between the different resources committed (see Fig. 12.2). Resources from the company, civil-society organisation or government authority should each add something new rather than duplicate the resources of others and should have a synergistic effect (i.e. benefits over and above the outcome if each resource were applied in isolation). Table 12.2 provides an inventory of the complementary competences available for managing the different social issues relevant to the extractive industries. The building of partnerships around each party's core complementary competences is about bringing together three distinct elements:

- Competences: these are the resources, roles, responsibilities or types of behaviour that are the true strengths of each party in contributing to the goals and objectives of the partnership.

- Complementary: these are the resources, roles, responsibilities or types of behaviour that add value to the resources, roles, responsibilities or behaviour of the other parties, in the context of achieving the goals and objectives of the partnership.

- Core contributions: these enable each party to meet its own organisational objectives.

Merging the core complementary competences of each partner increases the likelihood that each partner will meet its own objectives as well as enabling the overall goals of the partnership to be met. The reasons are:

- The building of tri-sector partnerships on core complementary competences increases the likelihood that the outcomes of the partnership will have direct relevance to the core objectives of each partner organisation.

- A partnership based on complementary competences highlights to each partner the potential value of the other partners.

- Partnerships based on core competences tend to require less investment in new capital, processes and mechanisms, relying instead on the use of existing capital, processes and mechanisms (i.e. the partnership incurs only incremental costs).

- Such partnerships minimise duplication (e.g. many of the community development activities of oil, gas and mining companies have tended to duplicate the activities of NGOs, local government, donor agencies or community-based organisations rather than adding something new).

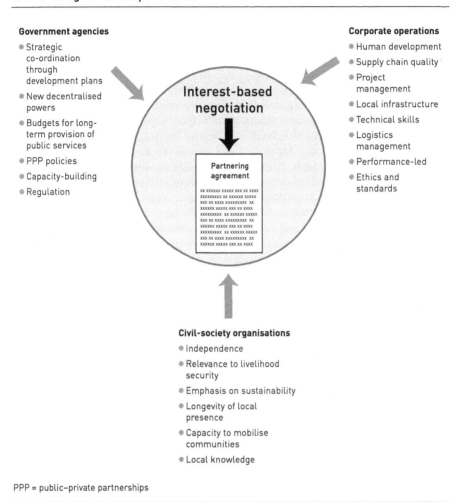

Government agencies
- Strategic co-ordination through development plans
- New decentralised powers
- Budgets for long-term provision of public services
- PPP policies
- Capacity-building
- Regulation

Interest-based negotiation

Partnering agreement

Corporate operations
- Human development
- Supply chain quality
- Project management
- Local infrastructure
- Technical skills
- Logistics management
- Performance-led
- Ethics and standards

Civil-society organisations
- Independence
- Relevance to livelihood security
- Emphasis on sustainability
- Longevity of local presence
- Capacity to mobilise communities
- Local knowledge

PPP = public–private partnerships

Figure 12.2 The fusing of core complementary competences

As noted in Box 12.4, part of the consultation exercise to find suitable partners should involve gauging the capacity of each partner to implement its likely roles successfully. With the objectives of the partnership agreed, resources committed and a joint work-plan developed, the last element of an effective partnership is to ensure that the partners' capacity to meet their commitments is adequate. If necessary, implementation of the tasks detailed in the joint work-plan should be delayed until measures have been taken to strengthen this capacity.

Partner

	Project–society interface				
	Infrastructure development[a]	Procurement, supply chain and local business development	Social impact mitigation[b]	Community development[c]	Long-term regional development
Corporation:					
Corporate level	Advisory services to operational managers to manage 'partnering' process. Examples of partnership approaches to infrastructure development from other successful projects	Examples of a partnership approach to secure the supply chain from other successful projects	Standards and benchmarking for impact mitigation. Provision of mentors to raise standards	Advisory services to operational managers to manage the partnering process	Sustainability policies that recognise the importance to corporate reputation of ensuring a positive regional economic legacy after closure of operations
Operational unit	Secondment of design engineers and infrastructure installation equipment. Capacity-building for municipalities or for SMEs in support of long-term infrastructure maintenance. Quality and safety assurance standards	Assistance in gaining import licences and customs clearance for components. Development of in-house policy to prefer supplies and services from locally owned SMEs, and alignment of this policy with other oil, gas and mining companies in the region	Implementation of policy that sees social impact assessment and mitigation studies as delivering not only the formal operating permit from environmental regulators but also the informal 'social licence to operate' from affected communities	Provision of logistics managers. Provision of water, sanitation and electrical engineers. Advocacy to leverage additional community development resources from municipal authorities and international aid agencies. Widening participation in company-owned community development foundations to include non-industry donors, and inclusion of NGOs, civil-society organisations and municipal authorities as members	Advocacy directed at state-owned parts of company, at regulators and at finance ministries to stimulate the distribution of resource rents to the region of operations. Driving multi-stakeholder dialogue on greater transparency of resource rent distribution

a Including rolling-out of operation-related infrastructure to the local populations (e.g. for water and electricity supply, roads, waste and so on).
b For example, on issues such as income restoration, health, displacement, and cultural and ecological impacts.   c Of the affected communities.

Table 12.2 **Core complementary competences in partnerships** (continued over)

Partner	Project-society interface				
	Infrastructure development	Procurement, supply chain and local business development	Social impact mitigation	Community development	Long-term regional development
Government:					
Industry regulators	When assessing concession bids, giving weight to partnership approaches to the development of local infrastructure	A willingness to relax the policy of tying selected employment quotas to the granting of concessions	Establishment of review panels with representatives from the company, local government and civil society to verify the effectiveness of mitigation plans	In assessing concession bids, giving weight to a partnering approach to the company's social investment programme	A willingness to recognise the long-term public interest for more visible and widely distributed resource rents in the region of operations
Municipal authorities	Strategic co-ordination of infrastructure development through local development plans Carrying out a 'public interest' and 'political' mandate to co-ordinate infrastructure development Sharing costs of infrastructure with the company Maintenance of infrastructure through cost-recovery schemes (e.g. through road tolls)	Capacity-building for SMEs in technical and business management Management of township or rural services put out to tender, thereby widening the market away from dependence on the company	Strategic co-ordination of various impact-mitigation measures with government programmes on agriculture, infrastructure, water, health, education and vocational training A willingness to integrate 'government-led' resettlement and land-compensation activities with 'company-led' negotiations on impact mitigation and employment opportunities	Taking a leadership role in 'smoothing' the introduction of new community development NGOs in project areas Through local development plans, undertaking strategic co-ordination of different community development programmes proffered by the company, NGOs and aid agencies	Acting as a driver of new strategic alliances between company and international aid agencies to develop regional infrastructure early in the investment cycle Showing great transparency in the distribution and use of resource rents Advocacy directed at international aid agencies to play an integral role in tri-sector partnership arrangements

Table 12.2 (from previous page; continued opposite)

Partner	Project–society interface				
	Infrastructure development	Procurement, supply chain and local business development	Social impact mitigation	Community development	Long-term regional development
Government (continued):					
Multilateral and bilateral (government aid) agencies	Offering favourable loan terms for municipal government to develop infrastructure, if seen to be partnering with the corporate sector (i.e. where there is a lower risk of cost overruns and corruption) Capacity-building for staff from municipal government (e.g. in contract management and cost recovery) Underwriting risks of the partnership approach to infrastructure development	Capacity-building for SMEs in technical and business management Contributing to venture capital finance for SMEs Provision of micro-finance funding for micro-enterprises that supply SMEs	Strategic partnering (i.e. linking all impact-mitigation and income-restoration plans prepared across a region over time, with the regional development plans of government authorities and international aid agencies)	Acting as a broker for partnerships Capacity-building for municipalities to be able to deliver on their commitments to the partnership	Formulating national and regional strategies of international bilateral donor agencies aligned with the infrastructure plans of municipal government and the company Providing political leverage, best-practice examples and capacity-building with municipal authorities to promote more transparent resource rent distribution at the regional level
Civil society:					
Community groups and leaders	Mobilisation of community participation in the design of infrastructure and 'workable' cost-recovery schemes Mobilisation of community volunteer work	Mobilisation of community participation in 'group-based' micro-finance schemes	Mobilisation of community participation in identifying potential impacts and mitigation measures	Provision of local knowledge, both biophysical and cultural Provision of local leadership and mobilisation of community participation in the design and provision of labour and facility maintenance	Participation in the design of transparent resource rent distribution mechanisms Community institutional participation in the 'bottom-up' management of community development programmes

Table 12.2 (from previous page; continued over)

Partner	Infrastructure development	Procurement, supply chain and local business development	Project–society interface		Long-term regional development
			Social impact mitigation	Community development	
Civil society (continued):					
NGOs	Design and management of community-based cost-recovery schemes Provision of capacity-building for infrastructure maintenance activities (either directly or through other NGOs)	Capacity-building for SMEs on contract, technical, business and management issues Design and management of micro-finance programmes, in particular community-based institution-building	Ensuring the relevance of impact mitigation to household livelihood security generally and to the most vulnerable groups in particular Linking individual impact-mitigation plans or resettlement plans with broader community development programmes aimed at the affected population	Providing state-of-the-art tools for community participatory planning Creating community project designs that take account of the most vulnerable groups Placing an emphasis on community organisations, community ownership and sustainability Making a long-term commitment to work in the project area	The commitment of international NGOs to co-ordinate and build the capacity of local NGOs to act as intermediaries between regional resource-rent-based public expenditure programmes and the household livelihood security needs of communities Providing the capacity to implement community development activities in the long term
SMEs	A willingness to employ and build the capacity of communities affected by the construction of infrastructure	Creation of local banks to reduce loan rates for SMEs, where the SMEs are engaged in capacity-building programmes in business management and/or have secured contracts with the company or municipalities			Establishment of project management and accountancy firms to provide transparency in resource-rent-funded public expenditure programmes

Table 12.2 (continued)

12.3 Partnership maintenance

Like any type of product, a partnership needs regular maintenance. Partnerships between companies, government and civil society are particularly complex and need careful and appropriate maintenance. As the partners begin to work together for the first time, there are bound to be tensions. This is normal. Indeed, in many of the partnership arrangements discussed in Chapters 3–11, within a matter of months the partners renegotiated certain aspects of their original set of agreements, including the types of resources committed, the key roles of certain partners or the addition of new objectives.

The need to adapt partnerships over time has four principal causes: namely (a) unanticipated behaviour of, or between, the different partners, (b) an insufficient capacity within the partner organisations to implement their commitments, (c) changes in the external business or political environment (e.g. a company's decision to suspend operations, or the onset of state elections) or (d) the completion of agreed 'milestones' in the work-plan (e.g. the end of the construction phase of a community project, the review of a 'pilot' or test case).

In addition to occasional renegotiations, the partners need to be in constant communication with each other, to resolve their differences, to prevent these differences from escalating and to solve problems jointly and creatively. The more the partners interact, the more likely it is that the partnership will be successful. If the original set of agreements governing the partnership has been properly structured, ensuring ongoing communication and transparency should be no more than a question of implementing agreed procedures.

At some point those engaged in executing the various work-plans and other agreements of the partnership will be required to show that these efforts are of practical value to their organisation. In short, they will be asked by their senior managers to demonstrate the benefits of the partnership model for managing social issues in terms of core business interests, social or community development goals or public-sector governance. Essential to this is the measurement of the impact of the partnership compared with the next best alternative, where the alternatives could be each organisation working alone, the company outsourcing to consultants or some other form of partnership (e.g. a company–NGO or a company–government partnership). It is this incremental contribution of the partnership over and above the next best alternative that lies at the heart of proving either the business case or development case for partnership. Chapters 13 and 14, respectively, consider in more detail the issues of monitoring and measuring partnerships.

13
Monitoring partnerships

Michael Warner

This chapter provides guidance on how to monitor partnerships to manage social issues in the extractive industries. The four discrete elements of monitoring are presented and discussed: (1) the business and social 'context' for the partnership; (2) the key factors in successful partnership development and maintenance; (3) the effectiveness of the governance rules and roles between the partners; (4) the outcomes of the partnership for business, communities and government.

There are a range of reasons why companies, other partners, facilitators and funding organisations wish to monitor the progress of partnerships. These reasons include raising awareness on key issues among the collaborating partners, checking the progress of partnership development or implementation against agreed milestones, maintaining a written record of activities and outcomes, learning from the experience in order to improve and replicate positive aspects in subsequent partnerships, measuring the impact of the partnership in relation to the intended objectives agreed by the partners and measuring the added value of the partnership over and above the alternatives available to the partners to meet their objectives. This chapter provides guidance on how to monitor partnerships. The issues of measurement are discussed in Chapter 14.

13.1 Applying the guidelines

The guidelines described in this chapter are intended to enable both the description (i.e. facts and perceptions) and the analysis of partnerships. In an effort to promote analysis, the overall style of enquiry used to prepare monitoring reports should be inquisitive. The broad questions that underpin such enquiries include:

- What was intended (i.e. what were the stated objectives and unstated motivations)?

- What happened (i.e. what are the impacts and outcomes)?

- How did it happen (i.e. what were the modalities)?

- How could things be improved?

- What should not be attempted again?

Because multi-sector partnerships are so complex, one-to-one interviews, though necessary to encourage freedom of expression, may also lead to inconsistencies of perception between the partners about what 'really' happened. Therefore, to complement the information that can be obtained from one-to-one interviews, short workshops can be used to develop consensus among the partners, sub-groups of partners or other stakeholders over what happened and to whom.

This guidance for the monitoring of partnerships is divided into the following five categories: (a) the business and social context for the partnership, (b) partnership generalities, (c) the process of partnership development and maintenance, (d) functionality and governance and (e) partnership outcomes. The issue of measuring partnership outcomes is considered in Chapter 14.

13.2 Business and social context for the partnership

Understanding 'why' business, civil-society and government organisations feel driven to collaborate on social issues, instead of working alone, should form part of the monitor report. From the business perspective, consideration should be given to:

- The types of business participating in the partnership process and their links to wider society in terms of issues such as employment, procurement, health, safety and environmental performance, human rights, the provision of infrastructure, customers and shareholders

- The stage in the project cycle of the participating business at the time of reporting, and the company's particular relationship to wider society at this stage

- The broader economic and political climate (past, present and anticipated) in terms of its relevance to the participating business moving towards a partnership approach to social management

- The main issues and challenges facing the company that are encouraging it to consider the partnership model (e.g. the need to comply with various environmental or social performance standards, to manage resettlement, to resolve local disputes, to contribute to regional development and to manage retrenchment)

- The current project management or strategic planning activities into which the partnership will 'hook'; examples could include pre-feasibility studies, due diligence studies, environmental and social impact assessment, political risk assessment, cost–benefit analysis, compensation and resettlement negotiations, public consultation, planning and financing approval negotiations, health and safety consultation and planning, environmental or social audits, and closure or decommissioning strategies

When looking at the social context for partnerships, consideration should be given to:

- The social and poverty characteristics of the resident population and the outstanding social development challenges and priorities of that population; for example their need for
  - Freedom from violence
  - Income
  - Healthcare
  - Secure land-tenure
  - Access to natural resources, education and training

- The security context (e.g. risk of conflict or disturbance), if relevant

- The physical environmental context, if relevant

The wider economic and political climate (past, present and anticipated) is often a critical influence on the willingness of civil-society groups and government authorities to move towards a partnership model for designing or delivering social programmes. Consideration should also be given to the current government, non-governmental organisation (NGO) or donor agency project management or strategic planning activities into which the partnership could 'hook'. From a government-authority or public-policy perspective, these activities could include municipal authority development plans, regional land-use plans, national sustainable development strategies, poverty-reduction planning (e.g. through use of poverty-reduction strategy papers), sectoral strategic planning (looking at healthcare, education, water supply, etc.), sectoral policy dialogue, programmes for decentralisation, and negotiations with official development agencies. For civil-society and donor organisations, possible initiatives into which partnerships could be hooked include household livelihoods assessments, community participatory assessments, participatory monitoring and evaluation, sectoral national and regional strategies, and programmes aimed at capacity-building and providing technical assistance.

13.3 Partnership generalities

Monitoring reports should include a description of the key characteristics of the partnership, including:

- The broad theme or topic of the partnership (i.e. the issue, or issues, that the partnership is seeking to address)

- The overall type of partnership being proposed or implemented (e.g. whether it is characterised as knowledge-sharing, consultative, informed-consent, contractual, shared-task, shared-responsibility or some combination of these)

- The partner organisations involved and the legitimacy of those 'sitting at the table' as representatives of their constituents

- How close the objectives of the partnership lie in to core business activities and the priority needs of communities.

13.4 The process of partnership development and maintenance

As discussed in Chapter 12, on getting started, the process of developing and managing tri-sector partnerships broadly falls into three stages: namely, exploration, building and maintenance. Monitoring the quality of activities undertaken to facilitate a partnership will require that each of the three stages is assessed.

13.4.1 Partnership exploration

For the partnership exploration process, consideration should be given to:

- How the needs of each party in terms of development impact and business benefit were identified

- How each party weighed the risks and costs of addressing these needs through tri-sector partnership against the opportunities and benefits

- The process of stakeholder consultation undertaken to bring potential partners into dialogue about forming a partnership

13.4.2 Partnership-building

When looking at partnership-building, the assessment should consider:

- The key actors (e.g. 'champions' and brokers) instrumental in bringing the partners together

- The underlying interests of each partner that had to be satisfied to reach an agreement to work together

- How the contribution of resources, the distribution of roles and responsibilities and the governance structure among the partners was negotiated and agreed

- The measures taken to strengthen capacity (institutional and human) to make the partnership work

- The measures put in place, both from the outset and subsequently, to manage and maintain the partnership over time

13.4.3 Partnership maintenance

Assessment of partnership maintenance requires that consideration be given to:

- The way in which partners communicate, make decisions and resolve grievances within the partnership (and with their respective constituents and other parties)

- The extent of satisfaction in the way the partnership is functioning

- The way in which the partnership responds to changes in the external environment (e.g. economic, political and environmental changes and changes relating to security) and to changes in the internal environment (e.g. in key personnel or management champions)

- How roles and responsibilities have altered over time

13.5 Functionality and governance

The experience with the case-study projects of the Natural Resources Cluster programme has shown the importance of partners reaching agreement on objectives, roles and rules for what the partnership will do and how the partners will interact. An analysis of how the resulting governance structure of the partnership functions in practice will assist in identifying gaps (e.g. in the capacity of particular partners to deliver on their commitments) or tensions between partners that need to be resolved (e.g. lack of transparency in the use of one another's resources).

Building on Box 12.6 on page 174, listing key elements of agreement in constructing a partnership, the following are key questions that need to be asked regarding the governance structure of the partnership:

- Have the legitimate representatives of the partner organisations been included?

- Have clear geographic boundaries and/or target populations for the partnership's social investment and/or community development activities been defined?

- Has a common vision for the partnership (e.g. a short 'vision statement') been agreed?

- Has agreement been reached on the partnership's objectives, including the shared objectives and those specific to individual partners?

- Has there been agreement on a joint work-plan for meeting the objectives, stating clearly
    - The key activities and tasks expected of each partner, including related schedules and performance indicators
    - The skills and resources brought by each partner to implement each activity, including 'tangible' resources (finance, human skills, etc.) and 'intangible' resources (access to vulnerable community groups, credibility with senior government officials, critical information such as surveys or databases, increased efficiency, etc.)
    - The division of roles and responsibility for each activity, and any associated funding arrangements

- Have the principles for decision-making (e.g. respect for different views, unanimous or majority voting) been agreed?

- Is there an agreed grievance mechanism to resolve disputes between parties?

- Are there agreed mechanisms for ongoing transparency and communication among partners and between partners and their constituents?

- Where appropriate, have measures been taken to ensure adequate capacity to negotiate, build and maintain consensus and to deliver on commitments?

- Have measures been adopted to mitigate the various medium-term 'threats' to the partnership (e.g. changes in key personnel, changes in commodity prices, political elections)?

- Is there an agreed monitoring and learning mechanism (e.g. are periodic progress reports produced, and facilitated reflection workshops held)?

The importance of monitoring and evaluating governance and functionality was shown in the Sarshatali case study (described in Chapter 4). Although the livelihoods assessment partnership was regarded, by all partners, as extremely successful, the early stages of the partnership were characterised by a lack of clarity and agreement on the roles and responsibilities of the implementing partners. The concerns raised by the company, Integrated Coal Mining Limited (ICML), were that reports did not arrive on time from the NGOs and the need for frequent proactive interventions to get the partners to pursue objectives. The concerns of the participating NGOs, ASHA and Suchetana, were somewhat different. ASHA observed that reports did arrive on time from Suchetana, and that it (ASHA) had to take full responsibility in the field-level work. Suchetana noted that there was no clarity in the role of ASHA as the facilitating NGO and that ICML interventions were mostly interfering. These concerns were identified as part of the ongoing monitoring of the partnership, and strategies were adopted to ensure that these difficulties and misunderstandings were addressed effectively.

At the time of inaugurating the Las Cristinas community health centre (see Chapter 5), a SWOT (strengths–weaknesses–opportunities–threats) analysis was undertaken to capture the lessons that had been learned to date and to provide input to the next stage of partnership activities. The results of the SWOT analysis are presented in Table 13.1.

13.6 Partnership outcomes

Perhaps most important in any monitoring regime is to record the outcomes being delivered by the partnership. These are likely to fall broadly into one of the following categories: business benefits, community development impact or public-sector governance. The categories of partnership outcome to be monitored include:

- The extent to which the partnership's intended impacts have been felt (i.e. whether joint and partner-specific objectives have been achieved)

- Unintended, unexpected or spin-off benefits to business, community development or governance

- Negative outcomes of the partnership for business, communities or governance

- Whether there is evidence that the partnership has 'added value',[1] in terms of its impact, over and above
  - The impact of other activities taking place at the same time that could have contributed to the same results
  - The impacts that would have accrued if the 'next-best alternative' had been implemented instead of the partnership

- Some indication of the cost of the partnership measured against the benefits (tangible and intangible)

- Evidence of institutional change either in the business, government agencies or civil-society organisations, such as
  - Institutionalisation of the partnership for the long term
  - Changes in micro-policy
  - Changes in incentive structures, such as in staff performance criteria, and reporting requirements
  - Changes in the overall attitude and behaviour of NGOs towards business, or of business towards NGOs

---

1   The measurement of added value is considered in more detail in Chapter 14.

Strengths

- The 'thirst' for learning among members and leaders of local communities
- The volunteer support created and developed
- The wider public recognition of the efforts of all involved
- The improved leadership of local team members within their communities
- The consolidation and capacity for effective action of the local team
- The success 'visible' in the new health centre
- The feeling of empowerment of being better organised by members of the community
- The establishment of new channels of communication with local businesses and local government institutions

Weaknesses

- The continuing under-development of local (community-based) partners, with continued dependence on a few dominant leaders
- The lack of a clear organisational and administrative structure for the health centre, and the lack of a clear legal scope of activities
- Insufficient communication between the health-centre sub-committees and other partners
- Insufficient participation in the project by existing local public-service health-workers
- Insecurity of funding for the second phase, (i.e. for centre operations and management)

Opportunities

- The willingness of local businesses and other companies to establish alliances
- Access to grants: if local communities can use partnership to demonstrate their ability to organise and manage funds, they may be able to access regional social development grants
- Future training opportunities for community leaders and other partnership members through the company
- Increased participation and empowerment for the community: community members of the partnership can use new knowledge and skills to strengthen their participation and influence in community affairs
- The creation of new channels of communication and an improved perception of competence between regional government and local communities
- Constitutional support: the type of community participation seen in the partnership is supported and promoted by the new Venezuelan Constitution
- Access to grants and funds: organised communities are more attractive to international funding agencies and NGOs

Threats or risks

- Lack of fulfilment of agreements by some institutions and other actors (e.g. an international NGO, provincial government and some community leaders)
- A misconception that healthcare will be free: a generalised perception of 'free health' is taking hold and may weaken the economic running of the health centre
- The influence of some people with a paternalistic and negative attitude
- Potential resistance from medical professionals, the government and other actors to the community managing the new health centre
- Lack of clarity of roles between communities and the NGO
- Potential for political community leaders to distort or mislead the aims of the partnership, in an effort to 'spoil' the process
- Lack of adequate security at the new health-centre facility (with the possibility of theft of equipment and materials), fulfilling fears of the NGO
- Lack of improvement in the infrastructure needed for health promotion (e.g. in drinking-water supply, waste disposal, access roads, etc.)

Table 13.1 **Example of the SWOT (strengths–weaknesses–opportunities–threats) analysis used to monitor partnership governance for the Las Cristinas healthcare partnership, Venezuela**

13.7 Conclusions and recommendations

If the monitoring report is to have utility, evidence-based conclusions will need to be formulated and, where appropriate, recommendations be made. As a minimum, monitor reports should consider the issues listed in Box 13.1.

Key issues to consider are:

- The key achievements of the partnership from the viewpoint of business, community development and public-sector governance
- Pressing and/or outstanding issues for the partners to address
- The immediate next steps to be taken for developing or maintaining the partnership
- The longer-term plan of action for the partnership
- Broader lessons for replicating the partnership approach

Box 13.1 **Key issues to consider in monitor reports**

14
Measuring the added value of partnerships

Jol Mitchell, Jill Shankleman and Michael Warner

This chapter sets out a methodology for measuring the impact of a partnership model of social management in the extractive industries. The emphasis is on measuring the 'added value' of a partnership approach, over and above the alternative ways in which business, government and civil-society organisations could meet their social objectives. The methodology is designed to be used in conjunction with the broader framework for partnership monitoring described in Chapter 13.

The purpose of the methodology is to facilitate the measurement of the 'added value' of partnership approaches to managing social issues in relation to the extractive industries. In particular, the aim is to measure the incremental contribution of a partnership approach to business interests, community development and public-sector governance, over and above that which could have been achieved though alternative approaches (e.g. though the corporation managing social issues 'in-house' or outsourcing the function to consultants, corporate foundations or non-governmental organisation (NGOs) or through government authorities, international donors and NGOs implementing social programmes alone).

The methodology was developed at a workshop held in London in May 2002 by the Natural Resources Cluster of Business Partners for Development (BPD). The workshop participants agreed a number of criteria that the methodology should meet. It should be:

- Affordable. It should be possible to apply the methodology during a 10-day field visit. Further, it should be possible if necessary to carry out the first phase of the methodology without direct contact with the partners and to carry out phases 2 and 3 with use of a single interviews with the partners.

- Repeatable. The methodology should provide a standard approach that can be consistently applied by different individuals; one caveat for this is that these individuals should have strong interviewing skills.

- Replicable. The methodology should provide a framework that should be applicable in a wide range of circumstances.

- Offer comparability. Consistent application of the methodology should, in theory, enable comparison. However, this will depend on the indicators chosen. In addition, it may well be necessary to compare qualitative conclusions as in many cases it may not be possible to place a monetary value on changes in the indicators.

- Independent. The methodology should enable one to isolate the specific causes and effects of the partnership.

- Non-intrusive. The methodology should be designed to optimise contact with the partnership parties, with secondary data-sources and key informants used where practicable.

This chapter is divided into four main sections, looking at:

- Phases
- Assumptions
- Tasks and responsibilities
- Guidance on application

14.1 Phases

The four phases in the methodology are as follows:

- Scoping, to identify the key indicators of partnership benefit relevant to each sector (corporate operation, civil-society organisations and government authorities) and the most appropriate methods of measurement of those indicators

- Data collection, to establish a baseline and to measure changes in the indicators selected

- Assessment of the incremental contribution, to calculate the effect of the partnership as measured by changes in key indicators and to assess the strength of the evidence for direct causation

- Assessment of value for money, to compare the evidence of benefits with the costs involved in the partnering process.

Table 14.1 summarises the key tasks and outcomes of each phase.

Phase	Tasks	Outcome
Scoping	• Through discussion with the partners, identify of a total of 10–15 indicators of partnership outcomes • Define and agree on methods of measurements for each indicator	A list of indicators and methods for their measurement
Data collection	• Collect relevant project data and interview the partners • Identify changes in the indicators	A list of indicators and methods for their measurement
Assessment of incremental contribution	Asses the incremental contribution of the partnership to changes observed in the indicators	A table outlining the contribution of the partnership to the changes observed in the indicators
Assessment of value for money	Measure costs in relation to benefits	A balance sheet

Table 14.1 Phases in measuring the 'added value' of partnerships

14.2 Assumptions

A key assumption underpinning the methodology is that the impact of tri-sector partnerships can be measured retrospectively by evaluating the extent to which partnership has delivered:

- Its intended outcomes (i.e. the original objectives agreed to by all partners, which should have been specified in the original memorandum of understanding, partnering agreement or charter between the partners)

- Outcomes that add value over and above the most likely alternative action a partner would have taken alone to achieve the desired objectives

- Other, unexpected, outcomes that are deemed by the partners to be either positive or negative

- A net positive ratio of 'partnership benefit' to 'cost of partnering'

The methodology proposed here focuses on the outcomes of the partnership as defined by each partner. It does not consider wider societal or business impacts unless these are explicitly determined as objectives of the partnership or unless these are revealed during the assessment as significant 'added-value' or 'unexpected' outcomes relating to the partnership. This limitation is intended to ensure that the methodology is quick and cost-effective to apply.

14.3 Tasks and responsibilities

The first task in measuring the added value of a specific partnership is to gather data from documents, interviews, workshops and direct observation. In general, this task is primarily for the assessor, with support from the partners to facilitate access (e.g. to particular documents or individuals). Following the data-gathering phase, the assessor and the partners are then responsible jointly for:

- Determining the outcomes attributable to the partnership in relation to the business, community development and public-sector governance

- Calculating the incremental contribution of these outcomes attributable to the partnership arrangement, as opposed to other social management activities taking place at the same time and as opposed to the most likely alternative to the partnership (i.e. to consider what each partner would have done to meet its objectives in the absence of the partnership)

- Identifying the costs of developing and maintaining the partnership (e.g. facilitation costs, logistics)

In relation to the costs of developing and maintaining the partnership, the assessment of the acceptability of these costs relative to the results achieved can be made only by the partners.

14.4 Guidelines for application of the methodology

14.4.1 Scoping phase

The overall objective of the scoping phase is to agree, with the key partners, around 10–15 key indicators of partnership impact and how these indicators will be measured. These indicators should cover the three categories of assessment: namely, business outcomes, community development impact and public-sector governance.

The first stage of the scoping phase (see Fig. 14.1) is to review the generic list of possible indicator categories and indicators. A comprehensive checklist of indicators of partnership benefits and outcomes has been prepared for each of the three

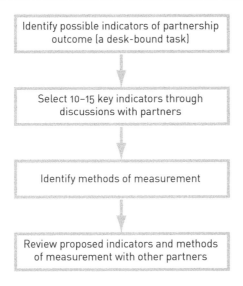

Figure 14.1 Scoping phase

sectors (see Appendix D). It is highly unlikely that all categories of indicators will be relevant to any one particular partnership, and the list of indicators should be shortened to exclude those that clearly are not relevant in the case under study. Other, more relevant, indicators may also be considered. Note that the process of selecting the indicators is an interactive desk-based exercise and requires knowledge of the nature of the oil, gas or mining project concerned and of the socio-economic context in which it operates.

The methods of measurement and the data sources for each of the key indicators should be identified in conjunction with representatives from the partner organisations and the assessor. The scale of measurement should be expressed precisely. Where possible, the scale should be quantitative and be capable of being expressed in financial terms (e.g. in terms of cost savings or cost leverage). However, in many cases it will be possible to apply only normative scales.

The resulting set of indicators and methods of measurement are likely to reflect a combination of the original objectives of each partner in entering the partnership (or, more specifically, the underlying interests behind these objectives) and unexpected outcomes, either negative or positive. Not only will different partners have different objectives for the partnership but also, within any one partner organisation, objectives will differ between individuals and their departments. It is important that these differences be captured when indicators are set. For example, in measuring the business case for partnerships, the project manager concerned with health, safety and environment may be interested primarily in obtaining environmental clearance from the regulatory authorities or investors, the production manager's main interest may be that scheduling milestones be met, and the

company's executive management may require that the company develop a reputation that attracts high-calibre staff.

Before the list of indicators is finalised it should be reviewed by other project
partners to bring their perspectives to the analysis. Where possible, community
stakeholders should also be consulted.

14.4.2 Data-collection phase

The overall objective of the data-collection phase is to identify the changes that
have occurred in each of the key indicators. The first step is to prepare a data-
collection plan to steer efforts towards the most relevant personnel and to allow
one to think through the best sources of information (e.g. documents, interviews,
workshops, observations, key informants). Data is needed not only on changes in
indicators during the partnership's life but also on the baseline conditions prior to
the partnership.

Data collected from the most relevant partner will need to be supplemented
through interviews with other partners as well as with representative stakeholders
such as the communities affected by partnership activities. The practical reality is
that, owing to time pressures, in many cases interviews will need to address all
areas of partnership impact (i.e. business benefits, community development and
public-sector governance) in a single meeting. The assessor needs to prepare
himself or herself accordingly.

The deliverable at this stage is a summary table identifying the magnitude of the
change in each indicator. The use of a predefined table and agreed indicators
fosters discipline in the data-collection and analysis process. Given the complexities of tri-sector partnerships, there is a real risk of developing increasingly deep

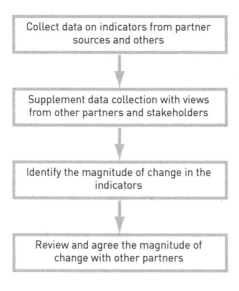

Figure 14.2 Data-collection phase

descriptions of the activities of the partnership at the expense of measuring its results. Figure 14.2 summarises the steps to be taken during this phase of the process.

14.4.3 Assessment of contribution

In order to evaluate the overall contribution of the partnership to changes observed in the key indicators, and in order to evaluate the reliability of the available evidence, an analysis should first be made of (a) external contributing factors and (b) each partner's most probable alternative method of achieving the desired objectives. This should then be followed by an assessment of both the incremental partnership and the confidence in the results obtained.

The assessment of external factors should include consideration of all relevant significant changes in the wider sociopolitical and economic environment that could affect the activities and outcomes of the partnership. This might include changes in political leadership, changes in the actual or anticipated return on project investment, delays to the project and related social investment programmes, changes in the local economy (e.g. the effects of privatisation), the effects of external disputes and political violence, the effects of social programmes implemented by non-partners and the effects of community groups' efforts to manage their own development.

A common mistake in evaluating the added value of partnership arrangements is to attribute all that is accomplished by the partners to the presence of the partnership. Not only are there likely to be external contributing factors but also, more importantly, each partner is likely to have had an alternative plan of action to achieve its objectives had the partners not come together. For example, instead of implementing a healthcare programme through a partnership arrangement, the company, communities, NGOs or government authorities may have attempted to undertake some of this work alone, though with different cost implications and different results. Care should be taken in identifying the 'most likely alternatives'. Although an organisation (company, government authority or NGO) may claim to have had in place plans to achieve some or all the results generated by the partnership, it is sometimes doubtful whether these plans would have been implemented in practice, in the same time-frame or to the same level of quality or sustainability as achieved by the partnership.

14.4.3.1 Calculating the incremental contribution

Once the value of the contribution of external factors and of the most likely alternatives have been identified (in monetary terms, where possible), the incremental contribution of the partnership is calculated as the value of the outcomes attributable to the partnership minus the sum of the values of the outcomes attributable to these factors and alternatives. This calculation can be represented as follows:

$$V_{added} = \sum [V_{partnership} - (V_{external} + V_{alternative})] \qquad 14.1$$

where

V_{added} is the added value of the partnership

$V_{\text{partnership}}$ is the value of the outcomes attributable solely to the partnership

V_{external} is the value of the outcomes attributable to external factors

$V_{\text{alternative}}$ is the value of the outcomes that could have been achieved had an alternative to the partnership approach been taken

The final step in this phase of the methodology is to provide an indication of the level of confidence in the reliability of the evidence used to make the calculation. The confidence limit can be simply characterised as 'high', 'moderate' or 'low'. The factors to take into account in making what is essentially an informed subjective judgement include the extent to which there is traceable data to support monetary values, whether published reports or personal quotes have been gathered to support subjective judgements, whether there is consistency in the different sources of information (including interviews) and the degree of consensus on the impacts both from the partners and from external stakeholders.

The key steps in this phase are summarised in Figure 14.3. An example of the deliverables from this type of assessment is given in Appendix E. The tables in

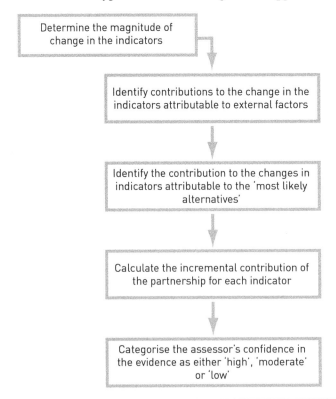

Figure 14.3 Assessing the contribution of the partnership to value added

Appendix E are drawn from the evaluation of the partnership arrangements at the Las Cristinas gold mine project in Venezuela (see Chapter 5).

14.4.4 Measuring costs in relation to benefits

The assessment of the 'value for money' of a partnership involves determining the total costs of the partnering process to each of the individual partners and comparing these costs with the monetary and other benefits achieved. The general process is presented in Figure 14.4.

The overall costs of resourcing, developing and maintaining the partnership arrangements will include direct costs (e.g. for the provision of equipment, funds and lodgings), indirect costs (e.g. for the provision of staff time and related opportunities forgone) and costs relating to the third-party brokering or maintenance of the partnership (e.g. travel costs and the fees of interpreters and facilitators). These partnership costs are then set against the added value of the partnership already calculated. The results of this value-for-money assessment can be compiled as a tabulated balance sheet, thereby enabling the costs and the incremental benefits to be compared directly. Wherever possible, values should be expressed in monetary or quantitative terms. This process will provide the partners with the information on which they can assess whether the results represent 'value for money'. An example of a balance sheet, taken from the perspective of the operating company, is given in Table 14.2. This balance sheet was prepared as part of the assessment of the Las Cristinas healthcare partnership, described in Chapter 5.

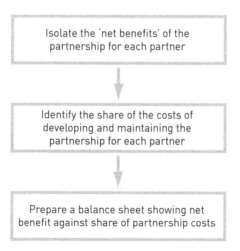

Figure 14.4 Cost–benefit

Partnership cost		Incremental benefit	
Description	Value (US$)	Description	Value (US$)
Management costs (costs of running workshops and for providing lodging and food for engineers, and fees paid for project management consultants and external visitors)	71,430	Positive reputation gains from improved relations with surrounding communities and other regional stakeholders	Intangible
Construction costs (costs of construction materials, equipment, furnishings, air-conditioning, a generator and staff time)	357,000	Marketing and competitive advantage gained through success	Intangible
Share of partnership facilitation costs	98,000	Licence to operate secured in the context of institutional uncertainty (less social liability)	Intangible
		Savings on lobbying expenditure	30,000[a]
		Leverage of additional investment from other organisations	2,079,538
		More cost-effective healthcare for future community-based employees	Intangible
Total	526,430	Total	2,109,538[b]

a Estimated   b Minimum benefit

Table 14.2 Costs and incremental benefits ('added value') of the healthcare partnership to Minera Las Cristinas, CA (MINCA), Venezuela

Part 3
Issues

15
Towards evidence of the costs and benefits of partnerships

Nicola Acutt with Ralph Hamann, Assheton Carter and Paul Kapelus

This chapter explores the costs of social issues, with a focus on the opportunities for cost savings or financial benefits that can be realised through partnership approaches to managing these issues. Specific reference is made to the measurement, from a business perspective, of the costs and benefits of partnering.

15.1 Social issues and partnerships

Oil, gas and mining companies are increasingly expected to take responsibility for addressing the social issues that arise as a consequence of their activities and operations. Partnerships involving working alongside government, civil society and local communities are seen as, potentially, an effective and efficient strategy to address complex social issues together with local environmental problems. Entering into partnerships as a means of addressing social issues, therefore, raises important questions about the anticipated benefits and the extent to which these benefits can be quantified or measured against the costs of the partnering process.

In assessing the business case for addressing social issues through tri-sector partnerships, the specific questions that arise are:

- What are the implications and potential costs of social issues?
- What opportunities do partnerships provide for cost savings?
- Can social costs and benefits be measured?

15.2 Implications and potential costs of social issues

Broadly speaking, social impacts can be divided into primary and secondary impacts. Primary impacts (e.g. disturbance to agricultural land, increased traffic on the roads, encroachment on spiritual and burial sites, cultural disturbance and the displacement of families or entire villages) are directly linked to the project and are typically addressed through mechanisms of compensation and mitigation. Secondary impacts include wider social and economic issues (e.g. the spread of disease, changes in migration patterns, changes in economic, livelihood and purchasing systems, economic dependence, inflation, competition for land resources, and healthcare practices) and frequently are more difficult to relate directly to a specific project or to the responsibility of a particular operating company.

The impact of social issues on mining, oil and gas projects represents a key category of risk that can be made worse by a failure to respond appropriately. A disregard for social issues (or an inadequate response to these issues) can create significant economic problems for companies resulting, for example, from large-scale protests by non-governmental organisations (NGOs) and consumer groups. Poor social responsibility can therefore compromise long-term commercial prospects, lasting regional development opportunities and, ultimately, profitability. The following examples highlight some of the more frequently cited risks and potential costs of failing to respond effectively to social issues.

15.2.1 Local community opposition

Local community opposition (from protest to sabotage) can cause costly delays in production, permits being challenged, increased inspection by officials, interruption to the smooth running of the project and even termination of production (e.g. see the case study on Shell Petroleum Development Corporation, Chapter 3). In some cases, local community dissatisfaction can lead to court action and costly litigation. Production delays are particularly problematic for 'just-in-time' supply chains and may mean that contracts are lost or terminated if the supply company is unable to guarantee delivery of its product (e.g. oil, gas, minerals).

15.2.2 Staff dissatisfaction

Local staff dissatisfaction, as a result of social concerns, can lead to antagonism, strikes and even rioting, which in turn can lead to productivity losses and human resource management problems. For example, Eastern Resource Capital reported that, as a result of not attending to local staff needs, annual staff turnover in the early 1980s at the Ok Tedi site in Papua New Guinea reached 150%.

15.2.3 Negative publicity on social impacts

The social impacts of a project can, potentially, be publicised on a global level, primarily by means of the Internet. An example is the Yanacocha Gold project in northern Peru where, in the early days of the project, NGOs roused the fears of local people over possible contamination of water sources. German Catholic groups working in local development projects raised the issue in Germany and involved German government authorities in an attempt to get German backing for the project withdrawn.

15.2.4 Consumer pressure

Some customers and consumers are becoming increasingly concerned about the production conditions surrounding the materials they purchase and are more likely to demand certification to recognised standards and indicators. Although certification is more prominent in the environmental arena (e.g. the ISO 14001 standard for environmental management systems), social performance certification standards are being developed (e.g. SA8000) and increasingly accepted by (and expected of) the extractive industries.

15.2.5 Community relations

The maintenance of good community relations is crucial for a company's reputation, which in turn is vital for the company's access to financial resources and government permits as well as to highly qualified and motivated staff. As information becomes more public and incidents are reported, the share price of listed companies can be affected as investors anticipate the enforcement of penalising legislation (although this may be less the case for the oil industry, where share price tends to be closely linked to 'assets', not production). Furthermore, unresolved social issues may require increased corporate financing to resolve (as illustrated by the Yanacocha Gold project described in Section 15.2.3). Failure to address social issues may compromise support from international financial or lending institutions as these may be less likely to invest in projects perceived to entail greater risk. As noted by one senior executive from a major extractive-industry company, 'the desire for a smooth development and operation process . . . can be jeopardised if local communities do not perceive themselves to have a true stake in the project. Their discontent can ultimately translate into regulatory and political problems.'

15.2.6 Health issues

Health problems and local conditions (such as the prevalence of malaria and of HIV and AIDS) can have significant implications for a company through high levels of absenteeism as a result of sickness or attendance to family crises. The financial costs include impacts on productivity as well as costs associated with labour replacement, training and recruitment. These issues and their potential impacts on the stability of the workforce were important drivers for the social development programme of Kahama Mining Corporation Limited, described in Chapter 8.

15.2.7 Summary

There is increasing evidence to suggest that corporate social responsibility initiatives (through mechanisms such as partnerships or investment programmes) can minimise the negative impacts and risks of social issues. The key elements of corporate social responsibility are:

- Consultation with local communities, beginning early in the project cycle and continuing through the entire project cycle

- The adoption of an open information policy, emphasising realistic expectations

- Communication with all groups, not just the authorities

- The provision of assistance to the community as an entitlement, not as a gift from the company

- The creation of local development funds, with support from the highest corporate and government levels

- Contributions to the development fund from the company being 'after tax'

- The provision of training and support to local communities to help them in negotiations (capacity-building)

- Efforts to diversify the local economy and lessen dependence on the company

- The conducting, as early as possible, of social and cultural baseline studies as well as social impact assessments

These corporate social responsibility activities require funding throughout the project cycle. This raises the question of the extent to which partnerships provide opportunities for cost savings or enable additional financial or development benefits to be achieved.

15.3 Opportunities for cost savings through partnerships

One of the most powerful incentives for companies to engage in partnerships is the potential for cost savings. Although the quantification and measurement of social costs remains difficult (for a discussion of the methodology that has been used in the case studies described in Chapters 3–11, see Chapter 14), there is growing evidence to suggest that there are opportunities for cost savings, or 'net benefits', across a variety of activities (e.g. through avoiding delays to project start-up, maintaining a good reputation and ensuring the smooth running of the project). Such benefits are not 'free goods' and there are additional cost considerations in addressing social issues through partnership approaches, including direct costs (e.g. partnership funding, travel and logistics expenses and the costs of hiring interpreters and facilitators) and indirect costs (e.g. management time). An example of the cost–benefit assessment for the Sarshatali livelihoods assessment and trust-building partnership is presented in Table 15.1.

Clearly, no two projects or partnerships are the same and the costs will necessarily vary according to local circumstances, the scale of the problems and the resources available to address the issues. Nevertheless, a sense of the nature and scale of costs and benefits involved in partnership development can be gained from the case studies presented in Chapters 3–11. The Sarshatali Coal Mining Project (described in Chapter 4) provides an example of the benefits and 'bottom-line' savings that can be realised in the context of operational uncertainty, delays to financial closure, rising community expectations and a fragile 'social licence to operate'. A summary of the costs and benefits of the livelihoods assessment and trust-building partnership to the company, Integrated Coal Mining Limited (ICML), is presented in Table 15.1 (for the measurable financial costs and benefits) and in Box 15.1 (for the qualitative benefits that were identified). Other opportunities for cost savings through tri-sector partnerships may include the leveraging of resources into community development (e.g. through the establishment of an independent development foundation) with the goal of winning support from other organisations, skill sharing, reduced dependence, and networking and collaboration.

15.4 Costs and benefits

The cost–benefit analysis drawn from the Sarshatali case study indicates that the financial benefits of partnering can be substantial. Similar results (i.e. significant financial and other benefits relative to the costs incurred) have been reported for many of the other case studies presented in Part 1. As well as demonstrating the business case for partnering, the analysis shows how developing and applying a systematic method of measurement can highlight strengths and weaknesses of the partnership, thereby providing considerable benefits for partnership management. It should be noted, however, that no clear lines of causality should necessarily be drawn between particular partnership elements or activities and specific cost savings. For instance, the substantial savings realised through the public–private partnership in road construction in the Sarshatali case might not have been possible without the trust and communication mechanisms established during partnership activities. In other words, the strength of a partnership lies in the fact that the whole is greater than its parts. This presents a further significant challenge to the measurement of costs and benefits.

Some of the most important benefits of partnerships are related to what partnering can help prevent, such as strikes by the company labour force or sabotage to production facilities. One monetary indicator of benefit here is to measure the cost savings resulting from a partnership in relation to security arrangements, both for

Costs of partnership development and management		Estimated savings and benefits of the partnership	
Description	Value (US$)	Description	Value (US$)
Facilitation costs:		Livelihoods assessment[a]	6,129
Initial field visits, August 1999	450	Trust-building and community development[b]	54,153
Exploratory workshop, September 1999	450	Road construction[c]	219,000
Partnering assessment, October 1999	1,350		
MOU formulation, November 1999	450		
Training and review meeting, April 2000	900		
Review meeting, July 2000	900		
Final evaluation, September 2000	450		
Sub-total	4,950		
Logistical costs:			
December 1999 to March 2000	50		
March to September 2000	213		
Final evaluation, September 2000	577		
Sub-total	840		
Total	**5,790**	**Total**	**279,282**

a   This is the difference between (a) costs incurred by the assessment of livelihoods as approved by the company–NGO–government partnership (US$18,871) and (b) the costs incurred by the most likely alternative assessment of livelihoods (i.e. consultants' fees to undertake a baseline socioeconomic strategy; US$25,000).

b   This is the difference between development costs incurred by the partnership and the anticipated size of the company's community development budget.

c   This benefit is attributable to the anticipated lower construction and maintenance costs of a mine link road resulting from a public–private partnership with the local authorities.

Table 15.1 Sarshatali coal-mining project: estimated net benefit of the partnership to Integrated Coal Mining Limited, January–September 2000

- Upgrading the socioeconomic baseline data. Compared with what the company would have spent on contracting external consultants, the cost saving of working through non-governmental organisations (NGOs) was around 25%.

- Resettlement. NGOs volunteered to assist the company in engaging households in designing aspects of the resettlement community. It is not possible to quantify the value in terms of risk prevention but the estimated saving against the cost of contracting external consultants to do the work was US$2,240.

- Trust-building and community development. In order to maintain the social licence to operate, the partnership was engaged in implementing 'low-cost' trust-building measures and began income restoration and community development initiatives. Although it is difficult to predict what the company would have invested in the absence of a partnership, an indication of cost savings can be gained by comparing the expenditure to the most likely alternative (which, in this case, would have been in-house recruitment and training measures as well as a proportion of the allocated community development budget for that period). The potential cost savings in this scenario amounted to about US$54,153 (89%).

In addition to the above-mentioned cost-savings, other benefits of the partnership included:

- Reduced risk of damage to reputation

- Reduced community dependence on the company in the medium term

- The creation of a holistic livelihoods assessment instead of a conventional socio-economic base survey

- Resettlement planning

- Community organisational development to manage income restoration

- Community development

- Cost sharing of operational infrastructure (for road construction)

- Greater visibility and responsiveness of government to local needs

Box 15.1 Sarshatali coal-mining project: cost savings for Integrated Coal Mining Limited from the livelihoods assessment and trust-building partnership

the company and for government agencies, such as the police. The business benefits of partnerships in reducing investment risks remain extremely difficult to measure. Nevertheless, risk reduction remains a core business activity and is thus a crucial element of the business case for partnering.

15.5 Emerging lessons

The following lessons are emerging:

- Failure to respond effectively to social issues can have significant economic implications for mining, oil and gas companies, such as protests, delays in permitting and project start-up, tarnished external relations, impeded project financing and problems with human resource management.

- Responding to social issues necessarily has cost implications, as additional resources are required for, among others, consultation, social investment programmes or partnership initiatives.

- Establishing partnerships to address social issues can provide significant benefits and opportunities for cost savings through, for example, the leveraging of resources, skill sharing, reduction of community dependence on the company, networking and collaborating, and maintaining a 'licence to operate'.

Further reading

Andrews, C. (1998) 'Emerging Trends in Mining Industry Partnerships', *Natural Resources Forum* 22.2: 119-26.

Humphreys, D. (2000) 'A Business Perspective on Community Relations in Mining', *Resources Policy* 26: 127-31.

McPhail, K., and A. Davy (1998) *Integrating Social Concerns into Private-Sector Decision-making* (Discussion Paper 384; Washington, DC: World Bank).

Utting, P. (2000) *Business Responsibility for Sustainable Development* (Occasional Paper 2; Geneva: United Nations Research Institute for Social Development [UNRISD]).

Web address

Global Reporting Initiative (which includes social reporting): www.globalreporting.org

16
Ownership and control of outcomes

Aidan Davy

A number of factors can influence the ownership and control of the outcomes of partnerships for social investment. In particular, the formal and informal obligations that each partner (or partnering organisation) has to other parties may present barriers either to assuming or to relinquishing responsibilities. This chapter describes six different models of partnership from the perspective of ownership and control and discusses options for dealing with such barriers. Specific reference is made to the obstacles to partnership faced by civil-society actors.

16.1 Why is the ownership and control of partnership outcomes an issue?

In the context of projects relating to the extraction and use of non-renewable natural resources, the decision to enter into a partnership for social investment raises important questions for all partners about the ownership and control of the outcomes. One such question is how the various partners are to manage their formal and informal 'obligations' both to internal and to external stakeholders (for examples, but not an exhaustive list, of the obligations between partners, see Table 16.1). For example, formal obligations for the company may arise from the need to comply with regulatory or policy requirements, whereas informal obligations encompass broader social responsibility and reciprocal considerations. As high-lighted by Table 16.1, some obligations may deter potential partners from engaging

Partner	Obligations		
	To government	**To business**	**To civil society**
Business:			
Formal	• Meeting requirements for environmental and social assessment, and public consultation • Complying with employment conditions • Supporting infrastructure development as part of the concession agreement • Undertaking monitoring	• Complying with group corporate policy (e.g. on sustainability) • Complying with policy of business unit (e.g. in relationship management) • Complying with loan conditions (e.g. with IFC requirements) • Ensuring subcontractors comply with policy provisions	• Obtaining the informed consent of indigenous peoples • Restoring livelihoods if resettlement occurs • Mitigating social impacts • Compensating for lost assets or access to resources
Informal	• Contributing voluntarily to the provision of social infrastructure • Developing capacity (e.g. for planning, revenue management)	• Meeting internal reporting requirements and key performance indicators • Transferring technology and skills locally • Maintaining credibility with internal staff (e.g. many engineers inside business units distrust NGOs)	• Obtaining and retaining licence to operate • Continuing dialogue with, and reporting to, external stakeholders • Maintaining credibility with external stakeholders
Civil society:			
Formal	• Recognising the role of government in strategic decision-making	• Meeting contractual obligations to business as a service-delivery NGO • Providing access to land in return for compensation and social mitigation	• Meeting contractual obligations to donors as a service-delivery NGO • Complying with the mission and values of the parent NGO

IFC = International Finance Corporation   NGO = non-governmental organisation

Table 16.1 **Formal and informal 'obligations' between potential partners**
(continued over)

Partner	Obligations		
	To government	To business	To civil society
Civil society (cont.):			
Informal	• Striving for transparency and accountability from government representatives	• Participating in dialogue or participatory development opportunities • Reconciling a campaigning and advocacy role with constructive engagement	• Representing local communities in a legitimate manner • Meeting expectations of financial supporters or constituents
Government:			
Formal	• Determining boundaries for the provision of social infrastructure at the regional and local levels • Supporting revenue distribution and capacity development at the regional or local level to discharge social responsibilities	• Defining requirements for social and environmental assessment and public consultation and involvement • Allocating concessions or exploration blocks (with or without social conditions attached)	• Creating enabling environment for NGOs to function and flourish • Ensuring representation of views in development decision-making
Informal	• Ensuring that decentralised government entities enjoy the support of central government	• 'Keeping up political appearances': promoting business interests in opposition to Western environmental or social NGOs (e.g. in the case of mining ministries) • Creating an enabling environment for corporate social responsibility	• 'Keeping up political appearances': supporting environmental or social NGOs regardless of credibility (e.g. in the case of environment ministries)

Table 16.1 (continued)

in partnerships or may hinder existing partners from assuming or relinquishing control of partnership outcomes.

A critical issue for corporations is ensuring they continue to meet their formal and informal social obligations within the partnership approach. This is particularly relevant when the risks to a company from not meeting its obligations are high. For example, the company may find itself in breach of legal requirements or loan conditionality as a result of an act or omission by other partners. For community representatives or non-governmental organisations (NGOs), maintaining independence from the other partners may pose internal difficulties in reconciling their more usual campaigning or advocacy role with one of constructive engagement with traditional 'adversaries'. Governments may perceive political risks associated with ceding partial control of under-performing social services and, subsequently, receiving little or no credit for improvements delivered through partnership arrangements. Governments may also be uneasy about blurring the limits of liability in the event of non-compliance with regulatory requirements that are being delivered through a partnership arrangement.

Partnerships are a means to an end, rather than an end in themselves. They enable collaboration towards mutually agreed objectives, with shared responsibility for outcomes, distinct accountabilities and reciprocal obligations. The challenge is to demonstrate how partners can overcome the potential pitfalls regarding ownership and control while maximising the benefits to the intended beneficiaries. This requires that consideration be paid to the different models of ownership and control that currently exist (and the relative advantages and disadvantages of each of these models) and the mechanisms that can be adopted to help potential partners overcome barriers to partnership entry, in particular those related to ownership and control of outcomes.

16.2 Existing models of ownership and control

Broadly speaking, at least six 'models' of partnerships are possible from the perspective of ownership and control:

- Nominal added value
- Subcontracting
- Build–operate–transfer (BOT)
- Shared work-plan
- Shared responsibilities
- Independent community development institutions

The following sections describe each model in turn, beginning with partnerships, where obligations are retained by individual partners, and moving progressively to more integrated models with greater equality of ownership and control.

16.2.1 Nominal added value

In this model, the participation of other partners adds value to existing programmes or activities, making innovation and synergies possible. The original promoter of the social programme for which the partnership has been convened retains ownership and control of the partnership outcomes. An example is a health-promotion partnership in the municipality of Maracaibo in the state of Zulia, Venezuela. In line with its electoral promise to extend the reach of health-care services, the municipal government searched for a more cost-effective approach than unilateral provision of traditional hospital and ambulance services. The idea of a mobile health clinic was proposed, with the municipal government providing partial funding and leadership. A range of private-sector partners contribute funding and other resources, and an NGO offers training for social workers, for the medical staff who travel with the mobile units and for community health workers. Although important productivity gains were achieved through adopting a partnership approach, the partnership contributed little to developing mutual understanding between the partners. This was due, in part, to the municipal authority's reluctance to share responsibilities.

16.2.2 Subcontracting

This model vests the responsibility for the social investment outcomes of the partnership in a service-delivery organisation (e.g. a local NGO, company or government agency). The other partners might have a financing, advisory or consultative role, but the main responsibility for delivering the outcomes rests with just one of the partners. This approach was used in the Kikori Delta in Papua New Guinea, where an NGO, Gulf Christian Services (GCS), was contracted to take over the running of a local hospital with the support of the local health authority and the oil company, Chevron. Within months of the hand-over, services improved dramatically (e.g. the number of outpatients treated rose from 800 per month to more than 5,000 per month). As a consequence of the improvements in the local hospital, Chevron pledged additional financial support to GCS and upgraded the facilities to district hospital status under Papua New Guinea's tax-credit scheme. The people of Kikori have benefited from the partnership between GCS, the Gulf Province health department and Chevron, but the coalition was initially somewhat fragile. The implicit failure of the health department to deliver an adequate service created tensions in the early stages of negotiation. Chevron's declared support for GCS exacerbated these tensions, as did Chevron's willingness to increase its financial support to GCS, in contrast to its reluctance to do so with GCS's predecessors. Further tensions were created following the failure of government to meet its share of the operational costs.

Overall, even though the subcontracting model may improve the quality of social provision in the short term, it often fails to facilitate learning or build trust between partners, both of which are primary factors in successful partnerships. In the Kikori example, despite the local health department nominally retaining control of the outcomes, the improved delivery of healthcare at Kikori by the NGO did little to increase the legitimacy of the provincial authorities. In fact, if anything, it highlighted their inability to deliver an effective service.

16.2.3 Build–operate–transfer

A variation on the subcontracting model, build–operate–transfer (BOT) contracts are increasingly used in developed countries for the provision of social and economic infrastructure. Here, non-public organisations are subcontracted to develop infrastructure or technical capacity for subsequent transfer to public ownership. This model has possibilities for adaptation to social programmes. For example, the healthcare facilities established for the Lihir gold-mining project in Papua New Guinea, which are available to the local community as well as to the mine workers, will be transferred to public ownership following mine closure.

16.2.4 Shared work-plan

In this model, the partners share the tasks of planning and implementing the partnership activities. The model is particularly well suited to local community investment initiatives in which each partner contributes to the process (e.g. with expertise, financing, commitment to meet operating and maintenance costs, materials or sweat equity). The partners share control of the way the outcomes are delivered, with the local government authorities or corporation retaining overall ownership. BP Amoco developed this approach for its community investment activities in Casanare. In the initial stages of the Casanare project, BP Amoco designed targeted community investments to obtain local access to certain sites, which led to disaffection and conflict. The establishment of a community affairs team in 1992 marked a significant change in the company's social programming and project implementation. Community affairs personnel held workshops and public meetings with communities to diagnose their development needs. Once development priorities were clear, a BP Amoco consultant assisted the communities to prepare individual project plans, specifying objectives, material requirements and costs. In almost all cases, projects were submitted to the appropriate municipal authority for approval, since BP Amoco's support was generally contingent on the availability of counterpart funding and community input (labour or materials). For each project, all partners (BP Amoco, the community and the municipality) signed an agreement detailing their specific tasks for planning, implementation or sustainable financing. The creation of a forum for discussion with communities and government fostered the capacity of both to negotiate and plan, which in turn improved the prospects for subsequent development projects.

A shared work-plan has the advantage of bringing the partners together in joint planning and decision-making. It engenders 'ownership' by community groups rather than simply 'participation', and improves their capacity to develop and implement projects.

16.2.5 Shared responsibilities

The downside to limiting a partnership to a shared work-plan includes the potential for imbalances either in power or in resources between partners and for the problem of 'free-riding' by one party or another. A partnership built on genuine 'shared responsibilities' for outcomes provides a means to ameliorate these imbalances. Shared responsibilities can include joint decision-making on goals, objectives and strategy, agreed equitable grievance mechanisms to resolve differences between partners and joint accountability for outcomes (e.g. joint production and release of partnership-monitoring reports). Even with shared responsibilities embedded within a partnership's governance structure, a company still may find itself accused of patronage in its choice of communities or government partners or in the projects it decides to support. This risk points to the need for an even more 'arm's-length' model of partnership, but one that enables the obligations of each partner to be fulfilled.

16.2.6 Independent community development institutions

Independent community development institutions, such as independent trust funds and foundations, offer both the institutional flexibility to react to community needs free of external influence and the potential for equitable representation in strategic decision-making (e.g. in the composition of the board). By providing a forum for equitable negotiation, such institutions can usefully redress imbalances in power or in resource capabilities between partners. Furthermore, because of their independence, they may more successfully leverage grants and finance from donors that are usually reluctant to directly fund the social programmes of private corporations. In practice, although many such community development institutions have been established in connection with oil and mining projects, the major influence in their administration has remained with the company.

Counter to this, the Foundation of San Isidro (FSI) in Colombia is an example of a company-inspired trust fund transforming into an autonomous foundation. The Foundation was originally formed with the aim of building relations between the Colombian mining company Cerro Matoso SA (CMSA) and people living near its nickel-mining operations. Over time, however, FSI evolved from delivering CMSA's social programmes (in areas such as education, health, water and sanitation) to playing a more independent development role. The foundation began to attract funds from other donors and formed alliances with other NGOs undertaking a range of small-scale economic activities. In collaboration with community groups and institutions such as the Red Cross, the FSI established a rotating fund (the San Jorge Fund) to finance micro-enterprise projects. The foundation also developed a participatory approach to community development, which now underpins all its activities.

16.3 Which of the ownership and control models is preferable?

Each of the six models of ownership and control of partnership outcomes has advantages or disadvantages, depending on the partnership objective. In some instances, those partnership models where one party retains the ownership and control of outcomes may be preferable (e.g. in helping to deliver much-needed improvements in social infrastructure). In this case, the financial risks can be managed only through legally binding and individually accountable contracts. At the other end of the spectrum, shared governance structures and joint account-ability, although not a panacea in all cases, can assist companies in sharing or ceding control of social investment programmes. In particular, such partnership models can help companies overcome allegations of patronage, prevent any one partner from exerting undue influence (such as a politically motivated NGO) and encourage broader participation of donors and more experienced NGOs.

16.4 Overcoming barriers to entry for civil society

For civil society in general, and NGOs in particular, retaining independence remains a critical issue and a potential stumbling block to partnering with private corporations and government authorities. Local and international NGOs frequently wish to be seen as separate from business and the state. In part, this reflects a traditional mutual wariness between these sectors, particularly between corporations and NGOs. For example, in past partnerships between Shell Petroleum Development Corporation (SPDC) and Living Earth in Nigeria, and between the World Wide Fund for Nature (WWF) and Chevron in Papua New Guinea, the NGO personnel working with community groups have been reluctant to be too closely associated with their private-sector partners.

This constraint is by no means insurmountable. For example, although fears of a loss of independence were partly behind WWF's decision not to join a consortium of Enron, Shell, Transredes and four conservation groups in developing an integrated conservation and development strategy in the vicinity of the Bolivia–Brazil gas pipeline, WWF did partner with Chevron to develop a similar integrated conservation and development project in Papua New Guinea. In the case of Papua New Guinea, Chevron Nuigini had developed its Kutubu project in the ecologically sensitive Kikori River basin, which supports diverse habitats of international significance. The company recognised that the potential social and environmental impacts of its operations extended far beyond the project area. In developing a partnership with WWF to mitigate these potential impacts through the Kikori Integrated Conservation and Development Project, both partners broke new ground.

Both partners recognised that they faced reputational risks. For example, some conservation groups have questioned the extent to which oil projects can ever be sustainable and, as a consequence, have been critical of WWF's involvement. Chevron has also received criticism of promoting one form of natural resource exploitation while tacitly supporting resistance against deforestation. Overall, the relationship between WWF and Chevron appears to have been positive for both organisations and for communities in the Kikori River basin. For WWF, the most obvious measure of success is that environmentally destructive activities such as large-scale logging have remained confined to a small fraction of the affected area.

16.5 Conclusions

The following conclusions may be drawn:

- Government, business and civil society have many formal and informal 'obligations' both to internal (organisational) stakeholders and to external stakeholders. These obligations, and the potential obstacles they present to forming effective partnerships, need to be identified and, if possible, mitigated before engaging with potential partners.

- At least six 'models' of partnerships are possible from the perspective of ownership and control. The spectrum runs from partnerships in which the obligations of an individual partner dominate the partnership activities, to more integrated models in which partners have greater equality of control of outcomes.

- One party's retention of the ownership and control of outcomes may be preferable in some partnerships (e.g. partnerships designed to deliver improvements in physical infrastructure where the financial risks can be managed only through legally binding, individual contracts).

- Where financial risks are low (or shared), joint governance structures can be a means of enhancing accountability within a partnership, thereby providing reassurance to all partners that the obligations of their respective organisations will be met.

- The desire to retain 'independence' is an important constraint on local and international NGOs entering into partnership with private corporations. Companies wishing to work with this sector will need to move from treating their involvement with NGOs as 'tokenism' to offering credible collaboration, adopting a flexible approach to meeting corporate obligations and enabling NGOs to meet their own aims and objectives.

Further reading

Murphy, D., and J. Bendell (1997) *In the Company of Partners: Business, Environmental Groups and Sustainable Development Post-Rio* (Bristol, UK: The Policy Press, Bristol University).

Web addresses

International NGO Training and Research Centre, Oxford, UK: www.intrac.org
The World Bank NGO and civil society web page, and a link to the Bank's NGO unit: www.worldbank.org/html/extdr/forngos.htm
Environment and Development Group, Oxford, UK: www.edg.org.uk

17
Companies in conflict situations
A role for partnerships?

Aidan Davy

Violent conflicts seem to be on the increase in mineral-producing developing countries. Yet the strategic importance of oil, gas and mining revenues for social and economic development ensures strong vested interests in maintaining production, even during intense conflict. Hydrocarbon and mineral resources are in fixed locations, and companies must invest large sums to exploit those resources. Disinvesting from such projects may be difficult or impossible. This chapter considers how partnerships between businesses, government and civil society can help deliver social investments in conflict areas or can transform the conflict and improve the social investment climate.

17.1 Violent conflict and the development of non-renewable resources

Violent conflict is common in many developing countries with oil, gas and mineral development potential and appears to be on the increase. The World Bank estimates that 90% of armed conflicts occur within nations (i.e. are 'internal' rather than 'external' conflicts). Hydrocarbon and mining companies are more likely to need to respond to internal conflicts. The reason is that, in conflicts between nations, the risks are usually too great for the private sector to remain. The origins of violent internal conflicts include ethnic or religious differences that prompt moves towards political autonomy, as in Sri Lanka and parts of Indonesia. Other factors are social and economic deprivation or the absence of representation, as in Burma. Whatever the circumstances of and reasons for the conflict, the suffering of the victims is universal.

The coincidence between non-renewable natural resources and internal conflicts poses practical and ethical challenges for natural resource companies. Almost inevitably, such conflicts lead to human rights abuses or infringements and raise questions about the companies' complicit involvement in such abuses. For example, oil and mineral rents to corrupt or repressive regimes can sustain conflict. In Angola, oil and diamond revenues help finance the conflict between the government (which controls oil production and export) and UNITA rebels (who control most of the diamond-producing areas). This violates an international 'arms and oil' embargo imposed by the United Nations in September 1993 and a similar embargo on diamonds, dating from June 1998. The illegal sale of diamonds by UNITA financed a return to open conflict in 1998 and the breakdown of a fragile peace accord between the warring factions.

Even where redistributive mechanisms direct a proportion of project revenues to local and regional development, conflict can still emerge. For example, the allocation of oil revenues in Colombia may have partly fuelled guerrilla–paramilitary–military conflicts in the departments of Casanare and Arauca. Companies almost inevitably risk becoming embroiled in such conflicts. Although the security of personnel or assets can often be assured, the reputation risks from allegations of complicit involvement in human rights abuses may be harder to control and are potentially damaging.

The strategic value of oil or minerals can also lead to localised conflicts where project-affected people's rights are infringed. In the vicinity of Freeport McMoRan's Grasberg mine in Irian Jaya in Indonesia, for example, concerns of non-governmental organisations (NGOs) have centred on human rights issues relating to indigenous peoples and environmental degradation. The abuses have resulted in part from loss and damage to ancestral lands (and the company's failure adequately to accommodate indigenous perspectives on landownership in the late 1960s) and in part from the Indonesian military's suppression of the Free Papua Movement.

Whether oil, gas and mining companies have a direct link to an outbreak or escalation of violence or whether they are simply passive observers, they will incur direct costs (i.e. affecting the company's bottom line or reputation) and indirect costs. The most obvious direct business cost is security provision—either in the hiring of security personnel or in the need to make payments to the state's security forces (possibly levied via a war tax or contractual arrangements). Other direct costs include risks to employees (from injury or kidnapping) and damage to assets or production materials. Indirect costs are those resulting from broader societal impacts (e.g. the destruction of human, social, economic, environmental and political capital), which generally lead to a breakdown in trust and governance systems, which in turn can increase the direct costs of conflict to the company.

17.2 The role of partnerships in transforming violent conflict

Any intervention in conflict situations requires an understanding of the conflict— its underlying and immediate causes, the stage of the conflict, its location and sphere of influence and the role of the protagonists and other affected parties. Figure 17.1 presents a framework for analysing the factors determining the role of business in conflict. Although the dynamic and complex linkages between the factors make a full and objective understanding of the conflict difficult, such analyses can identify possible interventions that lend themselves to partnerships. Perhaps most critically, companies need to recognise their part in the conflict, however indirect this may at first seem.

International Alert, a non-governmental organisation, defines conflict transformation as 'the process by which people change situations, relationships or structures so that they become less violent, less conflictual and less unjust' (International Alert 1998).[1] Conflict transformation addresses the root causes of conflicts and examines the processes by which such conflicts become violent. It includes measures to prevent violent conflict and maintain peaceful conditions (either before the conflict occurs or after it has ceased) as well as to resolve conflict by building relations among the protagonists and creating opportunities for reconciliation.

Broadly speaking, partnerships have a potential role to play at all stages—in preventing violent conflict, in resolving ongoing conflict and in promoting reconstruction and reconciliation after the conflict is over. The remainder of this chapter looks at whether and how such partnerships can contribute to conflict transformation by removing inequities in revenue distribution to promote good governance and by building social capital and trust among potentially conflicting parties to resolve the underlying causes of conflict. The chapter also considers the appropriateness of the partnership approach in undertaking social and community investment, securing human rights and delivering humanitarian assistance in conflict situations.

17.3 Improving transparency through revenue management

The management of resource rents (royalties and taxes) from hydrocarbon or mineral production offers the prospect of directing project revenues to socioeconomic development, as opposed to towards armaments. One potential model for linking revenue management to private-sector investment is that of the Chad–Cameroon pipeline project. The pipeline links the oilfields of the Dobra Basin in Southern Chad to a coastal terminal at Kribi, 1,100 kilometres away in Cameroon.

---

1   The web address of International Alert and those of other NGOs mentioned in text are provided at the end of this chapter.

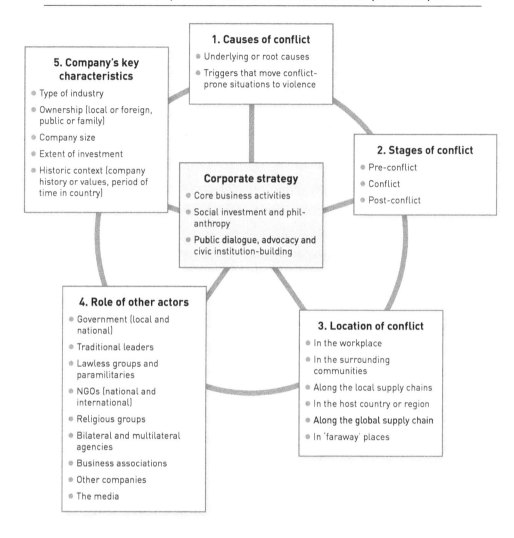

5. Company's key characteristics

- Type of industry
- Ownership (local or foreign, public or family)
- Company size
- Extent of investment
- Historic context (company history or values, period of time in country)

1. Causes of conflict

- Underlying or root causes
- Triggers that move conflict-prone situations to violence

Corporate strategy

- Core business activities
- Social investment and philanthropy
- Public dialogue, advocacy and civic institution-building

2. Stages of conflict

- Pre-conflict
- Conflict
- Post-conflict

4. Role of other actors

- Government (local and national)
- Traditional leaders
- Lawless groups and paramilitaries
- NGOs (national and international)
- Religious groups
- Bilateral and multilateral agencies
- Business associations
- Other companies
- The media

3. Location of conflict

- In the workplace
- In the surrounding communities
- Along the local supply chains
- In the host country or region
- Along the global supply chain
- In 'faraway' places

Figure 17.1 Factors that determine the role of business in conflict

Source: adapted from Nelson 2000

A consortium led by Exxon is promoting the project, and the World Bank has provided credits to the governments of Chad and Cameroon to take an equity stake in the project.

More than 80% of the people in Chad live below the poverty line. The programme of reconciliation and democratisation that began in the early 1990s marked the end of three decades of ethnic conflict, although human rights abuses are still reported. International NGOs have voiced concerns over the potential for project revenues to prompt a return to violence between the mainly Muslim northern population and the Christian south. Exxon views the World Bank's involvement as central to reducing the risks of investing in the region. The World Bank's structural adjustment programmes in both countries include measures to improve transparency, financial management and the judicial process. In addition, the World Bank has explicitly required the government of Chad to develop a transparent programme to direct oil revenues to poverty alleviation. The Chadian government's proposal includes segregating nearly all royalties and dividends in a dedicated special account and investing the balance in a 'future generations' fund, allocating most revenues in the dedicated special account to the priority sectors of health, education, rural development and infrastructure, having an oversight committee (including government, NGO, trade union and parliamentary representation) monitor the dedicated special account, and auditing and publishing the financial statements. The transferability of this model is unclear, owing to the pivotal role of the World Bank's requirements in Chad and Cameroon.

Another possibility is to improve government transparency where this and accountability are lacking. For example, Global Witness has called for oil companies in Angola to adopt a policy of full transparency whereby all payments must be published and made available in an easily understandable format to the Angolan population and internationally. Similarly, Human Rights Watch has urged oil companies operating in Angola to seek assurances that government will not direct the revenue from their operations to finance the civil war.

17.4 Building social capital to resolve conflict

Partnerships are a means to an end, rather than an end in themselves. They enable collaboration towards mutually agreed objectives. However, conflict resolution perhaps requires a slightly different model of partnership (as illustrated by the case study presented in Chapter 7 regarding oil and gas development in Azerbaijan). In conflict situations, trust building, mutual understanding and social capital formation can be the primary objectives of partnerships, albeit with outcomes that are difficult to measure. In this respect, the most important aspect of the partnership is the process, rather than the specific objectives. Clearly, the specific objectives matter, but the less easily quantifiable outcomes may also justify the relatively high 'transaction costs' of partnerships in conflict situations.

The erosion of social capital in conflict situations is inimical to sustainable social investment, and can profoundly affect the ability and willingness of civil society to participate in partnerships. The approach adopted for the World Bank's Magdalena Medio Regional Development Project in Colombia is strongly supportive of strengthening social capital, employing a partnership approach to bringing disparate organisations together to work towards collectively defined objectives of poverty alleviation and peaceful co-existence. The Magdalena Medio Region, the birthplace of the petroleum industry in Colombia, is one of the most violent parts of the country. The Magdalena Medio Regional Development Project builds on a two-year diagnostic and participatory planning phase (the Program for the Development and Peace of the Magdalena Medio Region), undertaken by a consortium of respected Colombian NGOs. ECOPETROL, the state-owned oil enterprise, is headquartered in the region and is contributing 15% of the project's costs. The regional development project primarily aims to foster the capacity of the consortium, local authorities, a citizens' network and other partners (including the private sector) to work together on programmes and projects to reduce poverty and violence, and to increase peaceful co-existence in the region. The project seeks to finance a number of sub-projects in strategic areas such as health, education and income generation, in order to test and document approaches that bring together community processes and disparate partners around specific goals. It will also enable ECOPETROL to evaluate its approach to community relations and outreach. To date, ECOPETROL's community engagement has been limited to municipalities and communities in the immediate proximity of its oil infrastructure, which can in itself create local tensions. While it is too early to judge the regional development project's eventual success, three aspects are worth highlighting. First of all, the two-year planning phase included a detailed analysis of the causes of the region's violent conflict, and its protagonists. Secondly, the role of the consortium in general and of popular key members such as independent facilitator/mediator Francisco de Roux (a leading Colombian civic leader) has been critical to the participation of all parties and initial efforts at building trust. Thirdly, the project has strongly emphasised participatory approaches to building social capital (which violent conflict has severely eroded over time) and promoting better governance (since the legitimacy of decentralised government is weak).

17.5 Appropriate approaches to social and community investment

The perception that one or more of the potential partners are directly or indirectly contributing to the conflict may constrain prospects for a partnership approach. For example, where government legitimacy is weak, private sector–civil society partnerships may be more realistic. During the apartheid era in South Africa, for instance, a number of hydrocarbon and mining companies (including BP and Rio Tinto) formed some enduring bi-sector partnerships in reaction to a government widely perceived as illegitimate. Responding in part to in-country revolutionary movements and the related threats to social and economic stability, Philippine Business for Social Progress and the Mexican Foundation for Rural Development adopted similar strategies. Such approaches often combine social responsibility with enlightened self-interest.

In some situations, the legitimacy of the company itself is in question, or the company's involvement in partnerships invites allegations of patronage. For example, as discussed in Chapter 3, in parts of the Niger Delta, Shell has attracted criticism despite the oil company's significant investment in community development. A more arm's-length model of engagement may be preferable in overcoming such allegations. One mechanism is for hydrocarbon and mining companies to pool community development resources, possibly through the creation of a trust fund. Offering greater legitimacy than the individual companies or their potential civil society partners, a board of trustees could administer the fund and allocate resources. An alternative approach could be to make financing available for social and community development on an unconditional basis to respected local NGO partners. Clearly, both options have downsides also, since they contribute little to building the credibility and legitimacy of companies as socially responsible partners.

Can partnerships help to bridge the divide? Can they deliver development benefits to communities experiencing conflicts despite the loss of trust between companies and communities? The answer may be a qualified 'yes', since examples of such partnerships in conflict situations are few (although the case study of oil and gas development in Azerbaijan presented in Chapter 7 provides some insights into the potential contribution of such partnerships). In Casanare, Colombia, BP's tri-sector partnership approach to community development may have helped to deliver mutual benefits and shared understanding at the local level (see Chapter 11). Despite the large number of local development projects that have resulted, however, guerrilla–paramilitary–military conflicts continue to weaken civil society and deplete social capital.

17.6 The contribution of partnerships to securing human rights

Violent conflict and human rights abuses are clearly interlinked. Can partnership approaches enable companies to use their influence to protect human rights in conflict situations? Increasingly, oil, gas and mining companies are adopting policies that explicitly refer to the protection of human rights. For example, Rio Tinto's Human Rights Policy specifically requires its operations to oppose infringements of the rights of employees and local communities. BP's Ethical Conduct Policy supports the principles set forth in the UN Universal Declaration on Human Rights and the International Labour Organisation Tripartite Declaration of Principles concerning multinational enterprises and social policy.

The provision of security in conflict situations offers a particular opportunity to advocate for human rights. Building on its experience in Colombia, BP has developed a partnership approach to security provision for the proposed Baku–Ceyhan Main Export Pipeline project, for the transportation of oil and gas from Baku in Azerbaijan, via Georgia, to Ceyhan in Turkey. BP has insisted on guarantees for the protection of human rights in the security contracts it has signed with each country. The guarantees commit each government to ensuring that its security forces comply with the company's Ethical Conduct Policy (including respect for human rights) and to providing adequate third-party monitoring of security forces.

One crucial question for companies is whether they will be able to conduct a dialogue with the host government. In some countries, the only contact with government is via the state-owned oil company. Legal provision for independent monitoring of human rights conditions may be lacking, or those doing such monitoring may themselves be victims of human rights abuses. If both these conditions prevail, the prospects for partnerships in support of human rights are poor.

17.7 Are partnerships the right approach to humanitarian assistance?

Humanitarian assistance is often desperately needed in conflict situations. Humanitarian assistance covers a broad range of activities such as helping displaced people, clearing landmines and educating people about them, and providing food, water and sanitation. But are tri-sector partnerships an appropriate vehicle for delivering humanitarian assistance?

Some NGOs argue that, as a general rule, support for humanitarian assistance is best delivered through multilateral and other non-governmental relief agencies, such as United Nations High Commission for Refugees, Oxfam or Christian Aid, in accordance with the International Committee for the Red Cross (ICRC) principles of impartiality and neutrality. The ICRC's Code of Conduct governing NGOs in disaster-response programmes emphasises the need for unimpeded access to affected populations and the provision of aid to relieve suffering regardless of ethnic origin or political and religious beliefs. The nature of tri-sector partnerships may make adherence to the ICRC principles more difficult: it may be impractical to expect a government to behave in an impartial manner, particularly where it is actively oppressing a segment of its people. However, this does not rule out companies providing unilateral and unconditional assistance to the victims of conflict. On balance, however, in such situations, contributions via relief agencies are preferable to a tri-sectoral approach.

17.8 Future challenges

The following challenges remain.

- The development of non-renewable resources in countries experiencing violent internal conflict poses practical and ethical challenges for companies. An understanding of the conflict's causes and area of influence of the company is essential for almost all social investment activities, whether delivered through partnerships or otherwise.

- In conflict situations, people may be less willing or able to participate in partnerships. Consequently, the process of creating a partnership and its subsequent role in building social capital may be more crucial than the physical components of community development.

- Partnerships that explicitly seek to prevent conflicts need to aspire to equal representation of all parties. In addition, facilitators or brokers of partnership arrangements must have the respect of all parties.

- Human rights are often under threat in conflict situations. Partnerships may help ensure that a company's security provisions include safeguards to protect human rights.

- Companies are less likely to participate in partnerships if society views the companies as being associated with the conflict in some way. Where company legitimacy is low, a more 'arm's-length' model of engagement is preferable.

References

International Alert (1998) *Code of Conduct for Conflict Transformation Work* (London: International Alert).

Nelson, J. (2000) *The Business of Peace: The Private Sector as a Partner in Conflict Prevention and Resolution* (London: Prince of Wales Business Leaders Forum, International Alert and Council on Economic Priorities).

Further reading

Amnesty International (2004) *The UN Human Rights Norms for Business: Towards Legal Accountability* (London: Amnesty International).

Frankental, P., and F. House (2000) *Human Rights: Is It Any of Your Business?* (London: Prince of Wales Business Leaders Forum and Amnesty International UK).

Human Rights Watch (1999) *The Price of Oil: Corporate Responsibility and Human Rights Violations in Nigeria's Oil Producing Communities* (New York: Human Rights Watch; www.hrw. org/reports/1999/nigeria).

Mitchell, J. (1997) *Companies in a World of Conflict: NGOs, Sanctions and Corporate Responsibility* (London: Earthscan Publications).

US Agency for International Development (1997) *NPI Resource Guide: New Partnerships Initiative: A Strategic Approach to Development Partnership* (Washington, DC: USAID; www.usaid. gov/pubs/npi/npiresrc.htm).

World Bank (1998) *Magdalena Medio Regional Development Project, Colombia: Project Appraisal Document* (Washington, DC: World Bank; www.worldbank.org/pics/pid/co46031.txt).

Web addresses

Amnesty International UK, Business Group, London: www.amnesty.org.uk/business

Global Witness, a London-based NGO that seeks to expose environmental exploitation and human rights abuses: www.oneworld.org/globalwitness

Human Rights Watch, a US-based international NGO dedicated to protecting the human rights of people around the world: www.hrw.org

International Alert, a London-based NGO committed to the just and peaceful transformation of violent conflicts: www.international-alert.org

International Business Leaders Forum, an NGO with a mission to promote socially responsible business practices in developing countries: www.pwblf.org

International Committee for the Red Cross, Geneva: www.icrc.org

18
Partnerships and local corporate foundations

Ralph Hamann, with Nicola Acutt and Assheton Carter

This chapter considers the application of a partnership model of social management to the development and management of corporate foundations. The main focus is on exploring the benefits and constraints of applying the partnership model with regard to the design, implementation, management and funding of foundations.

18.1 Corporate foundations and social development

Local foundations have, for some time, been seen as potentially effective agents for implementing voluntary social investments and development programmes. Foundations are usually created and funded by companies as separate legal entities, with the foundation's assets provided by an endowment from the donor company. They are instituted most commonly in the form of a trust fund or a company limited by guarantee, although the precise nature of such institutions depends on the jurisdiction under which they are established.

Corporate foundations can provide a dedicated focus for social issues and can build institutional capacity and relationships independent of the parent company. For these reasons, the organisational culture of foundations can overcome some of the problems typically associated with community development initiatives within companies, such as lack of motivation, conflict of interests, absence of specialised 'soft' skills and paternalism. Furthermore, a foundation may diminish community dependence on the company's presence in an area. This outcome is particularly important in the case of the eventual decommissioning of mining, gas or oil projects. Although there are many incentives for companies to engage in social development, there is a question surrounding why companies establish foundations when there may be other conduits for corporate social investment. From interviews and discussions with oil, gas and mining companies, the common reasons for establishing local foundations are one or a combination of the following:

- To demonstrate long-term commitment to communities, thereby improving company–community relations and facilitating a licence to operate

- To formalise the relationship between the company and the host government

- To comply with (or pre-empt) local, national or international law, treaties or conventions

- To administer compensation packages, financial proceeds from land sales or other rehabilitation and resettlement packages

- To enhance the image of the company, both internally and publicly (with other stakeholders)

- To solicit funds from other sources for social development

- To develop the institutional specialisation required for social development work

There are three broad types of foundation: namely, implementing or community foundations, development foundations and partnership foundations. However, most foundations display a combination of attributes, objectives and methods. Implementing or community foundations work directly with communities. They have their own staff that develop and implement local development initiatives together with community representatives. Such foundations are common in the mining, gas and oil sectors, where the foundation's projects are often targeted at communities directly affected by the activities of the sponsoring company, such as the Foundation of San Isidro set up by Cerro Matoso SA in Colombia or the community foundations instituted by Western Mining's Tampakan Copper Project in the Philippines.

Development foundations implement projects or initiatives that go beyond the scope of the communities affected by the parent company's actions, addressing issues that affect regions, countries or the globe. An example is the Anglo American and De Beers Chairmen's Fund set up in South Africa.

The main objective of partnership foundations is to establish, maintain and expand their interactions with government institutions, non-governmental organisations (NGOs), donor agencies and other businesses. Such foundations often see themselves as catalysts for development activities and capacity-building and are often at the centre of a network of institutional alliances. An example of a partnership foundation is the Asociación Yanacocha in Peru, the strategy of which has been to develop a network of alliances with external agents. For the company, this arrangement compensates for a lack of capacity in community development. For example, Yanacocha has a strong alliance with the NGO CARE International.

The management of the foundation does not take responsibility for the day-to-day implementation of development projects. Rather, through a team of five 'field co-ordinators' that interact with the foundation's partners, it guides, monitors and evaluates the development projects.

18.2 Emerging concerns

Although the advantages of foundations for delivering social investment are acknowledged, there are increasing questions and concerns regarding their impacts. For example, foundations have been criticised for reinforcing community dependence and for excluding stakeholders who might be able to contribute to improvements in the quality of development projects. Furthermore, foundations have been criticised for distancing the 'hands of responsibility' of the project managers from other operational company staff. Growing concern over the quality and long-term business benefits, as well as liabilities, of foundations raises the question of whether an approach based on the partnership model may help revive foundations as a legitimate and efficient means of delivering social development.

18.3 Partnerships and corporate foundations

There is growing interest in whether partnership approaches can help overcome some of the limitations of foundations, discussed above. The key characteristics of the partnership model include voluntary collaboration (turning relationships into partnerships, going beyond consultation to meaningful dialogue and participation), mutually agreed objectives (both shared and individual), the pooling of core competences and risk, added value to what each party could achieve alone and a consensus on the distribution of competences, resources, responsibilities, costs, risks and benefits.

How, then, can the partnership approach to social management be applied to the establishment and/or operation of a corporate foundation? In exploring this relationship, the partnership model could be considered as a means of:

- Involving key stakeholders in the design of the foundation's objectives and management rules

- Providing or soliciting resources for the foundation, by direct contribution or by the enhanced ability to obtain donor support

- Managing the foundation; for example, representatives from communities, local government, NGOs and development agencies could join staff from the company on the management board or management team of the foundation; examples of the foundation management structures that could be adopted include:

- The Rossing Foundation in Namibia, in which management comprises the foundation director, three company representatives (from Rossing), four government representatives and two 'good citizens'
- Community foundations in Tampakan, the Philippines, in which management consists of three company representatives (from WMC), two government representatives and three community representatives
- The Foundation of San Isidro in Columbia, in which management comprises the foundation director, the diocesan bishop, two company representatives (from Cerro Matoso) and one representative from the mayor's office

- Implementing and/or delivering the objectives and programmes of the foundation, whereby different organisations from civil society and government provide competences and resources that complement those of the company and whereby each of the partners contribute in a co-ordinated fashion to foundation activities

18.4 Benefits of applying the partnership approach

The main benefits of applying the partnership approach to local foundations are (a) the development of trust and the formation of relationships, (b) the pooling of resources and competences and (c) the provision of a mechanism for allowing transparency and accountability.

In order to identify the preferred foundation type and management structure for a given situation, sufficient time and resources should be invested in analysing the economic, cultural and social context of the foundation. In the case of the Yanacocha Association in Peru, before embarking on development work, managers spent 12 months undertaking a full diagnostic study of their locality, investigating, *inter alia*, demographic projections, cultural traits, stakeholder views and economic activity. At the Rio Tinto Indonesia Foundation in Kelian, the two-year social impact assessment was seen as a vital instrument fundamental to the success of the corporate foundation. In each example, mutually agreed foundation objectives and implementation structures were defined following an informed assessment of the situation of local communities. That is, these processes enabled the foundations to develop trust and relationships with the local communities, thereby enabling the foundation's activities to be focused on the real development needs of the local communities. The improved clarity and focus of a foundation's objectives formed through such processes, together with the creation of harmonious and trusting relationships between the foundation and key stakeholders, are likely to improve the foundation's chances of success.

In the design stage of foundation establishment, adoption of the partnership approach of voluntary collaboration may provide crucial benefits in the form of improved information provision, identification of development priorities and the creation of reciprocal relationships and trust between key stakeholders. Foundation design also entails the identification of key beneficiaries. Ensuring the equitable distribution of benefits is often difficult, and actual or potential inequalities can easily strain relations with local communities. A partnership approach can deal with such issues 'head-on' in a deliberative manner, thereby preventing, or at least pre-empting, disputes.

One of the clearest ways in which the partnership model may contribute to a foundation's objectives is by linking the foundation's activities to existing governmental or non-governmental projects or programmes. In this manner, the pooling of core competences can avoid duplication of effort, and opportunities for the efficient and synergistic division of labour can be explored. This is a crucial incentive for initiating partnerships for the purposes of foundation delivery. The benefits of such participation in the planning and implementation of development projects include improved information and knowledge transfer between stakeholders, increased community ownership of process and outcome and greater sustainability.

It is important that a foundation's operations and progress be evaluated and reviewed. This may be carried out internally by the company or by external auditors. In the partnership approach, community consultation is an integral part of the process of defining the evaluation criteria, measurement of indicators and communication. This partnership approach to the evaluation of operations may improve external accountability. In addition, the foundation's ability to solicit funds from a variety of sources, notably international donor organisations, can be enhanced. Through acting in alliance, groups can lever more funds for activities. Thus the 'added value' of the partnership approach can include the resourcing of a foundation's activities.

18.5 Constraints in applying the partnership approach

The key constraints in applying the partnership approach relate to the management and ownership of the foundation, the manner in which the operation of the foundation reflects local circumstances and the degree of community participation and representation.

The success of a foundation often rests on strong commitment from company management, shown by adequate budgeting that allows financial continuity for the foundation, and high-level representation on the foundation management structure. However, a certain degree of autonomy from the parent company is also an important success factor for foundations. A particularly important aspect of this is the proportion of non-company members on the foundation's governing body.

Adoption of a partnership approach to foundation management, through broad representation and collaboration, provides an opportunity for genuine shared governance, enhancing the implementation of foundation programmes and developing a long-term relationship between key stakeholders. However, the relationship between the autonomy of a foundation and ownership of outcomes affects the degree to which the partnership model may be effectively applied by corporate foundations, particularly with respect to foundation management. A key difficulty seems to be the high degree of company investment tied up in the foundation and the resulting reluctance of the company to share ownership and responsibilities. One consequence might be that implementation of a partnership for foundation management may be feasible only if every partner is also involved to some degree in the provision of foundation resources. Of course, this may only be possible if, for instance, local civil-society groups can obtain financial support from international donor organisations.

Another tension in the application of a partnership approach to foundation management may be the agreed-on preferential decision-making status for company representatives (e.g. through use of a veto). Such preferential status goes against the grain of a key principle of partnership: that of equal partners having equal stakes and equal access to decision-making.

There is no best model for a foundation. Rather, a foundation's form and nature should be determined with respect to local circumstances and in relation to the desired outcomes. Hence, the extent to which a partnership approach is feasible or desirable for a foundation will vary, depending on the local context. This may raise difficulties where, for instance, there are no accountable or legitimate local organisations or where there is deeply rooted conflict between local groups. In these circumstances it may be more desirable to establish an explicitly stand-alone foundation than a partnership foundation. If a partnership approach is applied in such difficult conditions, it may be better that it take the form of project design or implementation, rather than management of the foundation. In such situations, special resources will need to be made available for capacity-building and conflict-resolution mechanisms.

It is apparent that genuine and ongoing participation is an underlying principle and requirement for partnerships. However, the danger exists that the adoption of a partnership approach for the design, management and/or implementation of a local foundation may lead to the exclusion of local groups that are not represented by any of the partners. Hence, a partnership should not be seen as an exclusive club, and there should be a continuous search for groups that are not represented in the partnership.

18.6 Conclusions

The above discussion has considered how the partnership model can contribute to and enhance the design, resourcing, implementation and management of corporate foundations. Where partnering is to become an integral strategy, it is often desirable to institute the partnership as early as possible in the life of the foundation. For instance, if partnering is to support the implementation of the foundation's objectives, it is advantageous for the partnership to have a role in the foundation's design. Foundation management based on partnership will benefit greatly if the partnership provides a means of resourcing the foundation. This may be through the financial contributions of the partners or through the ability of the foundation to access financial resources (e.g. grants) that may not be available to the individual partners.

Although there are a variety of benefits that partnerships can bring to foundations, it should also be recognised that these benefits may not always be realised, depending, for instance, on the local context or the institutional capacity of government departments. What is required is an honest appraisal of the local context and of the capacities of potential partners, possibly linked to a thorough capacity-building programme. Before adopting a partnership model for foundation design, resourcing, implementation or management, the various advantages and disadvantages of partnerships, as summarised in Table 18.1, need to be carefully considered.

Advantages and benefits	Disadvantages and constraints
• Increased buy-in from a variety of stakeholders	• Where there are no accountable local organisations, or where there is local conflict, a partnership approach may disable the effective implementation of foundation objectives or require incommensurate resources for capacity-building
• Integrated needs appraisal and identification of objectives	
• Effective information exchange and co-ordination of implementation activities	
• Greater efficiency in the allocation of resources and less duplication of effort, with resulting cost savings	• The potential exclusion of stakeholders not represented by any of the partners
• Increased trust and capacity for conflict resolution	• The reluctance of company representatives to give up ownership of outcomes, on the basis of the high investments tied up in a foundation, presenting obvious difficulties for the adoption of the partnership model, particularly in foundation management
• Improved evaluation of foundation programmes and financial accountability	
• Increased access to resources, directly through contributions from partners or through greater ability to solicit external donor support	
• Ongoing capacity-building for community and government institutions	
• Greater longevity and self-perpetuation of development practices and impacts, leading to increased self-sufficiency and independence	

Table 18.1 Summary of advantages and disadvantages of adopting a partnership model to enhance corporate foundations

18.7 Emerging lessons and future challenges

18.7.1 Lessons

- The partnership model may complement and enhance the effectiveness of local corporate foundations as a means of delivering social development in mining, oil and gas projects.

- The advantages and disadvantages of applying the partnership model to corporate foundations can be assessed in terms of the implications for foundation design, resourcing, implementation and/or management.

- Within the context of corporate foundations, a partnership model may generate benefits, including:
  - Information provision
  - Better internal evaluation and external accountability
  - Authentic identification of development priorities
  - Creation of new, reciprocal relationships engendering trust between key stakeholders
  - The facilitation of more synergistic working relationships

18.7.2 Challenges

- There is often reluctance on the part of company representatives to give up ownership of outcomes, on the basis of the high investments tied up in a company-led foundation. This presents obvious difficulties for the adoption of the partnership model, particularly in the area of foundation management.

Further reading

Carter, A. (1999) *Mining Companies as Agents of Development* (PhD thesis; Bath, UK: Corporate Citizenship Unit, University of Bath).

Godfrey, D. (1997) *How to Run a World Class Corporate Social Investment Operation* (Namibia: Rossing Foundation,).

McPhail, K., and A. Davy (1998) *Integrating Social Concerns into Private-Sector Decision-making* (Discussion Paper 384; Washington, DC: World Bank).

Nigam, A. (1999) *Investing in People, Sustaining Communities through Improved Business Practice: A Community Development Guide for Companies* (Washington, DC: International Finance Corporation).

19
Managing community expectations through partnerships

Aidan Davy

Oil, gas and mining projects almost inevitably lead local communities to expect benefits and adverse impacts. Triggered in the earliest stages of exploration, these expectations evolve as the project proceeds. The type and location of the project and the communities' characteristics influence expectations, as do the interactions between stakeholder groups. This chapter examines the origins of adverse or unrealistic expectations and considers how partnerships between corporations, government agencies and civil society can contribute to mutual understanding and more realistic expectations.

19.1 The origins of community expectations

Communities near a project that exploits non-renewable natural resources often expect that the project will benefit or harm them in various ways. They may have experienced adverse impacts from mining, oil and gas development in the past. This was certainly true of communities near Shell's Camisea project in Peru, which had experienced a decade of oil exploration. It was also true at Placer Dome's Las Cristinas project in Venezuela, where two nearby communities consisted of illegal small-scale miners who had been cleared from the concession in 1990 (see also Chapter 5). At Western Mining's Tampakan copper prospect in the Philippines, the Marcos regime's historical allocation of logging concessions and military repression of indigenous Bla'an people had created local suspicion and resentment. In the Oriente region of Ecuador, indigenous communities responded angrily to

Arco's exploration activities in the 1990s, in part because of decades of environmental degradation by other companies.

Conversely, communities may expect significant benefits as a result of the state's stipulation that a proportion of project revenues be directed to regional or local development. If the state fails to deliver the social services or infrastructure it promises, the community may look to corporations for this support. Likewise, when state-owned enterprises, which traditionally took on some of the roles of local and regional government (e.g. in providing social services) are privatised, they may be expected to continue in these roles. For Zambian Consolidated Copper Mines (ZCCM) in Zambia, the potential social fallout from lay-offs and cutbacks in social services deterred some would-be investors. Even when all parties (government, civil society, non-governmental organisations [NGOs], companies, donor agencies, etc.) agree on the expected benefits in advance, a failure to deliver these promptly can contribute to escalating demands. In Papua New Guinea, for example, government delays in honouring agreements signed between the government, developers and landowners for Chevron's Kutubu petroleum project effectively shifted some of the responsibility for social mitigation from the state to the developer.

Despite no history of oil, gas or mining activity, many seemingly isolated communities are highly mobile. For example, a social assessment of a proposed uranium project in an isolated part of northern Malawi revealed that many of the local men had been migrant workers in the Zambian Copperbelt or South Africa. Their experiences elsewhere had shaped their predominantly positive expectations for local employment. Although usually modest in the early stages of exploration, expectations often increase during the project. For example, the willingness of exploration teams (often junior companies with short-term horizons) to 'buy' access to lands can often raise expectations. During construction, the cumulative benefits of large compensation payments, relatively high levels of employment and available cash can fuel expectations that prove difficult to manage during subsequent downsizing, temporary suspension of construction or operations and closure. In some instances, misdirected community investments by corporations in response to local pressures have led to escalating demands for compensation as well as to disaffection and protests.

The remainder of this chapter looks at the role of partnerships in managing these expectations of benefit. Four key measures that help build trust and mutual understanding needed for more realistic expectations are discussed, namely:

- Consideration of community dynamics and history
- Investment in community liaison capacity
- Enabling community participation
- Enhancement of social capital

19.2 Consideration of community dynamics and history

All too often, the community is viewed as a single entity, whereas the reality is often far more complex. It may comprise several groups with competing interests. For example, both spontaneous and sponsored migration from other areas of Indonesia have influenced the ethnic and cultural profile of the community around Rio Tinto's Kelian mine in East Kalimantan. The main division is between the indigenous Dyaks and other groups from outside the province, such as Javanese transmigrants and Buginese traders. The Dyaks themselves comprise a number of ethnolinguistic groups, with distinct systems of customary laws and beliefs. Not surprisingly, the many groups in the community have disparate interests. An understanding of the different groups and the dynamics between them is an essential first step to putting community expectations into perspective. Closely linked is the need to understand local governance (as opposed to government), and the legitimacy of representation within the community. The question 'Who is the community?' is perhaps better posed as 'Who are the stakeholders?'

Assessment of how a community's history has shaped negative expectations with regard to natural resource projects is vital. Before winning the exploration contract for Camisea in Peru in 1994, Shell had some exploratory work carried out in the mid-1980s. Conflicts between Shell and local indigenous people at this time had led the community to expect conflict and to demand that renewed exploration efforts be tied to a community development investment fund. An independent study revealed adverse local and international perceptions of Shell's prior involvement in the area. These findings, although negative, enabled Shell to better understand the community's perspectives and concerns, thereby assisting in the building of constructive partnerships between the company and the community (with later regional government buy-in to a broad development strategy).

At Placer Dome's Las Cristinas project in Venezuela (see Chapter 5), the initial discussions between Placer Dome and small miners had been dominated by the miners' assertions of what they saw as their rights and their desire to work without interference from either state or company-hired security forces. Conversely, Placer Dome sought to contain the risks to its operations from small miners. An independent evaluation of the concerns of small miners confirmed that their fears originated from their forced removal by the government, which had promised to build social infrastructure but had failed to do so. The evaluation proved a landmark in company–community relations, because it positioned the needs of small miners as of central concern (as opposed to being seen from the traditional perspective of the 'problem' of small miners). Over time, a partnership was forged between the company and the small miners' association, with regular meetings to resolve conflicts and with discussions evolving from being adversarial to collegial. During the same period, meetings with local communities gradually shifted from community representatives presenting an inventory of demands, to all parties recognising the need to work collaboratively. The outcome, the Los Rojas Small Miners' Project, has proved to be a successful company–community partnership that has generated a high degree of trust and mutual understanding, despite the absence of government as an active partner.

The expectation of benefits can also influence social and political dynamics. Corporations should recognise how their activities can contribute to local conflicts as different groups jostle for benefits. For example, in Ecuador's Pastaza Province, tensions already existed between two indigenous federations, which were broadly divided along religious lines and were struggling to obtain native land title. Arco's attempts to engage with communities exacerbated the tensions and precipitated the emergence of a third splinter group representing the interests of a cluster of families independently pursuing a community assistance agreement. At the Kutubu petroleum project in Papua New Guinea, the driving force for the emergence of numerous new subclans (and the related social disruption) was the potential for landowners to gain direct access to compensation, royalty and equity payments. Work with a coalition of partners may help to manage such dynamics. An evaluation of the Chiquita–Rainforest Alliance partnership in Costa Rica (aimed at promoting environmental and social responsibility among banana-growing enterprises) emphasised the value of building coalitions for successful partnerships. Coalitions can achieve broad representation from stakeholder groups and can overcome some of the risks of working on a one-to-one basis.

19.3 Investment in community liaison capacity

One of the linchpins for creating mutual trust (which helps form partnerships) and the basis for more realistic expectations is the community liaison capacity within field operations. In many junior oil, gas and mining companies, community liaison is either ignored or entrusted to exploration geologists as just one of many functions. Even in major oil, gas and mining companies the responsibility often falls to hard-pressed operational managers. Building sufficient skilled capacity (and at an early stage) and pursuing (or seeking out) partnership opportunities will strengthen the community liaison function.

Where community buy-in is seen as pivotal to a project's success, up to 20 or more staff may be employed in community affairs teams. This is the norm for natural resource projects in Papua New Guinea. At the height of BP Amoco's construction work at Casanare, Colombia, community affairs staff numbered more than 30 people. This is not to suggest that bigger is necessarily always better. Whatever its size, an interdisciplinary community liaison team should have a broad mix of skills, in particular in team-building, conflict resolution and participatory evaluation (such as participatory rural appraisal or beneficiary assessment).

Some companies structure their community affairs teams in line with local government offices to facilitate partnerships between the company and local government and employ staff dealing with health, education, agriculture and enterprise development. An emerging lesson from Shell's experience in Camisea, Peru, and from a number of evaluations, supported by the World Bank, of large natural resource projects, is the need to have community liaison personnel in place early on in the process so that they can participate and add value to processes such as environmental and social impact assessment, consultation and partnership formation.

At both Camisea and Rio Tinto's Diavik diamond mine in the Canadian Northwest Territories, the community liaison teams were empowered to identify and address underlying concerns in a participatory manner, rather than tackling the symptoms of such concerns through goodwill initiatives (which, in turn, can intensify expectations). At Diavik, for example, the exchange of indigenous traditional knowledge and technical project information embodied the principles of partnership.

The Philippine Business for Social Progress advocates involving community development experts at an early stage, to decrease the likelihood of generating charitable activities that fuel expectations. In addition, partnering with a local NGO is one mechanism for strengthening community liaison capacity. This has the attraction of providing access to in-depth local information, but has potential pitfalls if community liaison lacks a consistent approach. Consistency is critical to avoid the situation of potential partners receiving conflicting messages. Companies also need to find mechanisms to overcome internal resistance to partnering with NGOs. For example, in-house community development staff may view partnering with community-based organisations or other NGOs as a threat to their existence.

19.4 Enabling community participation

Civil-society organisations often see communities as the victims of unfair circumstances. This view hinders their involvement in dialogue and partnerships. In some respects, the victim perspective is understandable. Development of non-renewable natural resources is often thrust on such communities through an accident of geology, a distant government keen to exploit the resource potential or a willing and apparently very wealthy private-sector partner (often from another country). Heightened social sensitivity on the part of governments and corporations has, increasingly, resulted in communities being the recipients of compensation payments, social mitigation to offset adverse impacts, and community investment. Yet such benefits are all too rarely linked to any effort to harness community participation that in turn might improve people's capacity for self-determination. In part, this results from the simple expediency of giving and the ease of determining the associated costs, in contrast to the use of more participatory approaches, which are sometimes viewed with suspicion as open-ended commitments that are hard to quantify.

At times, the state and corporations assume the role of the repentant guilty party, making it difficult to challenge the manner of compensation. As noted by Edgardo Garcia, Programme Manager for Latin America, Living Earth, 'for the victim, it is all too easy to abdicate responsibility for one's own development.

Where this mentality prevails, it is important to promote protagonism—the notion that people have a role to play in determining their own development.'

Various approaches, including but not limited to, tri-sector partnerships can help overcome these assumed roles of victim and villain. For example, government can enable or facilitate the broader participation of its citizenry in determining the conditions for resource exploitation (and the benefits that accrue locally). In Papua New Guinea, the Development Forum Process provides landowners with a de facto veto over whether natural resource projects proceed, and mandates a tri-sectoral approach to decision-making. Although the Development Forum Process is conceptually sound, its application has also resulted in some adverse impacts. Specifically:

- Although the dictates of custom effectively exclude the involvement of anyone other than males of high social standing, the outcomes of the process often most adversely impact women.

- The boundaries of social and environmental impacts are unlikely to coincide with the arbitrary boundaries of subsurface resources and, as a consequence, many affected stakeholders may not be represented.

- The provision for individual enrichment enshrined in national law has caused conflict over benefits within and between clans and has created, rather than helped to eliminate, social inequities and unrealistic expectations.

- The landowners' power of veto highlights the state's inability to exert effective ownership over resources that the constitution defines as being for the benefit of the whole country.

In Casanare in Colombia, BP Amoco initially used traditional 'community development' as a means of gaining local access. However, the company soon shifted to a more participatory diagnosis of community development needs and priorities. A tri-sector partnership model was promoted to ensure that all community development initiatives were directly relevant to the intended beneficiaries. Additional aims of the partnership approach were to create a forum for developing mutual understanding, to foster the independence of communities and their capacity to negotiate and plan and to improve the prospects for the success of any follow-up development projects.

Issues of legitimacy can also concern potential NGO partners. Although corporations may see obvious attractions to partnering with an internationally respected NGO, resentment among local NGOs with an established presence in the area may result. In remote areas, however, bringing in an outside NGO in the absence of obvious local partners is often necessary. In Venezuela and Nigeria, the international NGO Living Earth has found that an effective approach is to emphasise its role as facilitator and to build local NGOs' capacity to develop and manage sustainable natural resources.

19.5 Enhancement of social capital

Social capital has been defined as the ability of people to work together for common purposes in groups and organisations. Although views on the concept and definition of social capital differ, all link the economic, social and political spheres and share the belief that social relationships affect economic outcomes. The ability to associate is a prerequisite for the formation of partnerships and can influence the ability of communities to benefit from revenue streams and economic opportunities and may contribute to the success or failure of community development initiatives. The Boston-based Institute for Development Research studied the role of social capital in creating co-operation across differences in power and culture in Asia and Africa. The Institute concluded that individuals and organisations who are widely trusted and who can help bridge divides are critical (e.g. when NGOs mediate between grass-roots organisations and state or corporate actors). Social capital also helps to explain the apparent paradox of how in some indigenous societies (such as Papua New Guinea), where traditional values, norms and culture are well preserved, the allocation and distribution of project benefits can be so divisive. Such family-oriented societies often have weak voluntary associations (compared with tribal or kinship ties), because unrelated people have no basis for trusting one another. This, in part, explains the unwillingness of people affected by natural resource projects in Papua New Guinea to involve other civil-society actors in development decisions.

In practical terms, how can social capital help in managing expectations? One emerging lesson from Camisea in Peru is that starting early with a 'social capital development process' minimises unrealistic expectations resulting from the company assuming a more central role in providing health services. The near-absence of health services in the lower Urubamba region is a serious problem, with NGOs, rather than government, sponsoring most healthcare initiatives. Shell was reluctant to undertake unilateral initiatives to improve the situation because its implied assumption of responsibility might prompt the withdrawal of the already limited government investment and because the company would assume the risk of being unable to satisfy intense demands. Rather than playing a surrogate role for absent public-service providers, Shell focused its resources on facilitating the involvement of key stakeholders in preparing and implementing an integrated regional health plan, thereby building the capacity of indigenous federations and local associations. The plan was envisioned as part of a wider strategy to develop social capital and a long-term commitment to sustainable development in the area. The aim was to provide net social benefit and to build local capacity. As a start, all partners collaboratively prepared a regional health baseline assessment, to establish priorities for achieving long-term sustainable improvements in public health. The partnership also leveraged financial contributions from regional government to match company support for the plan's implementation.

In conclusion, a robust and participatory consultative process assists in building trust between partners and in developing mutual understanding. At Diavik in Canada, Rio Tinto's project development team had observed the escalation of expectations around the nearby Ekati diamond mine and adopted a policy of involving community representatives from the outset, in part to ensure more realistic expectations. In extensive consultations with all aboriginal groups within the project's area of influence, the team identified and systematically responded to their concerns. Not all these concerns could be satisfactorily resolved, but the company's willingness to attempt this helped build trust with stakeholders. The company also went to great lengths to develop an informed awareness among aboriginal communities of the technical complexities of the project and the constraints under which the company operated, in parallel to capturing traditional knowledge to inform project decision-making. The enabling environment in Canada supported the participatory approach adopted at Diavik.

19.6 Emerging lessons and challenges

19.6.1 Lessons

- Through working in partnership with NGOs, community groups and government agencies, companies can strengthen their community liaison capacity, permitting consistent, realistic messages to be delivered to communities affected by the project.

- Where community groups have developed unrealistic expectations, partnerships may offer a 'clean slate', with the new personnel able to establish more realistic expectations and address the causes, rather than the symptoms, of discontent.

- Partnerships can help community groups acknowledge responsibility for their own development, thereby allowing them to move from being 'victims' of development to becoming full participants in it.

- An understanding of local dynamics (e.g. existing tensions, rivalry and legitimacy of representation) is advisable before attempts are made to build community relations. In certain cases, a trade-off between generating goodwill and fuelling tensions may be necessary.

- Social and environmental assessment should identify existing levels of social capital, both among community groups and between these groups and external agencies. This can indicate the potential for community groups to turn expectations into reality and may suggest the type of partnership that will best support the process.

19.6.2 Challenges

- As junior exploration companies with no long-term commitment to the project area frequently handle concessions before major oil and gas or mining companies begin development, the potential for raised expectations is high. Finding mechanisms to ensure that exploration companies act in a socially responsible manner (possibly through partnerships) is a significant challenge.

● Expectations of benefits, linked to high levels of employment during construction, are particularly problematic given the inevitable cutbacks that follow. Further research is needed on how partnerships can help mitigate such expectations and manage the consequences of these changes in employment.

Further reading

May, P. (1999) *Corporate Roles and Rewards in Promoting Sustainable Development: Lessons Learned from Camisea* (Berkeley, CA: Energy and Resources Group, University of California, Berkeley).

Mendez, S., J. Parnell and R. Wasserstrom (1998) 'Petroleum and Indigenous Peoples in Ecuador's Amazon', *Environment* 40.5.

Power, T., and P. Hagen (1996) 'The Escalation of Landowner Benefits in the Kutubu Petroleum Development Project', paper presented at the Third PNG Petroleum Convention, Port Moresby, Papua New Guinea.

Waddell, S. (1997) 'Market–Civil Society Partnership Formation: A Status Report on Activity, Strategies and Tools', *Institute for Development Research Reports* 13.2.

Web addresses

Institute for Development Research, based in Boston, which provides access to partnership-related research reports: www.jsi.com/idr/IDRReports.htm

Living Earth Foundation, an international NGO that encourages people to learn to work together to resolve the environmental issues that concern them: www.livingearth.org.uk

20
Learning from project partnering in the construction industry

Dom Verschoyle and Michael Warner

The construction industry in the USA started to develop 'partnering' as an approach to project management in the 1980s. The United Kingdom followed in the early 1990s. The use of partnering as a tool to manage social issues in the extractive industries is more recent, the first systematic piloting being that undertaken through the Business Partners for Development programme. This chapter examines the lessons to be learned by the extractive industries from the more established discipline of project partnering in the construction industry.

20.1 Drivers of project partnering

Project partnering in the Western world was founded in the desire to improve the low profit margins and project overruns inherent in the construction industry. The industry has few hurdles to entry and, as a consequence, in times of 'bust' contractors frequently bid 'at cost' (or below) to secure contracts, knowing that they will make a return by invoking claims for uncertainties such as inclement weather, client-induced delays, unforeseen ground conditions and so on. Compounding this, there is a tendency for the main contractor to outsource to subcontractors, leading to a cascade of claims, duplication of skills, project delays and a litigious work environment. In short, there is an ethos of conflict rather than co-operation.

Landmarks in the UK construction industry were the Latham (1994) and Egan (1998) reports. These reports reaffirmed what many already knew: namely, that the construction industry was inherently inefficient. They suggested there is a 30%

wastage on costs arising from a combination of employment of lawyers (to prepare for arbitration or adjudication), project delays and duplication of roles.

Part of the government's response was to shift public-sector tendering procedures towards 'best value' as opposed to 'least cost'. This shift was driven, in part, by a European Union directive on local government tendering. Project partnering between client, contractors and consultants can thus can be seen as part of this general move towards strengthening the 'value' side of project management in the construction industry. In broad terms, the key drivers for project partnering in the construction industry were as follows:

- The global reputation of the construction industry was at risk as a consequence of the adversarial nature of projects.

- The client was subject to unpredictable liabilities because of the contractor's dependence on claims.

- Cost overruns and project delays were commonly encountered problems because of the adversarial work environment between client and contractor.

- There was duplication of design, project management, quantity surveying and engineering roles.

In many ways, these drivers parallel the drivers for partnership in the extractive industries:

- The global reputation of the oil, gas and mining industries is at risk from the continued adversarial nature of projects, despite new corporate social responsibility policies.

- Companies are subject to unpredictable liabilities because of the dependence of communities on the company for social provision.

- The company receives reduced returns on core investments and experiences project delays because of an adversarial operating environment between companies and communities.

- There is duplication of social investment roles with government and civil society.

20.1.1 Definitions

Partnering in the construction industry has been defined as 'a management approach used by two or more organisations to achieve specific . . . objectives by maximising the effectiveness of each participant's resources'.[1] Tri-sector partnering in the extractive industries can be defined as a voluntary collaboration to manage social and local environmental issues based on an efficient allocation of complementary resources across business, civil society and government. Both

---

1   CSSC (Centre for Strategic Studies in Construction), 1995.

definitions emphasise practical co-operation based on an efficient 'pooling' of competences.

20.1.2 When to apply partnering

Project partnering works best, and repays the initial investment in time and resources, where the client accepts that the project will be both high-value and high-risk. High value and high risk are precisely the same characteristics displayed by many oil, gas and mining projects in the poorer areas of developing countries. The main difference is that the 'risk' element has less to do with managing cost uncertainties and more to do with managing social and political uncertainties. Drawing on a tool developed to help identify when to apply project partnering to a construction project (CIB 1997), Table 20.1 helps in addressing the question of whether to adopt a tri-sector partnership approach to managing social issues in oil, gas or mining projects. Because the tri-sector model seems to work equally well, if not better, when a company's resources for social investment are scarce, tri-sector partnering is recommended when conditions A or B are prevalent (rather than just conditions B, as in project partnering).

| | | *Value* | |
		Low	High
Risk	**High**	*Conditions A:* • Extensive poverty • Prior social unrest • Corruption in government • An unorganised civil society • Falling commodity prices projected • Assets are of low quality	*Conditions B:* • High levels of poverty • Prior social unrest • Corruption in government • An unorganised civil society • Rising commodity prices projected • Assets are of high quality
	Low	*Conditions C:* • Unpopulated location • Social licence to operate already secured • Political contacts secure • Falling commodity prices projected • Assets are of low quality	*Conditions D:* • Unpopulated location • Social licence to operate already secured • Political contacts secure • Community institutions are strong • Rising commodity prices projected • Assets are of high quality

Table 20.1 Company assessment of the need for tri-sector partnering

20.2 Which partners?

In construction projects, the usual partners are the client (public or private), consultants (the client's design and management consultants) and the main contractor and subcontractors. Auditors and regulators may also be project partners, although this is less common. In contrast, in extractive industry partnerships, the partners are generally drawn from corporate operations, community leaders, nongovernmental organisations (NGOs) and government departments (local and central). Other possible partners include international aid agencies, investors and regulators. It is interesting to note that construction industry partnering agreements rarely include community representatives or local authority departments (other than the client in the case of a public-sector contract). This seems to hold true even when the construction project in question has substantial community implications, such as the refurbishment of a housing estate or school complex. Usually, it is perceived sufficient for residents to be informed and the client (if public-sector) to voice the community view. Project partnering, therefore, seems to accept that community relationships are governed by the law and accepted norms of public consultation. This is understandable for construction projects where the community is not greatly affected. However, where communities are severely disturbed or where there are opportunities for exploiting the construction project as a catalyst for other local development (e.g. road rehabilitation and the provision of communication infrastructure and community facilities), community representation and/or the inclusion of other local government departments should be an option.

Usually, then, project partnering is a bi-sector model of partnership between a public-sector or private-sector client and a private contractor. In contrast, the model developed through the Business Partners for Development (BPD) programme is tri-sectoral, between a major company, local government and communities. What is particularly illuminating in terms of potentially strengthening the tri-sector model is that project partnering demonstrates the value of including contractors in a partnership arrangement. For the social investment programmes of oil, gas and mining companies this means that it might be possible to build notions of enhanced collaboration into the formal contracts between the oil, gas or mining company (i.e. the client) and subcontracting firms, be they construction companies or suppliers. Potential examples include requiring or encouraging contractors to use local employees, and use of the partnering ethos to improve the quality and reliability of local suppliers.

20.3 The partnering process

20.3.1 Project and strategic partnering

The search for suitable partners in project partnering usually begins with the tendering process. Tender documents increasingly require evidence of a track record in partnering, this being viewed as one feature of 'best value'. However, the detailed process of partnering (i.e. building the working relationship, defining roles and engaging in joint value engineering and management) commences only after the contract is awarded. The partnering arrangement then lasts only for the duration of the project contract.

It is recognised that, though this type of project-based partnering yields benefits to both client and contractor, further added value can be gained for both from the more strategic 'term-partnering'. Such partnerships are longer-term arrangements in which the client allocates successive projects to one of a small number of preferred contractors. The supermarket chains ASDA and Tesco currently work in this way with their main contractors, and the UK government has issued construction procurement guidelines (HMTCUP 1999) advising public-sector clients on the use of term-partnering. Through the application of partnering principles (i.e. agreement on a project vision, mission, objectives, roles, key performance indicators, share of benefits and losses, grievance mechanisms and so on) the added value of term-partnering is that performance improvements take place from project to project, with rolling contracts in which contractors and clients alike improve their performance by learning on sequential jobs. An illustration of this is provided by the Transredes–CARE partnership described in Chapter 6. CARE Bolivia was contracted to develop compensation arrangements for a major oil spill, on the understanding that it would be involved with Transredes in community development programmes across a wider region and population over time. It is precisely the long-term nature of the framework agreement between the partners that underpins the willingness of CARE Bolivia to be involved in what is essentially the oil company's responsibility. Without the prospect of future involvement in wider community development, CARE Bolivia would have been unlikely to have participated in the clean-up operations. As it is, this participation—because undertaken in line with partnering principles—added value to the community relevance of the compensation measures and also helped reduce the risks from the illegal 'tapping' and sabotage of pipelines and other oil infrastructure.

20.3.2 The importance of champions

In project and tri-sector partnering the commitment of senior management in the partner organisations is crucial. In project partnering, given the direct and total linkage between the activities of the partnership and core business (i.e. construction), all decision-making between the partners has an immediate operational impact. In tri-sector partnerships the impact is often less direct (though not necessarily less significant). In project partnering, not having the right champion at the right level of seniority reduces the efficiency of the working relationships and undermines the trust built between, for example, the clerk of works (client) and the foreman (contractor). There have been similar experiences where decisions made by the organisation's representatives were eventually vetoed (or needed to be renegotiated) because one party failed to secure 'buy-in' at a sufficiently senior level.

20.4 Third-party facilitators

Partnering is not currently natural to the construction industry. Workshops using trained external facilitators are often necessary to develop the new rules of behaviour, at least in the early stages. Not surprisingly, a dedicated consultancy and training industry has grown to service these workshops.

In tri-sector partnering, although the experience of the BPD programme is that third-party facilitation is indeed sometimes necessary, the expense, the huge diversity of human resource skills of oil and mining operations and the cultural characteristics of many societies in developing countries means that just as much emphasis has been placed on facilitation by a 'known insider' as on external, independent, third-party facilitation. A feature of term-partnering in the construction industry is that the need for third-party facilitation reduces over time as clients, contractors and consultants learn to work within the set of common partnering principles. For example, in the case of the Sarshatali coal mine in India (Chapter 4), although the livelihoods assessment and trust-building measures (LATM) partnership was brokered by BPD, subsequent partnership activities have been brokered by the partners themselves.

20.5 Joint risk analysis

Risk analysis is a standard management tool in the construction industry. What project partnering makes possible is joint risk analysis and joint risk management. To be fully effective, joint risk analysis needs to start before the contract agreement is finalised (e.g. at the stage of 'preferred bidder'). An excellent example of the importance of an early joint risk analysis is provided by the partnership arrangement in the United Kingdom for the Dudley Southern Bypass scheme, between Dudley Metropolitan Borough Council and Kvaerner Construction (now Skanska Construction Ltd).

The dual carriageway runs for 3.1 km through a brownfield corridor of contaminated land and over a network of worked coal seams. The client, Dudley Metropolitan Borough Council, called for tenders in late 1997, with a construction period to start in March 1998 and a completion date of March 2000. Kvaerner Construction put in the lowest tender, together with a proposal to manage the contract through 'partnering'. The Environment Agency and the client's auditor were involved from day one, leading to the 'fast-tracking' of problem-resolution efforts, with issues of contaminated land being dealt with as they arose and the rapid resolution of claims. Two subcontractors—M&L Civil Engineering (responsible for earthworks) and Hanson Construction Projects (responsible for applying the blacktop)—also joined the partnering arrangement.

The project contract was overlaid by a 'bolt-on' partnering agreement, and the partnering ethos was developed through a series of facilitated workshops. A single, combined, project office was set up with single filing, management, information technology (IT) and communication systems, with the contractor operating a single open-book accounting system approved by the client's auditors. A joint risk analysis was carried out before the contract agreement was finalised and led to the definition of risks, a 50:50 gain–loss incentive structure and a revised final overall scheme price of £47 million. The same arrangements were agreed between the contractor and its two main subcontractors. The 50:50 split was not only a commercial motivator but also a clear expression of the equality of the partners.

Joint earthwork designs and value engineering by the contractor in conjunction with the client's designers generated solutions that reduced costs and environmental degradation—for example, avoiding the removal of 66,000 m³ of contaminated material from the site, replacement of that material with uncontaminated material and 26,000 lorry movements. Partnering had the biggest impact in value engineering and value management. Solutions were developed between the client and contractors together, by sitting round a table in the shared office. An enhanced ability to manage uncertainty was demonstrated by a major variation in the design of the earthworks when, completely separately, a metro scheme was resuscitated by the council. The section of the bypass affected fell eight months behind programme, but the road opened in October 1999 five months early, with no outstanding claims.

A joint risk analysis and management procedure has merit in the tri-sector partnership model, not least because it will help to expose the fears of communities and NGOs in collaborating with the extractive industries and demonstrate that these concerns are being addressed. Although not explicitly referred to as 'risk analysis', the philosophies of risk assessment and risk management have underpinned most of the case studies presented in Chapters 3–11, where an integral part of the partnership exploration process was to solicit or identify the fears and potential risks of individual partners and to reach consensus on mitigation measures. These activities took place within the process of agreeing the objectives of the partnership, when identifying key 'assumptions' or when discussing how to manage potential threats. Further opportunities continue to present themselves during progress review meetings of the partners, through the application of SWOT (strengths–weaknesses–opportunities–threats) analysis.

Perhaps the lessons to be learned by the extractive industries from the construction industry regarding partnerships relate to the need to:

- Bring the process of identifying potential 'threats' higher up the agenda when constructing the partnering agreement

- Give greater emphasis to the 'joint' nature of the risk analysis process

- Link the results of the analysis to a joint incentive structure that reflects the need for risks to be shared

20.6 Legal and contractual basis

20.6.1 Partnering as a 'bolt-on'

Project partnering can be described as a step into the unknown. Clients and contractors alike have preferred the security of a traditional contract onto which is then 'bolted' the partnering agreement. Hence, in the construction industry, partnering is usually based either on a standard or modified contract, overlaid by a non-binding partnering agreement. The types of UK construction contracts (and their relationship to project partnering) have evolved from the early 1990s, when the standard bi-party contract was designed to stimulate collaborative working, through to the mid-1990s, when these contracts were amended to allow clients to elect to 'bolt on' separately developed partnering charters and agreements, to the present, where the standard contract allows 'designer' partnering agreements to provide everything needed to create a full partnering process around the designers, contractors, subcontractors and supplies as well as the client and other key stakeholders, with a strong emphasis on pain–gain incentives and the freedom for partners to join at any stage and leave as their part of the work is completed, or at other times agreed by the partners. However, as articulated by one participant in April 2000 in a virtual debate on partnering hosted by the UK Construction Best Practices Programme (CBPP): '[partnering] is not a contract, or a substitute. It is a mutual agreement between the interested parties to work together. It is effective teamwork, for the benefit of "best practice" completion of the project.' In other words, purpose-designed partnering contracts are not sufficient on their own—a change of mind-set is needed.

20.6.2 Partnering charters

Both project partnering and tri-sector partnering promote early joint workshops to generate a shared vision, mission statement and set of objectives between the parties. In the current model of extractive industry partnerships, these 'charters' are generally embedded within a wider partnering agreement or memorandum of understanding. In the Dudley Southern Bypass example, discussed in Section 20.5, the discussions led to the development of a partnering charter, where the agreed vision for the partnership was stated as: 'We agree to work together on-site to implement the intent of the Partnering Charter and to achieve the most successful outcome we can. We want to be proud of being part of a quality product.' The specific mission was 'to complete the Dudley Southern Bypass within time and below cost by working together as *one* Team'. The vision statement and mission were supported by a series of common objectives, namely to:

- Promote honesty, openness and trust
- Complete the project within target cost and time
- Ensure a safe site for all
- Provide a quality product to be proud of

- Provide value engineering through innovation

- Maintain good public relations

- Ensure productivity through efficiency

- Promote effective communications

- Adopt a proactive management approach

- Maintain a positive attitude to the environment

- Seek the effective involvement of affected parties

- Minimise waste

20.7 Partnership structure

20.7.1 Value engineering and value management

For over ten years the concepts of value engineering and value management have provided a set of tools for improving the design and management of construction projects. Until recently, the usual approach was for an external consultant to review the project 'in its totality' to find areas of duplication and synergy from which costs could be saved or value added. With its collaborative working philosophy, project partnering can maximise the opportunities for value engineering and value management by enabling duplication and synergies between the contractor and client to be revealed on a rolling basis. Joint problem-solving, finding the 'best person for the job' and the rapid resolution of disputes all feature as aspects of value engineering and management gained through project partnering.

20.7.2 Integrated organisation

A key component of the Dudley Southern Bypass partnering experience was a single, integrated site office, with responsibilities based on 'the best person for the job', combined IT, communications and management systems, and with the contractor operating a single accounting system with the approval and rolling validation of the client's auditors (see Section 20.5). This suite of collaborative practices allowed project solutions to be developed between the client and contractors together, faster and with cost savings. The close working relationships that emerged acted to prevent and rapidly resolve disputes. The accounts were closed without claims or litigation.

The parallels here with the tri-sector partnership model are clear. The tri-sector model seeks an assignment of roles based on 'core complementary competences' or, as has been described in terms of project partnering, 'the best person for the job'. One of the principal reasons why the tri-sector model is of interest to international oil, gas and mining companies is that these companies have learned through hard experience that their core competences rarely stretch to sustainable community development. Far more meaningful to them is to partner with NGOs, community-based organisations, local government authorities and international donors (i.e. those organisations that are tooled up to address issues of poverty and international development). Conversely, though, local government, NGOs and donors are increasingly looking to the unique competences (e.g. in employment, infrastructure development, improving supply-chain and marketing opportunities, political advocacy and business ethics) presented by the presence of major oil, gas and mining corporations to help eradicate poverty.

20.7.3 Decision-making

In project partnering, the combination of a single management office, a high level of senior management 'buy-in' and the fact that the activities of the partnership impact wholly and directly on the core business provides the basis for rapid decision-making. Private-sector construction industry partners, in particular, usually have efficient decision-making systems and the ability to import skills and resources, when necessary, to solve problems. They are able to assess situations and to resolve internal conflicts quickly and in a matter of weeks can reach decisions that commit them to new activities. The client side of project partnering (particularly where this is a public authority) is often more constrained. Public authorities may be bound by legal or transparency requirements or by external factors such as finance or planning permission. These problems are compounded still further in the tri-sector partnership model, where the involvement of NGOs and community groups can mean extended periods of ratification with partners' constituents.

Two elements of the Dudley Southern Bypass partnering process (see Section 20.5) offer ideas for improvement in the decision-making processes of tri-sector partnerships. The first is that a single management office for the partnership's activities might help parties to present a uniform position where measures to ameliorate the different underlying interests and fears of constituents have already been taken into account. (The alternative is often a drawn-out process of shuttle diplomacy.) The second is that 'buy-in' from senior managers and community leaders to their own partnering charter can help delegate responsibilities to field staff, thereby reducing the need to ratify ad hoc decisions.

20.8 The benefits of partnering

Construction industry partnering has been established as a method of reducing costs and of making outcomes more predictable. The cost savings quoted in many published papers are substantially larger for term-partnering than for single-project agreements. However, the relatively short Dudley Southern Bypass project (for details, see Section 20.5) is generally believed to have provided savings of 20–25%, achieved largely through the complete integration of the project office and extensive value engineering and management. Other documented benefits include improved quality of the project, the ability to handle setbacks and changes, and greater staff satisfaction.

Similarly, there is now evidence that tri-sector partnerships can deliver a range of benefits for all parties in terms of increased business benefit, reduced development impact and good governance. In the tri-sector model, from the company perspective, the cost savings involved, though potentially substantial as a proportion of the overall cost of social investment programmes, are not so significant when set against the expected cash flow of the oil, gas or mining operation as a whole. However, as can be seen in Box 20.1, providing a summary of potential benefits, oil, gas and mining companies are looking just as much at long-term risk management and global reputation as they are at project costs, and, against these criteria, the tri-sector model offers significant benefits. Specifically, the tri-sector model is proving itself as a cost-effective way for business to manage relationships with communities and local government and of securing a social licence to operate. It also can provide better outcomes for business and communities than those provided simply by meeting the minimal compliance requirements of investors or regulators and can enhance stakeholder relationships further and in a more sustained way than can the use of external social consultants.

It is also important to recognise that the benefits listed in Box 20.1 are not guaranteed. In each type of partnership the benefits are dependent on good management, preparation and identification of suitable partners. Tri-sector partnerships are not risk-free for NGOs, the community, local government or for the

---

Project partnering

- Benefits to the client:
  - Cost savings through reduction of duplication of roles and through reduction of conflict and claims
  - Greater predictability of project costs
  - Greater certainty of completion date
  - Reduced delays as a result of improved co-operation and access to and sharing of ideas and information
  - Reduction of claims and litigation
  - Strengthening of the concept of 'best value'
  - Provision of a 'quality control measure' in a non-standardised industry
  - Creation, in the United Kingdom, of more effective private finance initiative and public–private partnership arrangements
  - Strengthening of value engineering and management through use of joint problem-solving
  - Development of the experience of contractors within the project and capture of that experience for use in repeat projects
  - Reduction of project and reputation risks
  - Generation of a more rewarding experience for staff

Box 20.1 **A comparison of the benefits of project partnering in the construction industry with those of tri-sector partnering for social investment in the extractive industries** (continued over)

- Benefits to the contractor:
  - Creation of competitive advantage in the bidding process
  - Increased possibility of repeat work
  - Improved health and safety performance (reduced number of incidents)
  - A more even distribution of risks and profits (pain and gain) between client and contractor
  - Increased chance of achieving bonuses through pain–gain arrangements
  - An enhanced reputation
  - Generation of a more rewarding experience for staff
  - Quicker settling of accounts after completion of the project
- Benefits to the consultant or to the project manager:
  - Improved design through contractor input
  - Reduction in role

Tri-sector partnership

- Benefits to corporate operations:
  - Securing of long-term social licence to operate
  - Better management of risk to public and community relations
  - Provision of evidence of compliance with social reporting requirements and with criteria for receiving funds for socially responsible investment
  - Reduction in costs of social investment (or increased value added)
  - Increased opportunities to leverage government resources
- Benefits to non-governmental organisations (NGOs) and communities:
  - Provision of a pathway to modify oil, gas and mining projects to reduce negative impacts
  - Improved outcomes for poverty reduction, increased livelihood security and increased sustainability of the affected population
  - The provision of a means to address risks and the fears of affected communities
  - A strengthening of the position of NGOs and community leaders
- Benefits to central and local government:
  - A means to demonstrate the response and responsiveness of public office to community needs
  - An opportunity to deliver on legal requirements and to develop plans and policies
  - Improved governance of public office
  - Greater transparency in use of resource rents and public-sector budgets
  - An opportunity to transfer skills and to gain experience
  - Enhancement of reputations and strengthening of the democratic process (i.e. provision of an opportunity to be seen to be discharging civic duties)
  - In the United Kingdom, increased access to public–private partnership arrangements (e.g. for infrastructure) that involve civil society

Box 20.1 (continued)

corporate operation. However, the process does provide a tool for managing the risks inherent in the social complexities of oil, gas and mining activity, complexities that must be addressed one way or another in order for economic globalisation to be seen to be beneficial for all.

20.9 Conclusions

The following observations can be made regarding project partnering and tri-sector partnering:

- The project partnering and tri-sector partnership methodologies share the same key drivers: namely, the desire to reduce adversarial behaviour between parties, to minimise cost overruns and delays, to avoid duplication of roles, to better predict liabilities and to improve the reputation of the wider industry.

- Project partnering demonstrates the feasibility of including SME (small and medium-sized enterprise) subcontractors within tri-sector partnerships to improve supply-chain opportunities.

- The term-partnering model (strategic agreements whereby contractors improve by learning on sequential jobs) offers a possible entry strategy for NGOs reluctant to be involved with companies on a one-off basis.

- Undertaking a joint risk analysis, and incorporating this within a partnering agreement, can reduce the fears of NGOs, community groups, company managers and government officials alike over the loss of ownership and control that partnering implies.

- A key principle of project partnering is that it reduces duplication and ensures the 'right person for the job' is chosen. This reflects one of the key principles of the tri-sector partnership model: namely, that roles should be allocated on the basis of each organisation's 'core complementary competences'.

- The evolution of construction contracts to encapsulate partnering principles and to allow for partners to join and leave explodes the myth that NGOs can engage in tri-sector partnerships only through voluntary, non-contractual, arrangements and provides an example to companies and others of how to reduce the longer-term liabilities of partner interdependence.

References

CIB (Construction Industry Board) (1997) *Partnering in the Team* (London: Thomas Telford).

Egan, J. (1998) *Rethinking Construction* (London: The Stationery Office).

HMTCUP (Her Majesty's Treasury Central Unit on Procurement) (1999) *Government Construction Procurement Guidance 4: Teamworking, Partnering and Incentives* (London: The Stationery Office).

Latham, M. (1994) *Constructing the Team* (London: The Stationery Office).

Part 4
Conclusions

21
Conclusions

Rory Sullivan and Michael Warner

21.1 Overall assessment

The key lesson from the work of the Natural Resources Cluster (NRC) of Business Partners for Development (BPD) is that partnerships between extractive companies, government and civil society can, under the right conditions, yield better results for communities and for business than alternative approaches to community development. The business benefits have been directly associated both with community development (e.g. more cost-effective community development, greater leverage of resources into community development, better-quality outcomes) and with broader and somewhat more intangible benefits such as improved social licence to operate, improved business climate (e.g. reduced risk of conflict, greater policy certainty). The community development benefits have been not only those traditionally associated with community development activities (e.g. the provision of infrastructure or health services) but also an improvement in the quality of community development activities, greater sustainability and increased community capacity to manage its own development and to negotiate effectively with government and with the private sector. Public-sector governance can also be enhanced, through greater government accountability and transparency, the provision of a forum where the different parties can meet and through enabling government to deliver on policy commitments in areas such as health, education and poverty alleviation. The evidence from the partnerships presented in this book is that these benefits will be maximised when partnerships are built on core complementary competences, and where the participants' activities, contributions and benefits are aligned with their core activities.

However, partnering is not a panacea, and there may be situations where other approaches to community development are preferred. For example, in the discussion on conflict zones (see Chapter 17), partnerships with the private sector may prove ineffective or may exacerbate existing situations. It may also be that the time and cost associated with negotiating effective partnerships may outweigh the expected benefits. That is, before entering into a partnership, it is critical that all potential partners carefully consider the costs and benefits of partnering against the other approaches to community development that are available.

Finally, the work of the NRC has led to the development of a series of management tools to assist organisations to explore, develop and maintain successful partnerships. This book is one of those tools. Others include detailed case studies on the impacts of partnerships for each of business, communities and public-sector governance, working papers, sample memoranda of understanding, and training modules. A list of the key publications of the Natural Resources Cluster is provided in Appendix F. All the materials can be found on the BPD website, www.bpd-naturalresources.org.

21.2 Specific themes

In Chapter 1, key social issues faced by the mining industry were identified as:

- Maintaining community relations during periods of investment uncertainty

- Contributing to community development

- Securing the social licence to operate

- Preventing and resolving disputes with communities and non-governmental organisations (NGOs)

- Creating local employment and managing retrenchment

- Contributing to long-term regional development

- Managing the closure of projects

The NRC has enabled conclusions to be drawn about the manner in which partnership approaches can contribute to addressing each of these issues.

21.2.1 Maintaining community relations during investment uncertainty

Uncertainty and delay in investment decisions are a common characteristic of many natural resource projects. Examples include uncertainty over whether exploration will lead to project development, delays in finalising development or investment agreements or in obtaining permits and permissions, and staff-level downsizing or project suspension related to falling commodity prices. At the same time, the physical presence of an oil, gas or mining company raises community expectations. However, the financial controls imposed on companies during periods of investment uncertainty often constrain the company's ability to meet those expectations. Investment uncertainty therefore places a particular stress on company–community relations. Common community concerns during such periods include a lack of clarity over what employment will be created, for whom and when, indecision and delays in planning resettlement and fear over who will be affected. In addition, the community may have unfulfilled expectations arising from delays in implementing the results of socioeconomic studies and public consultation or community development planning processes and may face uncertainty over when action will be taken to stop agricultural activity on land already acquired by the company. Such stresses fuel mistrust and can jeopardise both the company's long-term social licence to operate and the overall value of a concession.

Partnerships (in particular, partnerships between the company, local or central government and civil society) offer a new way to generate benefits for communities affected by investment uncertainty. Partnerships built on the principles of pooled resources and shared responsibilities can provide benefits such as:

- Rapid action to mitigate social impacts and promote community development prior to final investment decision-making

- A sharing of the costs and risks of social management

- The creation of a multiplier effect from the partnership on the social investment efforts of the company (e.g. by increasing the quality of community development and improving its reach and scope)

- Reduced community dependence on the company arising from the opportunities for communities to engage with other actors from government and civil society

- Protection of the company's reputation by ensuring a legacy of community development activity performed by the 'other' partners, in the event that the company should decide not to proceed with the project

An example is provided by the outcomes achieved by Placer Dome at its Las Cristinas project in Venezuela (see Chapter 5), where the partnership approach to the construction of the community health centre enabled the company to provide development benefits and enhance its reputation, even though the mine did not go ahead. At the Sarshatali coal mine in India (see Chapter 4), despite the uncertainties surrounding the project financing, partnership approaches enabled Integrated Coal Mining Limited (ICML) to develop the infrastructure (link road) necessary for mine operations and to complete a livelihoods assessment.

The key success factors for adopting a partnership model during a period of investment uncertainty include:

- Openness and clarity from the company, when negotiating with potential partners, regarding its underlying interests for wishing to work in partnership, be they cost sharing, maintenance of its social licence to operate or minimisation of reputational risk should the asset not be developed or the concession sold

- Recognition by government, NGOs and civil society that the company's core business activities (project management, technical skills, leadership, access to heavy equipment, etc.) can make a significant contribution towards social management in addition to cash contributions; that is, partnerships can be based on these other core competences, not just on the company's potential financial contributions

- The willingness of each partner to work with partners with complementary capacities and with long-term commitment to the project area

- The willingness of each partner to renegotiate roles and resource commitments within the partnership if uncertainties continue

21.2.2 Contributing to community development

The major contributions that natural resource projects make to the development of local society are through the payment of taxes and royalties, the provision of employment and the access to procurement opportunities. Other contributions are through compensation for land acquisition and the measures adopted to mitigate the project's social and environmental impacts. Many companies are finding that these 'conventional' measures are insufficient. It is becoming clear that, in order to secure their 'social licence to operate', manage social risks and enhance local reputations, companies need to play a more active role in supporting local communities. However, companies face real challenges in achieving this, including:

- The risk of raising community expectations and demands to a point where the cost of contributing to community development becomes excessive

- The danger of creating community dependence on the company for the provision of basic services (a situation from which the company may find it hard to exit; e.g. during periods of economic slowdown or at closure)

- A lack of 'in-house' expertise in community development skills, leading to community projects that fail and/or lead to jealousies and disappointment between community members

Common business approaches to community development (i.e. social investment) include donations to 'good causes', such as education and youth development, and the establishment of company-funded foundations, trust funds or local NGOs. In recent years, some companies have shifted from company-led approaches to community development to programmes managed through partnerships with established NGOs and community groups. The concept of tri-sector partnerships (voluntary partnerships to promote community development involving the company, civil-society organisations and local and/or central government) are an extension to this idea. Some of the potential roles for the different partners are listed in Table 21.1.

Company	Government departments	NGOs and church groups	Community groups and leaders
• To act as a catalyst • To provide employment and procurement opportunities • To 'roll out' infrastructure (e.g. roads, electricity) • To provide technical skills and heavy equipment	• To take a leadership role • To provide strategic co-ordination • To provide leverage of departmental budgets • To provide vocational training	• To undertake community project planning • To facilitate community participation in decision-making • To ensure project efficiency and sustainability • To give long-term commitment to the project	• To bring local knowledge to the partnership • To provide local leadership • To mobilise community participation and labour

Table 21.1 **Partnerships for community development and social investment: roles of partners**

A partnership can help a company contribute to community development in a number of ways, including by:

- Ensuring that the profile of local government remains high, such that the company is not expected to take on tasks properly belonging to government

- Drawing on the skills of NGOs and community organisations so that community projects more accurately reflect community needs

- Recognising that, in relation to community development, a natural resource company can serve as a catalyst for community development without taking on 'all' responsibility

- Leveraging resource commitments from others (e.g. local government, communities and international development agencies) and so achieving greater returns on its social investment than it could have achieved alone

- Widening the range of community benefits; for example:
  - Broadening the 'reach' of NGO and government programmes
  - Strengthening the negotiating capacities of community leaders
  - Improving the 'visibility' of government

- Speeding up delivery of benefits to communities (e.g. making it possible for government development plans to be implemented faster)

- Enabling the company to focus on those aspects of community development that it is best placed to deliver; for example:
  - 'Rolling out' operational infrastructure to communities
  - Extending employment and procurement opportunities
  - Provision of skilled staff and heavy equipment

There are a number of critical factors for the success of a partnership approach to community development. The first is that the company should undertake an early assessment of the resources, skills and technologies it has to offer, including the level of cash contributions it intends to invest in social programmes and those areas of core business where changes in design or procedures could increase the opportunities for the company to contribute to community development. The company should remain firm over the objectives it wishes to achieve (compliance with investment agreements, meeting deadlines, 'capping' social investment expenditure, etc.) but should be flexible in how to achieve these objectives. The company should then find partners who have complementary (not duplicate) resources, skills or knowledge and should inform regulators and investors of the company's intentions to secure their support in the event that the partnership causes deviation from commitments made in formal social or environmental management plans.

21.2.3 Securing the social licence to operate

Environmental impact assessments (EIAs) are carried out for most large-scale facilities prior to construction or to other major activity (e.g. oil and gas field developments, new or expanded mine sites, laying of major pipelines and the construction of processing, storage or waste management facilities). The EIA is commonly required by local regulators (ministries of environment, energy, minerals, etc.), corporate environmental management systems and investor institutions. EIAs frequently lead to improvements in project design in the form of the location of facilities, pollution abatement, hazard management and wildlife conservation. However, conventional EIA fares less well as a tool to manage the negative social impacts of projects (e.g. on the health, livelihoods and physical environment of local communities) and often fails to ensure that the project is acceptable to local communities.

A key challenge facing companies in the extractive industries is whether the EIA process can be improved so that it delivers not only the 'formal' environmental operating permit from the regulators but also the 'informal' social licence to operate from the affected communities. Alongside expansion of the scope of the EIA study to fully include social impacts and to ensure a more effective public consultation, partnering with community leaders and groups, NGOs, local government authorities and international aid agencies offers a way for a company to improve the contribution the EIA process makes to securing its social licence to operate.

Certain stages of the EIA process lend themselves to partnering. These include:

- Baseline data collection. Partnerships between the company, research institutes, communities and government authorities can improve the accuracy, reliability and public credibility of environmental and social baseline data used in EIA studies.

- Scoping. Short-term partnerships (one to two months) may be convened to set the 'scope' and terms of reference for the EIA, thereby potentially beginning:

- To address the lack of trust that often arises between community and company over what is included in the EIA studies
- To mobilise community participation to more accurately identify potential impacts
- To ensure that the methods of assessment are relevant to those affected
- To help manage community expectations of what an EIA can deliver

- Impact mitigation working groups. These can work on specific impact categories or topics (e.g. biodiversity, water-resource management, community health and socioeconomic issues), thereby providing greater community relevance to the studies, credibility in the results and ownership by communities in the choice of mitigation measures.

- Linking the environmental management plan (EMP) to community development.

- EMP monitoring. This is carried out to verify the effectiveness of EMP implementation.

The factors that are critical to the creation of a partnering process that enhances the role of EIAs in securing the company's social licence to operate include: (a) choosing partners with knowledge and expertise that are credible with and trusted by the affected communities, (b) choosing partners whose collective expertise covers all aspects of community expectations regarding the new facility, both in terms of the negative impacts (e.g. on livelihoods) and in terms of the benefits (e.g. of jobs and community development) and (c) recognising where the objectives of different partners might conflict (e.g. the time-scales of the company in contrast to those of community groups).

21.2.4 Preventing and resolving disputes with communities and non-governmental organisations

Natural resource projects frequently introduce conspicuous wealth into regions of extreme poverty. Further, such projects are often accompanied by

- The acquisition of land or other assets traditionally used by communities

- Involuntary resettlement

- Employment prospects insufficient to meet local expectations

- The involvement of shareholders and government authorities with vested interests in keeping projects on schedule and operating at peak production

- Scrutiny by NGOs and the media

Given these potential sources of local grievance, it is not surprising that the operators of extractive industry projects sometimes find themselves embroiled in disputes with communities and NGOs.

Disputes with these groups can affect the financial return of the company and the regional reputation and competitiveness of the company. For example:

- Verbal and physical assaults on company staff can add security costs and impede community liaison staff from discharging their duties.

- Road blocks by communities can delay project schedules and reduce the volume of materials exported from site.

- The sabotage of facilities can add significant costs through repairs, lost production and compensation.

- The theft of materials and vehicles, and illegal 'tapping' of ancillary infrastructure such as pipelines and electricity supplies, can severely disrupt production and, in some cases, endanger lives.

- Hostage-taking often leads to ransom demands, negative international publicity and staff recruitment problems.

- The armed suppression of aggrieved communities by police or the military can escalate disputes, increase security costs and entangle the company in allegations of human rights violations.

The escalation of disputes into violence is often underpinned by other contributing factors. An understanding of these 'externalities' helps companies and affected parties to design strategies to prevent or resolve disputes. These external factors include the legacies of past projects, implemented at a time when social safeguards were less rigorous, countries in transition from state control to market liberalisation (resulting in, for example, increased unemployment from privatisation and political violence), ineffective regulations for the distribution of resource rents, popularist political movements, especially during elections, inter-cultural conflicts, either among ethnic groups or between communities and foreigners and issues of indigenous rights.

Contributing to social programmes through partnership approaches means bringing together the unique competences of the project operator with those of government authorities and civil-society organisations. Through working closely together, these non-traditional parties can build an understanding of one another's motivations and constraints, enhance transparency and trust and establish a network of new communication channels. Partnerships are thus a new and deeper set of relationships that can be applied in areas beyond their original design to prevent local misunderstandings and grievances.

A more direct application of partnerships in dispute prevention is to use the approach to 'roll out' project-related infrastructure (such as roads, power, telecommunications) to local communities. Business partnerships with government authorities (to share capital costs) and with communities and NGOs (to collaborate on maintenance) can create a level of interdependence on infrastructure that engenders a sense of shared ownership and that mitigates against the risk of sabotage and theft.

Another use of partnerships to prevent disputes is to establish a partnership forum in the region of operation. The forum ideally should comprise all regional extractive companies (with representatives from management at the executive level, and from departments dealing with health, safety and environment, external and government affairs, and engineering), government officials and industry regulators, representatives from affected communities, and engaged NGOs. Initiated at the inception of the project, and supported by mediation and partnership brokering capacity, the forum can act as a platform for preventing disputes and exploiting partnership opportunities.

Once local disputes have escalated to the point of delaying projects or fuelling violence, it is likely that the 'triggers' of the dispute are being compounded by contributing factors. In these cases, project-level tri-sector partnerships should *not* be deployed as the sole vehicle for dispute resolution. Instead, project-level tri-sector partnerships could be used to consolidate agreements arising from a 'prior' process of grievance resolution or to call on the authority of a regional tri-sector forum to provide mediation.

21.2.5 Creating local employment and managing retrenchment

Poor communities in a cash economy need income. From their perspective, it is often the prospect of permanent employment from the presence of oil, gas or mining projects that most fuels their expectations. Resource extraction projects can contribute to local employment directly (e.g. providing manual and semi-skilled labour during the construction phase, and, during the operational phase, providing jobs to manage and maintain production, in processing and transportation and to operate ancillary equipment) and indirectly (e.g. though employment with subcontractors, providing construction, components or services). Despite these opportunities, the employment expectations of local populations are rarely met in practice. The common barriers include:

- Local populations having education levels insufficient to gain employment in an industry that is inherently technology-intensive, highly skilled and dependent on quality and security of supply chains

- Trade unions that source employees on a national basis, to the detriment of local communities

- The use of 'turn-key' contracts for construction work, over which the operating company has little influence regarding the prioritisation of jobs to local subcontractors

- A lack of business management skills in local small and medium-sized enterprises (SMEs)

- Prohibitive loan repayment rates at local banks, which are frequently in excess of 50% per year

- High transaction costs and delays associated with business start-ups

- Expediency in the process of subcontracting, with local companies unable to participate in 'call-down' lists

- The practice of companies either sourcing worldwide based on cost and quality or giving preference to their home country

There are various stages in a project when retrenchment is necessary; for example: at start up (privatised companies invariably shed excess capacity during the transition from construction to full production, when the demand for manual and semi-skilled labour decreases); when changes in commodity prices require downsizing; in response to fluctuating operational priorities; and, inevitably, at project closure.

Management of fluctuating levels of retrenchment over the life of the project and removal of the barriers to market entry are two sides of the same coin. If local business can be stimulated, both in relation to servicing the project and independent of the project, local communities and retrenchees will stand the best chance of securing a lasting income. Working alone, the operating company is limited in its capacity to achieve this goal. This limitation is magnified during the transition from construction to operations, when downsizing and at closure—each of which are points in the project when the corporate focus is on minimising activities external to core business. At this time, a partnership approach to stimulating local business development can bring the strengths of the operating company alongside the complementary skills, resources and market opportunities provided by others in society. Examples of partnership innovation in local business development include the company:

- Using its advocacy capacity to encourage local authorities to extend market access for the company's suppliers to the construction and maintenance of public utilities—the aim being to broaden the base of the company's subcontractors and to create local business opportunities that last beyond the life of the project

- Working with local NGOs and international donors that have expertise in providing technical and business management training, establishing micro-finance and linking local business to new market opportunities

- Establishing funds (e.g. in partnership with international investors) to provide SMEs with equity financing and/or to underwrite local bank loans

- Developing strategic alliances in a region to ensure a 'level playing field' of access to opportunities for locally owned suppliers (in the case of major companies)

21.2.6 Contributing to long-term regional development

Ensuring the distribution of project benefits across the wider region of operations is critical in order to prevent conspicuous disparities in wealth that can lead to local jealousies and hostilities and stimulate migration towards the economic 'growth pole'. There is therefore a need to encourage public policy and legislation to attract foreign investors, to build regional competitiveness by demonstrating to host governments the added development value of the investment for the wider region and to promote regional development not dependent on the project in order to mitigate against the reputation and cost liabilities often associated with site closure (e.g. the collapse of the economy, and mass unemployment).

However, the current 'package' of resource rents and compensation, environmental and social safeguards (EIA, environmental management systems, social reporting, etc.) and local voluntary social programmes is no longer sufficient. The reasons include:

- Failures in regulatory frameworks for revenue distribution to distribute wealth to communities across the region of operations

- The focus of environmental and social safeguards on securing permission to operate and compliance with investor requirements, which tends to lead to a management focus on minimising localised negative impacts on rather than adding development value

- The targeting of compensation, employment opportunities and voluntary social programmes at communities most affected by operations (i.e. those losing assets or involuntarily resettled) rather than at the regional level

A number of different elements are required to ensure that natural resource projects add development value on a regional scale. The first requirement is for a comprehensive vision and plan for sustainable regional development, within which the potential economic and poverty reduction effect of the resource project can be assessed and optimised. The second requirement is for equitable and visible gains for companies, communities and governments. This requires transparency, legitimacy and efficiency in the use of resource rents by regional government authorities and the provision of incentives and capacity development in local government and civil-society organisations across the region to ensure that revenues 'reach' communities. The third requirement is for community development opportunities that are accessible across the region and sustainable beyond the life of the natural resource project.

A partnership forum, comprising leadership organisations from across the region, is one way for extractive industry companies to begin to deliver on this vision. The forum should include representatives from national regulators, regional and local government authorities (e.g. from finance departments, public works bodies and social welfare departments), project operators from the extractive industries, other corporations (e.g. agri-business), employee unions, trade associations, regional corporate foundations and national NGOs as well as regional church and community leaders (e.g. chiefs). The functions of such a forum could include the provision of a platform for negotiating strategic partnerships that optimise co-ordination and resource leverage across the corporate, civil society and international donors sectors (in support of the government's development plans and community poverty-reduction strategies), the authority to convene project-based partnerships, a 'level playing field' for negotiating voluntary codes of conduct among regionally competing corporate operators (e.g. in providing market access for local suppliers, and agreeing equitable terms and conditions for employment and compensation) and a 'safe space' for resolving grievances (e.g. regarding companies 'poaching' staff from the local civil service, and the maintenance of public roads used by project vehicles).

Such a forum works best in supporting long-term regional development, when:

- There is sufficient political capital inherent within the programmes it promotes to ensure the release of resource rents by government.

- The forum is supported by administrative and brokering or mediation services.

- The role of project operators in social programmes consists of short-term inputs (e.g. standard-setting, project management or technical skills) such that neither local society nor the company are caught in a 'dependence trap'.

- The forum is composed of members, from across the region, that give it legitimacy.

- Consideration is given to utilising existing forums in the region.

21.2.7 Managing the closure of projects

Extractive industry projects generally have a medium-term to long-term presence in society—lasting 10 to 30 or more years. Some investments date to a time when the state-owned company would contribute substantial social benefits and services both to the workforce and to the local population. More recent investments, for example in support of privatisation programmes, tend to be characterised by a less paternal relationship with local society, comprising essentially employment, social and environmental safeguards and an assumed redistribution of taxes. In either case, the question of how to achieve the socially responsible closure of a project presents a challenge.

For the business, the management of social issues at project closure centres around mitigation of the risks of withdrawal (i.e. ensuring continued regional access to business opportunities), and protecting corporate reputation.

From the perspective of local society, the issues of project closure include:

- A decline in regional economic activity

- Loss of local livelihoods

- Loss of community services

- Long-term environmental risks

- Unresolved grievances

At least three closure scenarios lend themselves to a partnership approach:

- Forward planning, where the issue of closure is considered early in the life of the project and where partnerships are convened to help ensure a positive legacy

- Retrofitting, where consideration of the consequences of closure are deferred towards the end of the project's life and where partnerships offer a means to rapidly retrofit measures to manage the impending transition

- Grievance management, where the onset of project closure stimulates the emergence of past grievances among the local population that can, in part, be managed through partnerships

In the poorer countries of the world the most secure way to manage project closure is to align the investment with regional public policy for economic development from the outset. One way to achieve this is to convene a multi-stakeholder regional-level forum at the time of project planning (involving government, other businesses and civil-society groups) and to continue the dialogue at intervals throughout the life of the project. Such a forum has at least two functions:

- To align the direct employment, supply-chain and distribution opportunities presented by the investment with other economic opportunities and markets in the wider region and with public-sector programmes for enterprise development and vocational training

- To facilitate the development of local-level partnerships between the operating company, district-level government agencies and community groups in order to align parts of the operational infrastructure and fixed assets of the business with the strategic infrastructure needs of the region or district

The strategic objective of such a forum is to link the project to sustainable economic regional development while concurrently building local capacity to manage and maintain the project's infrastructure legacy in the longer term (see Box 21.1).

The Tanzanian government recently opened its mining industry to the private sector. KMCL, part-owned by Barrick Gold, is the developer of a gold–copper mine in the Shinyanha Region of Tanzania. Looking ahead to when the mine will close, the company has been proactive in aligning parts of its operational infrastructure (staff housing, water supply and road construction) with the government district development plan.

A district-level partnership forum has been established to agree how to ensure that the alignment benefits both the business and wider society; to agree the basis for 'cost recovery' and to build the capacity of local government, community groups and local enterprises to maintain the infrastructure in the long term. (See further Chapter 8.)

Box 21.1 Kahama Mining Corporation Limited (KMCL), Tanzania

Where early planning for closure has not been possible, a regional or district-level partnership forum, dedicated specifically to closure issues, can be convened as a means to rapidly agree a closure plan. The components of such a forum include:

- A steering committee, consisting of
  - Representatives from the company (at the corporate and operational levels)
  - Government officials (from provincial and national levels)
  - Legitimate community leaders

and tasked with

- – Defining the objectives of the closure plan
- – Selecting the closure themes
- – Developing criteria to appraise closure options

- Theme-based working groups, covering such topics as:
  - – Site use and asset transfer
  - – Environmental risk management and rehabilitation
  - – Local business development
  - – Regional sustainable development

and charged with

- – Selecting between options
- – Developing design parameters
- – Allocating roles and agreeing resource commitments
- – Defining targets and standards

The impending closure of a mineral extraction project can trigger local actors to raise a variety of grievances, not least for fear of missing the chance to secure compensation before the company departs (see Box 21.2). The origins of many of these grievances may lie not so much with the current business but with: shifts in political power during the period of the project and with the historic regulatory environment where levels of social and environmental accountability within both government and company were less stringent. As discussed in more detail in Chapter 12, to resolve many of these grievances it is first necessary to implement a dedicated and mutually agreed process of grievance resolution. The aim is to generate sufficient trust for the disputing parties to be willing to then come together into a partnership forum to develop a closure plan.

Grievances that arise in the community at closure of a project include:

- Inadequate or inappropriate levels of compensation for land acquired to develop the operation
- Allegations of human rights infringements, such as violence by company security staff and/or local police, and sexual misconduct by contractors
- Unfulfilled commitments to provide development projects to communities affected by the project, such as healthcare, power and water supplies
- Redundant operational facilities and infrastructure, posing a local health risk
- Continuing environmental pollution, such as gas emissions or leaching of overburden
- Perceived inadequate retrenchment packages

Box 21.2 Common local grievances arising at closure

Appendix A
Example of a grievance-resolution process

One of the common issues with partnership projects is the need to address pre-existing grievances or issues. This appendix presents a process that was recommended at an early stage of the Shell Petroleum Development Corporation (SPDC) case study, described in Chapter 3. Although some of the details clearly are specific to the case study the overall process is generally applicable to situations where disputes need to be addressed.

A.1 Preamble

On 6 September 2001 a number of government, Shell Petroleum Development Corporation (SPDC) and community stakeholders agreed to arrange a meeting for 4 October 2001 to be held in Iko Town (the principal settlement affected by the proposed Utapata and Oil Mining Licence [OML]-13 redevelopment project). The objective of the meeting was to reach consensus on a partnering agreement for stakeholder involvement in the environmental assessment studies of the Utapata and OML-13 redevelopment project.

On 10 October 2001 the Business Partners for Development (BPD) Secretariat was informed by the SPDC facilitator that the meeting had been halted by the youth of Iko town on the following grounds:

1. The 'youths' had not been informed of the meeting and had not been formally invited.

2. The community members in the working group were unable to fully represent the communities as a whole.

3. The meeting as currently constituted was perceived to be inadequate for taking care of the present and future needs of the concerned community.

4. Issues concerning the past activities of SPDC in the two communities (Iko and Emereoke) that were perceived to have caused hardship and suffering to the communities had not been seriously addressed by the company.

5. There was an unsettled legal case with the Emereoke community.

6. SPDC had failed to complete existing community projects in the communities.

The youth also added that further progress in discussions or negotiations with SPDC on the new redevelopment project proposals would be hindered by failure to address points 5 and 6 and by failure to involve representatives nominated by the youth.

A.2 Business Partnership for Development Secretariat recommendations

The Secretariat suggested that for the subsequent few months the process of partnering needed to be undertaken by external professional facilitators (i.e. individuals with experience both in partnering and in dispute and conflict resolution). Over the subsequent few months, and working with the SPDC facilitators as mentors or buddies, the external facilitators would execute the following work programme.

A.2.1 First visit of external facilitators: November 2001

A.2.1.1 Status review

The aim was to determine the status of the Natural Resources Working Group and Community Issues Working Group (although it was assumed that the planned meeting of the Community Issues Working Group was at that point on hold).

A.2.1.2 Wider stakeholder analysis

The aim was to broaden the inventory of stakeholders already identified and, from this, to determine a 'strategic' set of stakeholders relevant to moving the environmental impact assessment (EIA) process forward. The starting point was a list complied at the stakeholder workshop held from 3–5 September 2001 in Port Harcourt. It was considered important to add to new knowledge about the youth groups of the OML-13 area, their recognised leaders if any and each party's core underlying interests or issues. The plotting of a graph of 'influence' against 'support' (i.e. a risk analysis) was suggested by the facilitators as being potentially useful.

A.2.1.3 Initial grievance process design

The aim was to design a 'process' of dispute resolution to address the needs of the youth leaders that dovetailed with efforts to introduce partnering principles into the EIA studies. The concerns raised by the youth at the 4 October 2001 meeting offered a clear way forward here. For example, the facilitators suggested it may be possible to set up a new working group (or forum) explicitly designed to resolve outstanding grievances with regard to, at a minimum:

- The redundant facilities

- Past negative effects of activities

- Incomplete community projects

A.2.1.4 Company 'buy-in'

The aim was to discuss this grievance resolution process, agree the level of participation and commitment from senior SPDC managers and identify the 'limits to negotiation' for SPDC.

A.2.1.5 Community 'buy-in'

The facilitators suggested first discussing with stakeholders the design of an acceptable 'process' for addressing the outstanding grievances. These discussions should be held with relevant community representatives, including youth leaders (and state or local government agencies if applicable). This exercise would involve a visit to the field and small one-on-one or group discussions with a wide range of youths, chiefs, committee chairpersons and so on. Agreement with these parties should be reached on:

- Who will represent the youth and other community groups in resolving the outstanding grievances and in the existing two working groups

- A final design for an acceptable process of grievance resolution and, if possible, how this will be dovetailed with the partnering efforts within the EIA studies; options for dovetailing would include:
  - A separate working group on grievance resolution (running in parallel with the other two working groups, or in advance if youth objections remain too strong)
  - A sub-working group of the existing Community Issues Working Group (again, preferably in parallel)
  - A completely separate forum, driven primarily by the design requirements of the youth (again, preferably in parallel)

A.2.2 Second visit of external facilitators: December 2001

A.2.2.1 Facilitation of grievance resolution

The task of the facilitators was to provide professional facilitation of the forum or working group within which the community grievances were to be addressed. It was considered likely that this first meeting would achieve the following outcomes:

- Confirmation of who will represent the youth and other community groups in the forum or working group

- Agreement on the 'level' at which different types of grievance would be resolved (e.g. through legal means; as joint venture partners; with recourse to state-level government; through discussion between senior SPDC managers, youth leaders and chiefs; through discussions between SPDC community development managers, chiefs and youth leaders; or through customary conflict-resolution mechanisms)

- Clarification of the location and nature of particular grievances

- Agreement on the decision-making rules (i.e. what criteria to apply to judge that a resolution of a grievance is 'fair')

- Agree a series of meetings or forums to resolve the outstanding grievances and agree who will act as facilitators, mediators or arbitrators

- If there is time, gain clarification of the grievances (e.g. locations, affected parties, scale of impact)

A.2.2.2 Mentoring of environmental impact assessment partnering agreements

The task was to continue to mentor and advise SPDC facilitators on developing the partnering agreements for the Natural Resources Working Group and Community Issues Working Group in relation to the EIA studies for the Utapate redevelopment.

A.2.3 Third visit of the external facilitators: February 2002

A.2.3.1 Review

The task was to review the progress of the work, both to resolve the outstanding community grievances and to agree the partnering agreements for the Natural Resources Working Group and the Community Issues Working Groups in the Utapate OML-13 redevelopment EIA.

Appendix B
Example of a partnership memorandum of understanding
The Sarshatali Coal Mining Project
Partnership for the Construction of a
Metalled Link Road from Rasunpur
Forest Area to Barabani Railway Yard

B.1 Preamble

This memorandum of understanding (MOU) is proposed as the basis for a partnership to construct a link road from Rasunpur Forest area close to Sarshatali coal mine up to Barabani Railway Yard, covering a total length of 10.5 km. The programme is to cover the period July 2000 to March 2001.

This MOU is not a contractual document and carries no legal obligation on any party. The overall partnership described by this MOU is a working arrangement and is intended to provide mutual benefits for all parties.

This MOU reflects the common understanding of the following parties:

Party	Integrated Coal Mining Limited (ICML)
Signatory	Kallol Basu, Vice President, ICML
Date	12 July 2000

Party	Zilla Parishad, Burdwan
Signatory	Nurul Absar, Addl. Executive Officer, Zilla Parishad
Date	12 July 2000

Party	Barabani Panchayat Samity
Signatory	Mithu Chatterjee, Sabhapati, Barabani Panchayat Samity
Date	12 July 2000

B.2 Assumptions

- Financial closure for the Sarshatali coal-mining project is scheduled to be completed by September 2001.

- The budget allocated by ICML for the proposed road construction will be made available on financial closure. An interim/ad hoc budget, if necessary, will be made available before financial closure, depending on the progress of work.

- The budget allotted by Zilla Parishad for the proposed road construction will be made available from 'remunerative assets schemes' of the 10th Finance Commission to complete the work within the agreed time schedule.

B.3 Objectives of the partnership

This partnership combines a series of 'shared' objectives, with objectives 'specific to individual partners'. An initial set of shared and individual objectives for the proposed partnership were agreed at the different meetings between ICML, Zilla Parishad, Burdwan and Barabani Panchayat Samity including affected Gram Panchayats. These are as follows.

B.3.1 Shared objectives

Vision Statement: this road-building partnership will help business and also provide benefits to effected communities in remote areas and have direct impact towards successful development.

- The construction of the road will be completed within December 2001 and ready for use by all the partners.

- Creating an example of effective 'business-case' benefits both the government and the corporate sector through tri-sector partnerships. If successful, a similar partnership arrangement may be adopted in other areas.

- Undertake inclusive and continuous community participation in the formulation of road design and alignment, widening and construction till the completion of work.

- Benefit to the local villagers of five villages for quick communication to important places such as Kelejora Hospital, School and market by an all-weather metal road. Increase in trading and commercial activities.

- Increase in railway traffic and revenue earnings by movement of additional coal wagons through Barabani Railway Station (at present extremely low goods traffic density).

- Social risks better managed, including effective grievance mechanism.

- For [the above six items], supplement and complement similar work being authorised and undertaken by government and/or other agencies, to avoid unnecessary expenditure and duplication of effort.

B.3.2 Individual objectives

B.3.2.1 Integrated Coal Mining Limited

- Utilising the existing village road by widening and strengthening/new construction wherever required to transport coal from mine pit to Barabani Railway siding until the completion of railway link from mine pit to Barabani Eastern Railway line.

- Containment of ICML commitment to community development and mitigation measures within predetermined/budgeted project viable limits.

- More cost-effective risk management (pollution, natural disasters, utilising technical and administrative know-how of Zilla Parishad).

B.3.2.2 Zilla Parishad, Burdwan

- Zilla Parishad will impose a 'toll tax' on the road from general traffic as per the approved rates of Zilla Parishad. The Zilla Parishad will also impose a 'licence fee' on ICML for using the road as per the same rate as already prevailing for similar nature of activities by other joint sector company.

- From fifth year onward the Zilla Parishad will impose a 'toll tax' for vehicles of ICML as per the rates which the Zilla Parishad will be charging to other traffic.

- Build trust and confidence with communities in the area.

- Addition of road infrastructure in the rural area to boost business with support from company.

- Integration of new link road with the district road development plan.

B.3.2.3 Barabani Panchayat Samity and Gram Panchayats (Jamgram, Punchra, Barabani)

- Panchayat Samity will assist ICML and Zilla Parishad to develop and construct the proposed road according to the work-plan with a view of longer-term sustainable development in the rural area.

- Social and economic benefits to the local villagers, by the way of access to the new road to hospital, school, market, business area, etc.

- The road will be built as per the acceptable standard with bitumen blacktop and good environmental practices by developing a green belt along the roadside.

- Panchayat will assist and extend co-operation to ICML in carrying out land payment for the additional area required to widen the existing village road.

- The link road will create opportunities for the local villagers to work in the road construction activities.

- Construction of a high brick wall along the roadsides of the Jamgram High School building and Kelejora Hospital to minimise the pollution effect.

- Construction of a new road from Jamgram High School up to Domohani road bus stand for easy and safe communication by the students.

- Construction of two new classrooms in the existing Jamgram High School building. Assisting the School Managing Committee for electrification in the school building from nearby power sources.

- Existing village road at Natundih village will be improved at the crossing of the proposed link road.

- Street lights will be provided at important road crossings. Power will be arranged by State Electricity Board. Panchayat will pay the electricity bill and maintain the system.

- Community development projects will be undertaken in consultation with the Gram Panchayats and Field Committee.

- Collaborating with the implementing partners to supplement and complement similar work to avoid duplication of effort and unnecessary expenditure.

B.4 Schedule

This construction work will cover the period July 2000 to December 2001. The detailed break-up will be included in the work-plan.

B.5 Scope

The geographic boundary for the road upgrading, widening and construction activities is in Barabani Block of Asansol Subdivision, Burdwan District covering Mouzas Rasunpur, Sarshatali , Kapista, Jamgram, Kelejora, Punchra and Barabani. The link road will be constructed to suit heavy traffic movement throughout the year.

Zilla Parishad will contribute and construct the link road work from ground level up to sub-base level and ICML will contribute and construct the balance portion of the work including base level, bituminous, Premex® carpet and seal coat and cross-drainage work.

B.6 Work-plan and performance-monitoring indicators

A work-plan for the metalled link road construction is to be mutually agreed between ICML, Barabani Panchayat Samity and Zilla Parishad. A core committee will be formed for overview of the tasks and finalisation of a detailed work-plan. A field committee will be formed at grass-roots level to co-ordinate the land payment and also provide technical support to the contractors during the construction period. Performance-monitoring indicators have to be established for all parties against which progress till completion of work can be measured.

B.7 Funding and contractual arrangements

B.7.1 Funding

- The Zilla Parishad will make funds available from 'remunerative assets schemes' of the 10th Finance Commission and will do the work up to sub-base level investing around Rupees One Crore (Rs 10,000,000); exact amount will be ascertained on finalisation of the detailed estimate for the work.

- ICML will contribute resources for the road construction, investing around Rupees Three Crore + (Rs 30,000,000) from base level up to final seal coat; exact amount will be ascertained on finalisation of the detailed estimate for the work.

B.7.2 Contractual agreement

There will be a separate contract agreement for the purpose.

B.8 Responsibilities and accountability

- ICML and Zilla Parishad are jointly responsible for meeting the requirements of road design, development, construction and completion within the agreed time-schedule.

- The implementing partners are responsible for contributing to the objectives of this MOU, implementing the work-plan of activities. The work-plan is to be agreed on a mutual basis between ICML, Barabani Panchayat Samity, the Field Committee and Zilla Parishad, Burdwan.

- The road for the first four years, after the construction period, will be maintained by ICML after which the same will be handed over to Zilla Parishad, Burdwan.

B.9 Internal communications and reporting

- Throughout the period of construction, Zilla Parishad, Burdwan, Barabani Panchayat Samity, the Field Committee and ICML officials will regularly meet to exchange views and monitor the progress of work.

- Each month a progress report will be prepared, distributed and compared with the work-plan. Any significant gap will be identified and accordingly corrective action will be undertaken to fulfil the commitment.

- Upon completion of work, a final report will be prepared and distributed for future reference and for use as maintenance guidelines.

B.10 Dispute resolution

All parties agree that in the event of a grievance of any one party, all parties will jointly meet at Zilla Sabhadhipati's office, Burdwan, for mediation:

- The Sabhadhipati will first seek to build a new consensus between the parties.

- In building a new consensus, the objectives of this MOU will be the principal guiding consideration.

- An addendum to the MOU may be added to reflect the new consensus. All parties to the original MOU must agree to the addendum before it is included.

- If a new consensus cannot be reached the Sabhadhipati will weigh the arguments and provide a recommendation.

- If this recommendation is not accepted by all parties, then this MOU will be treated as automatically void and all further financial disbursements will cease in accordance with the contractual arrangements. However, funds already invested by the Zilla Parishad would be mutually shared between the parties as decided by the Core Committee and the decision of the Core Committee will be final and binding.

B.11 Managing threats

If financial closure of the project or fund availability from Zilla Parishad is delayed, the implementing partners will continue their presence in the work area towards fulfilment the objectives of this MOU. ICML and Zilla Parishad will explore different avenues to provide the minimal financial and in-kind resources necessary to continue the work.

If construction work at the site is interrupted due to local problems, all the partners will work together to resolve the issue.

Appendix C

Example of a partnership charter
Charter of the Kelian Mine
Closure Steering Committee

C.1 Overview

The work of the Mine Closure Steering Committee (MCSC) is to provide a consultative forum to promote responsible mine closure by Kelian Equatorial Mining (KEM). The MCSC is designed to create an enabling environment for negotiated outcomes derived from a diverse range of stakeholders. The committee tasks working groups to consult with their constituents and identify and address issues as directed in a scope of work.

The MCSC operates under the joint chairmanship of the Bupati, West Kutai and the President Director of PT KEM. Its composition balances representation between government, the company and civil society (community groups and NGOs [non-governmental organisations]). Membership consists of one representative from each stakeholder group. Usually, members hold positions within their own organisations which incorporate the responsibilities and interests associated with mine closure and carry out much of their MCSC functions as part of their normal work. Other members are also appointed from areas such as academia or technical institutes. The tenure of members is reviewed annually. The MCSC has appointed a Project Officer, heading a Secretariat, to manage its affairs.

Members of the MCSC and working groups are expected to exercise the highest integrity in all of their dealings and are to deal fairly, equitably and openly with all interests represented in mine closure issues. Conflicts of interest, existing or incipient, are to be declared by all members for consideration by the MCSC. Conflicts of interest may limit some participation in, but not necessarily totally preclude members from, MCSC activities. Members are paid an honorarium by way of a sitting fee for meetings attended, as well as some expenses. No honoraria are paid for other work done as this is generally part of the members' usual working responsibilities.

MCSC decisions are arrived at by consensus in the spirit of *musyawarah untuk mufakat* (reaching agreement by consensus). Proposals made by the MCSC membership or the MCSC working parties, if approved, are promoted to the appropriate instrumentality (e.g. a government department, PT KEM, community organisations, NGOs, etc.). The fostering of these proposals is managed by the MCSC through the aegis of its appropriate members in concert with others as required.

The MCSC convenes quarterly to consider proposals and reports from its MCSC working parties and members. A record of proceedings is prepared and distributed to all working interests and a communiqué is issued within a week of meetings to inform the community at large of developments and to foster public consultation.

The MCSC is cognisant of the weighty responsibility it bears to help ameliorate the economic, social and cultural effects of the closure of the PT KEM mine for all stakeholders; and particularly the communities living in the region of the mine. Every effort is made to ensure that these stakeholders, through the MCSC, are empowered to negotiate development options and outcomes for themselves.

1. Duties and responsibilities of MCSC members:

   1.1 Members of the MCSC are expected to be of the highest integrity. Their duties are to conduct the business of the MCSC to achieve beneficial outcomes based on fair and equitable negotiation between all represented parties.

   1.2 MCSC members are expected to represent the views of their stakeholders fairly and honestly.

   1.3 Their mandate is to be legitimate and authoritative representatives of their stakeholders. The office of each stakeholder group, not the individual, holds MCSC positions.

   1.4 If a committee member is not available an alternate representative should be nominated and that office should remain the same throughout and have the authority that the usual/main member has. This is to ensure consistency of representation on the MCSC.

   1.5 A principal role of MCSC members is to provide direction and terms of reference for the working groups and ensure that sustainable solutions are implemented to the satisfaction of all stakeholders.

   1.6 The MCSC commits to the timely review of proposals submitted to them by working groups against agreed criteria and agrees to secure decisions and commitments from stakeholders in order to implement agreed options.

2. MCSC eligibility and term of office:

   2.1 Representatives of stakeholders who are affected by, or who can affect, the closure of Kelian Mine are eligible to become MCSC members. The composition of the MCSC aims to balance representation from business, government and civil society—including advocacy groups and universities. This balance is essential to promote negotiated outcomes.

    2.2 Good practice suggests that the number of committee members is kept to a minimum. It is important to be clear about the distinction between members on the committee and the working groups.

    2.3 Only one representative from each stakeholder group may be a member.

    2.4 The term of office for an MCSC member shall be reviewed annually.

3. Management of power imbalances between the members in order to prevent the dominance of one or two parties:

    3.1 Members of the MCSC approve decisions by consensus and have commitments to each other to carry out decisions agreed by the committee.

    3.2 Appropriate time (set by the working groups) must be made available for effective public consultation and socialising information within stakeholder groups before final decisions are taken.

    3.3 In the event of a deadlock, the co-chairmen are empowered to seek suitable compromise proposals in consultation with stakeholders. These proposals can then be submitted for approval by the MCSC.

    3.4 A record of meetings will be kept. In addition, a communiqué will be made available to the public and distributed to local communities. It will be also posted on a website in both languages: Bahasa Indonesia and English.

4. Time commitments required of an MCSC member:

    4.1 Four quarterly MCSC meetings are scheduled each year for at least the next three years. Each meeting requires two days' input. It may become necessary to hold extraordinary meetings from time to time.

5. Fees and expenses of MCSC members:

    5.1 In recognition of their inputs, MCSC members are paid a daily sitting fee plus travel expenses. No other allowances will be made.

6. Measures to ensure public confidence in the integrity of MCSC members:

    6.1 All conflicts of interest must be declared by MCSC members prior to the negotiation of any issue. Undeclared conflicts of interest, evidence of fraudulent activities or criminal convictions will result in the replacement of any MCSC member.

    6.2 If a conflict of interest is declared then the MCSC members should decide any limitations that may apply.

7. Accountabilities of MCSC members:

    7.1 MCSC members are individually accountable to their stakeholders and to other members of the committee. Members are collectively accountable for achieving MCSC objectives and to the working groups.

7.2 The MCSC will develop performance targets and monitor progress on a regular basis. The MCSC commits to make its progress towards targets fully transparent and open to public scrutiny.

7.3 Performance targets will be a combination of process- and output-oriented targets (e.g. proportion of meetings held, attendance rates, number of recommendations received, number of consensus decisions made, number of proposals reviewed).

7.4 The business of the MCSC will be reported on the Internet and through an annual, publicly available report which will be independently audited.

7.5 A statement of operational expenses will be included as a line item 'cost of operations' in the annual report.

8. Implementation of MCSC decisions:

8.1 At times implementation will be the responsibility of KEM, but some decisions are likely to require joint implementation between KEM and external partners such as the government or local institutions.

9. MCSC budget:

9.1 The MCSC has an operating budget but not an implementation budget.

9.2 The budget will be prepared annually and resourced by PT KEM.

9.3 The MCSC recommends actions to external agencies and checks on their progress against agreed targets. It does not implement these activities itself.

10. Internal and external communication protocol of the MCSC:

10.1 Internal communication is co-ordinated by the Secretariat and will include monthly reporting on progress of the working groups, and a record of each meeting.

10.2 In addition, external communication will comprise an agreed communiqué that will be produced for local distribution. The agreed communiqué will provide an authoritative and consistent source of information.

10.3 Publicly available documents will be posted on a website and will be released to the media.

C.2 Terms of reference for the working groups

11. Duties and responsibilities of the working groups:

11.1 Working groups are established by the MCSC in response to defined needs. Four working groups are currently proposed, but these groups may evolve and change. New groups may be required as issues of importance to stakeholders arise.

11.2 Members are expected to act in the interests of defined beneficiaries and exhibit honesty in all matters.

11.3 Working groups are responsible for using criteria and their terms of reference to develop appropriate proposals. They are also expected to identify constraints.

11.4 Working groups are expected to identify pertinent emerging issues with their stakeholders and bring these to the attention of the MCSC.

11.5 Working groups are responsible for identifying the timetable and requirements for the transition of issues and assets to appropriate authorities.

11.6 Working groups prepare work programmes and performance objectives with targets that are directly linked to achieving the programme of good mine closure.

11.7 Working groups are required to prepare an analysis of tasks and intermediate goals, and this is used to measure success and progress.

11.8 Working groups will consult with the public and local communities over the development of their plans.

12. Eligibility and term of office for working group members:

12.1 MCSC members are responsible for the appointment and replacement of working group members. Working groups may propose additional members as necessary for approval by the MCSC.

12.2 Working group members may be drawn from all sectors of society, including business, government, civil society and research institutes. The composition of each working group should be balanced to reflect the legitimate interests of stakeholders.

12.3 The term of office of working group members is based on performance against measurable targets and will be defined by the MCSC in accordance for work to be carried out.

12.4 Leadership of the working groups should be joint or combined. The process for the appointment of working group leaders will be determined on a case-by-case basis.

12.5 The following criteria will be used for selecting working group members:
   (a) Stakeholder
   (b) Relevant to MCSC objectives
   (c) Expected to be able to actively contribute and have the diversity of skills and expertise appropriate to the needs of the working group
   (d) Integrity
   (e) Must have authority from their stakeholders

13. Guidelines to assist working groups to develop suitable proposals for consideration by the MCSC:

13.1 Stakeholders, through the MCSC, give their authority to the working groups to proceed with their tasks.

13.2 The MCSC will develop publicly available criteria which will be used to judge and approve proposals arising from the working groups.

13.3 The terms of reference for the working group will be representative of the needs and considerations of the MCSC stakeholders.

14. Fees and expenses of working group members:

14.1 Sitting fees and travel expenses will be paid for meetings attended. No further payments will be made. Follow-up work for government representatives are considered a part of the ordinary duties. Work done by unfunded local community groups will need to be defined and financed accordingly.

15. Measures to ensure the effectiveness of working groups:

15.1 Working group members may be released if they do not achieve agreed targets.

15.2 In addition, working groups will be disbanded once agreed tasks have been completed satisfactorily.

16. Accountabilities of working group members:

16.1 Working group members are expected to report on any activities related to the MCSC to their own stakeholders/departments.

16.2 In addition, working group members are accountable to the MCSC.

C.3 Terms of reference for the Secretariat

17. Duties and responsibilities of the MCSC Secretariat:

17.1 [The Secretariat will] conduct the business of the MCSC, co-ordinate meetings, publish a record of the meeting and ensure efficient communication between the MCSC and the working groups.

17.2 The Secretariat will distribute an annual schedule of meetings to all participants in December of each year.

17.3 The Secretariat will be responsible for compiling and circulating a monthly progress report to the MCSC and other working groups.

17.4 The Secretariat will be responsible for the production of an approved communiqué (containing key points and outcomes for public release) and report. The communiqué should be released immediately. The report should be released within a week.

17.5 The Secretariat will also disseminate information in the local community to ensure that public opinion is fed back to the MCSC.

17.6 The Secretariat will maintain a website and ensure that it is fully updated.

18. Accountability of the Secretariat:

18.1 With regard to everyday duties, [it is accountable] to the MCSC co-chairs.

Appendix D
Checklists of impact indicators

This appendix provides an extensive list of indicators that can be used for measuring or assessing:

- The business outcomes of partnerships (aimed specifically at oil, gas and mining corporations)
- The community development outcomes of partnerships
- The governance outcomes of partnerships

D.1 Indicators for measuring the business outcomes of partnerships

D.1.1 Indicators at the project and operational level

D.1.1.1 Overall efficiency of production

General

- Scheduling targets and milestones met (or anticipated to be met)
- Budget targets met (or anticipated to be met)
- Quality and cost of suppliers (e.g. of maintenance services)
- Management of political and social risks
- Costs of security and criminal activity
- Costs of insurance
- Accessibility of sites
- Staff morale

- Disaster management (relating to pollution, natural disasters and violence)

- Effectiveness of staff training

- Quality of grievance mechanisms to contain social and political risks

Exploration and feasibility

- Attainment of permits

- Speed and quality of procurement of human and physical resources

- Management of community expectations during periods of uncertainty and delay in investment decisions

- Dependence of community on company for social provision

- Foundations laid for long-term stakeholder engagement

- Impacts on communities have been accurately identified and measured (e.g. scoping in environmental and social impact assessment, impact prediction)

- Equitability and transparency in distribution of economic and social costs and benefits (i.e. 'packaging' of positive and negative social impacts)

Construction

- Sensitivity of construction workers to cultural norms

- Levels of employees sourced locally

Operations

- Production targets met or exceeded (e.g. the impact of social unrest and tensions on production)

- Distribution of social benefits beyond project 'footprint' (i.e. beyond project-affected people)

- Availability of partners to sustain social investment activities when projects experience delays, temporary 'downsizing' or suspended operations as a result of market pressures

Closure

- Community dependence on company for public-service provision, economic opportunities and environmental management after closure

- Risk to global corporate reputation of an economic or political vacuum following closure

D.1.1.2 Effectiveness of social investment

General

- Cultural sensitivity of social investment programmes

- Effective and early resolution of disputes with communities

- Consistency and frequency of 'messages' to communities that help to manage community expectations

- Durability (shock-resistance) of 'social licence to operate'

Employment

- Local sourcing and procurement of labour, products and services

- Opportunities for the most affected households to gain long-term employment through the project

- Level of skills and/or transferability of skills of local employees

- Integration of project skills with skills needed for the social or economic programmes of the government and donors

Impact mitigation

- Accuracy of scoping and impact prediction

- Relevance of impact mitigation studies to household livelihoods

- Transferability of relationships built during consultation for environmental or social impact assessments into long-term stakeholder relationships

- Quality and sustainability of social impact mitigation (e.g. trust built; expectations managed; use of responsive and meaningful consultation; establishment and maintenance of ongoing and culturally relevant communications; participation of affected parties in scoping, design, implementation and maintenance of impact-mitigation measures; resolution of grievances; existence of adequate organisational capacity in local institutions to sustain mitigation)

- 'Time-to-benefit' of interventions for affected households

- Effectiveness of social impact mitigation (including resettlement and management of inward migration) through alignment and integration with government, NGO and donor programmes and institutional structures (e.g. by linking income restoration to a government training programme, or through offering advice on 'best practice' in micro-finance)

Community development beyond direct social impact mitigation

- Quality and sustainability of community development programmes (e.g. trust built; expectations managed; establishment of responsive and meaningful consultation; establishment of ongoing and culturally relevant communications; participation of affected parties in scoping, design, implementation and maintenance of development projects; resolution of grievances; existence of adequate organisational capacity in local institutions to sustain projects)

- Cost burden of social programmes

- Risk burden of social programmes

- Rate of return on social investment (e.g. does it offer a faster 'time-to-sustainability' or more cost-effective projects?)

- 'Shock-resistance' of community development projects (e.g. to natural disasters or economic events)

- Medium-term to long-term community dependence on company

- Efficiency (e.g. less replication and fewer gaps) in the roles and responsibilities of the company, government agencies and civil-society organisations in relation to public-service provision

- Efficiency in apportioning of costs (human and capital) for public-service provision between company, government and civil society

- Geographical and population 'reach' of company's community development programmes (e.g. obtained through alignment with government and donor programmes)

- Impact of existing government, NGO or donor community development programmes coincident with the project area (e.g. increased participation of communities in government local health programmes)

Regional development

- Transparency in tax and royalty revenue flows

- Visibility of company's contributions in the region of operations to the creation of long-term, sustainable economic opportunities not dependent on the extractive industry

- Leverage of all oil and mining companies operating in the same region (or country) in relation to tax revenues and contributions to regional development

D.1.1.3 Compliance: legal, contractual and policy requirements for social performance

- Minimisation of the cost of meeting various legal, contractual and policy compliance requirements

- Compliance with the social requirements of regulatory authorities and investors

- Quality of environmental and social impact assessments

- Quality of ongoing political and social risk assessments

- Evidence of compliance with corporate policies on community participation and external stakeholder relations

- Capability of senior staff to meet social investment targets embodied in 'performance contacts', 'scorecards' and so on

- Compliance with social reporting requirements

D.1.1.4 Enhancing local reputation and competitiveness

- Transferability of licence and permits (i.e. absence of social tensions)

- Visibility and equity of regional benefits from tax and royalty revenue streams

- Competitive advantage in bidding for concession tenders (i.e. absence of social tensions)

- Meeting corporate (group-level) criteria for internal investment (i.e. the 'right to growth')

- Co-ordination between social, community and public-affairs units within the company in terms of utilising stakeholder relations

D.1.2 Indicators at the corporate (group) level

D.1.2.1 Increased shareholder value

- Informed national and regional risk assessment (e.g. use of scenario planning)

- Demonstrable capability of portfolio of business units and operations to manage social impacts and risks, and communication of this competitive edge to financial analysts

- Risks of public exposure on sensitive social issues (human rights, labour conditions, issues relating to indigenous peoples, biodiversity, bribery and corruption)

- Public credibility of social reporting and audits

- Risks to marketing, sales and share price associated with perceived poor management of social impacts

- Global competitive advantage from showing leadership in management of social issues

- Cross-operational learning (e.g. partnership structure and processes providing replicable 'models' for good practice)

D.1.2.2 Marketing and sales

- Success stories of partnerships on which to draw for advertising and marketing strategies

- Sponsorship alliances with international NGOs

D.1.2.3 Staff recruitment and retention

- Attractiveness to graduates

- Morale of existing staff

D.2 Indicators for measuring the community development outcomes of partnerships[1]

D.2.1 All indicators

D.2.1.1 Environment, where households exist

Natural resources

- Community-level assets, forest and non-forest products, aquatic resources, etc.

- Use made of the commons: grazing, fuel

- Tree ownership

- Availability of land

Infrastructure

- Adequacy of transportation (access, seasonal reliability, sustainability)

- Adequacy of water supply and sanitation

1   Compiled with the assistance of A. Roderick, Programme Manager, CARE International UK.

- Adequacy of electricity supplies

- Adequacy of telecommunications

Economy

- Sustainability of income sources

- Access to markets and employment

- Division between on-farm and off-farm activities

- Reliability and affordability of agricultural inputs (e.g. fertilisers) and infrastructure (e.g. irrigation)

Culture

- Ethnic or cultural groupings

- Propensity to social vices: drunkenness, witchcraft, violence

Social differentiation

- Participation in community decision-making

- Wealth ranking

- Vulnerability to conflict

Institutions

- Effectiveness of community administrative structures

- Evidence of community institutions taking initiative for development

- Evidence of community institutions able to 'tap into the organs of the state'

Political environment

- Intra-community disputes

- Efficiency of community decision-making

D.2.1.2 Household livelihoods

Nutritional security

- Weight in relation to 'healthy' weight for age

- Height in relation to 'expected' height for age

- Type of feeding practices between mother and infant or child

Food security

- Percentage of population consuming minimum standards of required nutritional intake
- Number of meals consumed per day
- Percentage of food safety net funded from domestic sources

Health security

- Recent illness patterns
- Health service utilisation (distance from residence, time to travel to service, affordability of service)
- Utilisation of obstetric care services
- Utilisation rate of pre-natal services
- Average personal consumption of water
- Access to affordable potable water
- Access to affordable sanitation facilities

Economic security

- Value of household productive assets
- Value of household liquid assets
- Business management skills
- Applicability of vocational or technical skills to available employment opportunities
- Proportion of household income earned by women
- Percentage of small loans given to women
- Production levels, crops, livestock
- Dependence on 'middle men'

Educational security

- Percentage of children enrolled at primary school
- Educational achievement of young adolescents
- Adult literacy
- Quality of educational services

Environmental security

- Access to quality land
- Soil and biodiversity conservation practices
- Access to and management of renewable natural resources critical to livelihoods
- Rate of local deforestation

Habitat security

- Percentage of families with adequate housing
- Percentage of families with adequate waste disposal
- Crime rates

Social network security

- Level of active household participation in community organisations
- Level of democratisation of community organisations
- Mutual support of kin and friends in neighbourhood or community
- Access to organisations and services that offer any types of social service
- Community influence on local or regional government social programmes
- Participation of local people in the management of 'common goods'

Personal empowerment

- Enhancement of life skills (financial management, negotiating skills, time management)
- Capability skills (interpersonal, systemic and judgemental skills)

D.3 Indicators for measuring the governance outcomes of partnerships[2]

D.3.1 All indicators

D.3.1.1 'Visibility' of public office in discharging its civic duties for social development

Effectiveness of social programmes

- Timely implementation of stated development policies, plans and programmes

- Reach of government programmes (total populations and particular groups)

- Long-term sustainability of government social programmes

- Leverage of additional resources from non-government sectors

- Linkage between donor-supported poverty-reduction strategies papers and the social programmes actually implemented

- Degree of interaction or negotiation between communities and local government service providers

- Accessibility of government services to the 'poor' (e.g. healthcare, primary education, public radio, telecommunications, water supply, transportation)

Transparency and accountability

- Government participation and monitoring of community land and asset compensation evaluations (e.g. resettlement, health and safety breaches)

- Civil-society participation in the design of government's social programmes and poverty-reduction programmes, including local development plans (e.g. evidence of government responsiveness)

- Physical presence of government extension staff in areas of poverty

- Linkage between political mandates (secured during free and fair elections) and delivery of social programmes

- Evidence that resource rents from extractive industry are reaching:
    - Project-affected people
    - Populations in the wider region of operation

- Existence of published figures on the relationship between resource rents and public spending

---

2   Adapted from Kaufmann *et al.* 1999.

- Civil society is informed of changes in the rules and policies governing access to social programmes
- Business is provided with a platform to express views over changes in laws or policies

D.3.1.2 Capacity of public office to manage resources

Effectiveness of resource management

- Capacity of regional and local government to mange large-scale injections of capital from resource distribution
- Existence of bureaucratic delays to resource rent redistribution (e.g. amount of staff management time spent with bureaucrats)
- Extent of corruption: in particular, extortion for contracts or the release of disbursements
- Loss of government civil-servant capacity to extractive industries
- Turnover of government staff that lowers the quality of the government's personnel
- Incentives (political, reputational, staff promotion, financial, etc.) to ensure resource rents reach affected communities
- Civil service free from political influences

Effectiveness of regulations

- Evidence of regulators embracing 'development additionality' in concession tendering
- Government-related transaction costs of setting up new businesses
- Effective and fair regulatory framework for resource rent redistribution
- Efficiency of government customs and excise departments
- Implementation of tariff and non-tariff trade regulations
- Degree of burden on business of social and environmental regulations
- Effect of deregulation policies
- Effects of government wage and price controls
- Government intervention in capital flows
- Government intervention in the banking system
- Effect of regulations or restrictions on business or equity ownership by non-residents
- Effect of foreign currency regulation on business development

- Effect of tax system on the willingness of extractive industry corporation to partner with government on public-service provision

D.3.1.3 Effectiveness of laws and institution designed to protect the public interest

Rule of law

- Frequency and cost of crime
- Frequency of kidnapping (e.g. of foreigners)
- Willingness to enforce private and pubic contracts
- Levels of corruption in the banking system
- Extent of black market
- Enforcement of property and infrastructure rights (including access to 'common' resources)
- Predictability of judiciary and local courts
- Government support for 'customary' dispute and punishment systems
- Protection of intellectual property rights

Assurance of political stability

- Fair and free elections
- Orderly change in government following national elections
- Transparency, accessibility and perceived fairness of legal system
- Quality of civil liberties: freedom of speech, assembly and demonstration
- Extent of press freedom
- Extent of local demonstrations, road blocks, violence, riots, insurgency and rebellion, military coups, political terrorism, political assassination and civil war
- Evidence of reductions in ethnic tensions and divisions
- Presence of local government representatives as arbitrators of intra-community disputes
- Risk of unconstitutional changes in government

Levels of corruption

- Effectiveness of anti-corruption initiatives in government
- Corruption in the political system as a 'threat to foreign investment'
- Frequency of 'additional payments' to 'get things done'

- Irregular, additional payments connected with import and export permits, business licences, exchange controls, tax assessment, police protection, loan applications, etc.

Reference

Kaufmann, D., A. Kraay and P. Zoido-Lobaton (1999) *Governance Matters* (Washington, DC: World Bank).

Appendix E

Examples of impact tables
The Tri-sector Healthcare Partnership, Las Cristinas Gold Mine, Venezuela, December 1999 to January 2001

This appendix provides a series of 'impact tables' demonstrating how the costs and benefits of partnerships can be assessed in practice. For each of the key performance indicators, an assessment is made of:

- The impact of the partnership on the indicator
- The assumed most likely alternative strategy to partnership
- The incremental construction of the partnership
- The confidence in the evidence

The examples presented are from an evaluation of the Las Cristinas healthcare partnership described in Chapter 5.

Indicator	Impact of partnership on indicator	Assumed most likely alternative strategy to partnership	Incremental contribution of partnership	Confidence in evidence
Corporate reputation:				
Improvement in relationship with local stakeholders	Channels of communication and trust between MINCA and the local stakeholders improved significantly though the process of constructing the CHC. BPD workshops improved relations between previously adversarial Creole and indigenous communities. Reduced need for security measures on-site.	Community development programme of MINCA would have tended to have been more piecemeal (e.g. through modest donations to existing state-run clinics plus other small-scale development activities), with no single focus (other than artisan mining) for developing collaborative working relationships with local communities and reducing hostilities between community groups.	Benefit of a positive corporate reputation from improved community relations and evidence of an innovative approach to managing social issues.	High
Competitive advantage:				
Competitive advantage gains for maintaining existing (or winning future) concessions	During a period of uncertainty over the future of its mining operations, MINCA was able to demonstrate to government regulators and corporate managers that it could maintain its social licence to operate at reasonable cost. The partnership model was also used by Placer Dome as a demonstration of good social management to help strengthen its tender for a new mining concession in another Latin American country.	Cost of alternative social investment programme in Las Cristinas area was likely to have been comparable but less likely to have generated the same lower levels of community dependence on MINCA.	The partnership model may have contributed, in part, to extensions to MINCA's existing concession agreement for the Las Cristinas mine. The model also provides marketing opportunities and evidence to enhance future bids for new concessions.	Low

BPD = Business Partners for Development   CHC = community health centre   MINCA = Minera Las Cristinas CA

Table E.1 **Business outcomes** (continued opposite)

Indicator	Impact of partnership on indicator	Assumed most likely alternative strategy to partnership	Incremental contribution of partnership	Confidence in evidence
Investment risk:				
Reduced dependence of communities on company as sole provider for social investment resources	Noticeable increase in self-confidence among key local stakeholders Improved capacity of communities to engage in negotiations and build alliances with other organisations with which there was previously no contact (e.g. with the Director of Environment, Bolivar State, and the Foundation Tierra Viva) Involvement of other parties and resources in the CHC partnership Transfer of new management and construction skills from MINCA to other parties	Without the partnership model, the likelihood is that MINCA's community development programme would have generated greater dependence on the company for community development funding and related skills, leaving the company exposed to the liabilities of escalating community demands during a period when funds were scarce.	The security of MINCA's investment in the Las Cristinas area (either in 'care and maintenance' mode or future operations) is less exposed to community dependence on the company for social provision (i.e. there are fewer social liabilities).	Moderate
Cost-effectiveness of social investment programme:				
Leverage of additional social investment resources from 'other' organisations	Organisations other than MINCA committed resources to manage and maintain the CHC: ● Ministry of Health and Social Development and Tumeremo Hospital: medicines, materials, salaries, training of CHC staff (US$9,200) ● ISP: medicines, materials, training, salaries (US$397,500) ● Mayor's office: including salaries (US$125,400) ● Community: volunteer construction hours (equivalent to US$77,138) *continued over*	Little investment in health facilities was expected from the government during the period of the partnership (although the assumption is that some items may include existing government budget allocations, from past experience these allocations are unlikely to have been disbursed during this period). Similarly, no investment to improve water services or healthcare education and training was anticipated during the same period.	The leverage of social investment from other sources during the period was valued at US$2,079,538	Moderate

BPD = Business Partners for Development   CHC = community health centre   ISP = Instituto de Salud Publica (government health institute)
MINCA = Minera Las Cristinas CA

Table E.1 (from previous page; continued over)

Indicator	Impact of partnership on indicator	Assumed most likely alternative strategy to partnership	Incremental contribution of partnership	Confidence in evidence
Investment risk (continued):				
	from previous page			
	• HMRF: medical equipment, training, technical assistance (US$1,428,500) • CVG: water services (US$10,500) Additional contributions: • ABB: trucks, engineering, supplies (US$8,200) • Edelca: engineering services (US$14,200) • BDC: construction (US$4,000) • Others: equipment, etc. (US$4,900) Collective contribution: US$2,079,538			
Cost-effectiveness of healthcare for future employees at the mine	In the event of the mine being developed, future employees and their families will have access to high-quality local healthcare at low cost and will be positively affected by other preventative measures (e.g. improvements to potable water supplies).	Company would normally provide quality healthcare and related administration at the mine site for employees.	Reduced cost to company of providing healthcare to future (community-based) employees	Moderate

CVG = Corporación Venezolana de Guayana   HMRF = Humanitarian Medical Relief Foundation

Table E.1 (continued)

Indicator	Impact of partnership on indicator	Assumed most likely alternative strategy to partnership	Incremental contribution of partnership	Confidence in evidence
Access to health services:				
Improved access to essential local health services for the wider community	Access to preventative healthcare facilities, technical medical equipment, healthcare information and education, village worker training. Outreach healthcare was improved for a population of 12,000. Opportunity cost of health problems (loss of time for farming, caring for children, trading, etc.) lowered for communities as a result of improvements in disease prevention and in emergency treatment. Upgraded health centre facility, with positive implications for management autonomy and size of budget	No locally accessible blood laboratory, no dentistry, no X-ray facility, no surgery Without the CHC approximately 5,000 people per year would have to incur additional cost and time to travel to hospital in Tumeremo for treatment.	Improved local accessibility to quality healthcare, estimated at US$52,122 per year (based on a figure of US$9.52 per day per person in travel costs) Reduced losses to livelihood as a result of improvements in curing preventable diseases Potentially increased medical budget for CHC as a result of government agreement to upgrade the designation of the CHC from Rural II to Urban I	High
Time to benefit:				
Faster time-to-benefit of social investment programme	Functioning CHC completed in 11 months	MINCA would have been expected to have contributed modest donations to existing state-run clinics. Though these improvements would have been rapid, they would not have been comparable in terms of quality to the types of medical services provided by the CHC.	High-quality health centre constructed and functioning in 11 months, accessible to a population of 12,000	Moderate

CHC = community health centre   MINCA = Minera Las Cristinas CA

Table E.2 Impact on community development (continued over)

Indicator	Impact of partnership on indicator	Assumed most likely alternative strategy to partnership	Incremental contribution of partnership	Confidence in evidence
Sustainability of healthcare provision:				
Long-term maintenance of CHC without presence of MINCA	Process of CHC construction generated new local capacities for community leaders and local government, including: • Group decision-making, organisation and management skills • Capacity of communities to raise funds without MINCA (as demonstrated by the securing of funds for a community information centre) • Exploration of new relations and partnerships (e.g. with the Director of Environment, Bolivar State authorities and the NGO Foundation Tierra Viva)	There would have been less-extensive training and capacity-building opportunities for community leaders (e.g. it is unlikely to have included BPD training and partnership-building experience, or hands-on experiences of the executive committee in constructing the CHC). It is likely healthcare would have remained state-managed.	Improved community organisational and leadership capacity to sustain CHC management in the long term without the presence of MINCA	Moderate
Improved infrastructure:				
Improvements in supply of potable water	CVG and community have improved the maintenance regime of existing water supplies, with a rolling programme to increase supplies to communities.	No community involvement in monitoring improvements in water service provision was anticipated during the period prior to the process of agreeing the first CHC MOU.	Improvements in reliability of supplies of potable water to local communities	High

BPD = Business Partners for Development   CHC = community health centre   CVG = Corporación Venezolana de Guayana   MINCA = Minera Las Cristinas CA   MOU = memorandum of understanding   NGO = non-governmental organisation

Table E.2 (from previous page; continued opposite)

Indicator	Impact of partnership on indicator	Assumed most likely alternative strategy to partnership	Incremental contribution of partnership	Confidence in evidence
Improved infrastructure (continued):				
Improvements in road access to CHC	Proposed paving of CHC access road and repair	It is unlikely that the road would have been paved and repaired during the time-period.	Improved road infrastructure access to CHC	Low
Capacity-building and community participation:				
Community participation in its own development, and evidence of collaborative problem-solving	High levels of voluntary participation (4,000 hours in meetings and co-ordination, and 30,000 hours in construction of the CHC) Improved dialogue skills through participation in community executive committee (negotiations, advocacy and joint decision-making) Community executive committee fostered joint decision-making between Creole and indigenous communities Creation of new relations and joint working relationships with CVG through community water-management committees	There would have been less-extensive opportunities for learning negotiation and decision-making skills between competing community groups and between these groups and regional government (although an artisan mining initiative of MINCA continued during this period).	Sense of community empowerment improved considerably, not only for managing the CHC but also for initiating and securing funding for new community development programmes.	High

CHC = community health centre   CVG = Corporación Venezolana de Guayana

Table E.2 (continued)

Indicator	Impact of partnership on indicator	Assumed most likely alternative strategy to partnership	Incremental contribution of partnership	Confidence in evidence
Improved visibility of public authorities:				
Visible participation of government agencies in successful community development project	Notwithstanding relatively small investments through the CHC partnership, central and regional government agencies have been associated favourably with a tangible improvements in community health provision in the Las Cristinas area.	Visibility of government authorities participating in improvements to health services are likely to have been negligible during same period.	Improved reputation of government agencies with local communities, in particular: • Local municipality (mayor's office) • ISP (government health institute) • Ministry of Health • Tumeremo Hospital (regional health authority)	Moderate
Increased agency interaction:				
Increased interaction between government agencies	CHC partnership provided a platform for joint action around issues of common concern to a number of different government actors: On health issues: • Local municipality (mayor's office) • ISP (government health institute) • Ministry of Health • Tumeremo Hospital (regional health authority) On artisan mining issues (including key issues such as small-scale mining): • Ministry of Energy and Mines • Ministry of Environment and Natural Resources • CVG	Genuine collaboration between authority over health provision for Las Cristinas area was unlikely.	Collaboration between government agencies to provide health services	Low

BPD = Business Partners for Development CHC = community health centre CVG = Corporación Venezolana de Guayana
ISP = Instituto de Salud Publica (government health institute) MINCA = Minera Las Cristinas CA

Table E.3 **Impact on public-sector governance** (continued opposite)

Indicator	Impact of partnership on indicator	Assumed most likely alternative strategy to partnership	Incremental contribution of partnership	Confidence in evidence
Responsiveness of government to local need:				
Communities more satisfied with government public programmes	Through CHC executive committee and sub-committees, increased interaction and transparency between local government and community groups to address local needs for healthcare and water supply Direct and continued community participation through community water committees in the CVG water supply and maintenance programme	No anticipated direct involvement of communities either in healthcare provision or in the water supply and maintenance programme	Permanent forum (i.e. the community executive committee) created for ongoing exchanges between government health agencies and community groups	Moderate
Cost-effectiveness of public spending:				
Resource leverage	Contributions of resources, materials and labour from other sectors for the improvement of public service delivery: ● MINCA: construction and facilitation (US$456,000) ● Mayor's office: a proportion of salaries (US$125,400) ● Community: volunteer construction hours (equivalent to US$77,138) ● HMRF: medical equipment, training, technical assistance (US$1,428,500) ● ABB: trucks, engineering, supplies (US$8,200) ● Edelca: engineering services (US$14,200) ● BDC: construction (US$4,000) ● Others: equipment, etc. (US$4,900) Total contributions from other sectors: US$2,100,000 approximately	Contributions in absence of partnership: ● MINCA: most likely contributions to existing state-run clinic: US$150,000 ● Mayor's office: US$0 ● Community: US$0 ● HMRF: US$0 ● ABB: US$0 ● Edelca: US$0 ● BDC: US$0 ● Others: US$0 Total likely contributions from other sectors: US$150,000	Contribution of resources for improved public service delivery of healthcare over and above what government would have delivered during same period: US$1,940,910	High

CHC = community health centre   CVG = Corporación Venezolana de Guayana   HMRF = Humanitarian Medical Relief Foundation   MINCA = Minera Las Cristinas CA

Table E.3 (from previous page; continued over)

Indicator	Impact of partnership on indicator	Assumed most likely alternative strategy to partnership	Incremental contribution of partnership	Confidence in evidence
Cost-effectiveness of public spending (continued):				
Decreased need for clinical treatment of preventable diseases	Through CHC, rolling provision of education and training programmes on preventative medicine to a population of 12,000 people, including malaria prevention (likely to decrease government expenditure on clinical treatment of preventable diseases by 30–50%).	Government likely to continue current level of expenditure on clinical treatment of preventable diseases: e.g. annual cost of US$141,900 for malaria treatment in Sifontes district (3,300 people, at US$43 per person per year).	Reductions in malaria expenditure of at least US$42,300, based on a 30% reduction in disease	Low
Lower water-maintenance costs	Reduced need for high maintenance because of greater community participation (e.g. CVG water service delivery and maintenance visits reduced)	Reliable figures not available	Maintenance savings	Moderate

CHC = community health centre   CVG = Corporación Venezolana de Guayana

Table E.3 (continued)

Appendix F
Publications of the
Natural Resources Cluster

F.1 Website

The Natural Resources Cluster website (www.bpd-naturalresources.org) hosts a wide variety of guidelines and case-study material to help 'get started' with the process of partnering. The materials available include:

- Evidence of the business case for a tri-sector partnership approach to social issues management

- Evidence of the impacts on poverty alleviation and sustainable development of tri-sector partnerships

- Case studies from around the world

- Tools and training modules to assist in the exploration, building and maintenance of partnership arrangements

- Examples of the different types of deliverables in the partnering process (e.g. terms of reference, partnership agreements, progress reports)

F.2 Case studies

The following case studies have been published by the Natural Resources Cluster of Business Partners for Development and are available from the website of the Natural Resources Cluster.

Copeman, V., and E. Rivas (2002) *Transredes/CARE Partnerships—Managing Oil Spill Compensation: A Case Study*.

Garcia Larralde, E., and R. Sullivan (2003) *BP Exploration Company Colombia—Long-term Regional Development in Casanare: A Case Study*.

Hamann, R. (2002) *Kelian Equatorial Mining, Indonesia—A Partnership Approach to Mine Closure: A Case Study*.

Killick, N. (2002) *Case Study: Oil and Gas Development, Azerbaijan*.

Ladbury, S., and H. Goyder (2002) *The Micro-Credit Scheme for Agricultural Development (MISCAD)—SPDC, Nigeria: A Case Study*.

Sullivan, R. (2002) *Kahama Mining Corporation Limited, Tanzania—Social Development Programme: A Case Study*.

Sullivan, R., and S. Porto (2002) *Sarshatali Coal Mining Project, India: Update*.

Sullivan, R., and M. Warner (2002) *Partnering and EIA—SPDC, Nigeria: A Case-Study*.

Sullivan, R., and M. Warner (2002) *Konkola Copper Mines, Zambia—Partnerships for Local Business Development. A Case Study*.

Tull, J., E. Garcia Larralde, A. Mansutti and S. Porto (2001) *Las Cristinas Gold Mining Project, Venezuela—Healthcare Partnership: A Case Study*.

Warner, M. (2001) *Sarshatali Coal-Mining Project, India: A Case Study*.

F.3　Working papers

The following working papers have been published by the Natural Resources Cluster of Business Partners for Development and are available from the website of the Natural Resources Cluster.

Acutt, N. (2001) 'Working Paper 10: Towards Evidence of the Costs and Benefits of Tri-sector Partnerships'.

Davy, A. (2000) 'Working Paper 3: Emerging Lessons for Tri-sector Partnerships: A Review of Four Case-Studies'.

Davy, A. (2001) 'Working Paper 5: Tri-sector Partnerships for Social Investment: Ownership and Control of Outcomes'.

Davy, A. (2001) 'Working Paper 8: Managing Community Expectations through Tri-sector Partnerships'.

Davy, A. (2001) 'Working Paper 9: Companies in Conflict Situations: A Role for Tri-sector Partnerships?'.

Grzybowski, A., D. Johnston, N. Macleod, R. Roberts and M. Warner (2001) 'Working Paper 7: Training Modules'.

Hamann, R. (2001) 'Working Paper 11: Corporate Foundations and Tri-sector Partnerships'.

Mitchell, J., J. Shankleman. and M. Warner (2002) 'Working Paper 14: Measuring the "Added Value" of Tri-sector Partnerships'.

Verschoyle, D., and M. Warner (2001) 'Working Paper 12: Learning from Project Partnering in the Construction Industry'.

Warhurst, A. (2000) 'Working Paper 4: Tri-sector Partnerships for Social Investment: Business Drivers'.

Warner, M. (2000) 'Working Paper 1: Overview of BPD and the Natural Resources Cluster'.

Warner, M. (2000) 'Working Paper 2: Tri-sector Partnerships for Social Investment within the Oil, Gas and Mining Sectors: An Analytical Framework'.

Warner, M. (2001) 'Working Paper 6: Guidance Note for 'Getting Started': Tri-sector Partnerships for Managing Social Issues in the Extractive Industries'.

Warner, M. (2002) 'Working Paper 13: Monitoring Tri-sector Partnerships'.

F.4 Briefing notes on tri-sector partnerships

The following briefing notes have been published by the Natural Resources Cluster of Business Partners for Development and are available from the website of the Natural Resources Cluster.

- Briefing Note 1: Overview of Tri-sector Partnerships (2002)
- Briefing Note 2: Overview of the Partnering Process (2002)
- Briefing Note 3: Managing Community Relations during Investment Uncertainty (2002)
- Briefing Note 4: Contributing to Community Development (2002)
- Briefing Note 5: Environmental Impact Assessment (EIA) as a Tool to Secure the Social Licence to Operate (2002)
- Briefing Note 6: Preventing and Resolving Disputes with Communities and NGOs (2002)
- Briefing Note 7: Managing Retrenchment and Contributing to Local Business Development (2002)
- Briefing Note 8: Contributing to Long-term Regional Development (2002)
- Briefing Note 9: Managing the Closure of Projects (2003)

F.5 Publications: training modules

A series of training modules have been developed for those likely to be engaged in, or the facilitator of, partnerships between companies, governments and civil society. The training modules that have been developed are:

- Senior Manager's Overview (1 hour)
- Partnership Route Map (1 day)
- Internal Assessment (1 day)
- Consultation and Communications (1 day)
- Consensus-Building (2 days)
- Facilitation (2 days)
- Management Tools (1 day)

These training modules have been published by the Natural Resources Cluster of Business Partners for Development and are available from the website of the Natural Resources Cluster.

F.6 Books and reports

PricewaterhouseCoopers (2002) *Putting Partnering to Work* (London: Business Partners for Development).

Warner, M. (2003) *The New Broker: Brokering Partnerships for Development* (London: ODI).

Editors and contributors

Editors

Dr **Michael Warner** is a Research Fellow with the Overseas Development Institute (ODI), London. For three years he managed the Secretariat of the Natural Resources Cluster (covering the oil, gas and mining sectors) for the World Bank's Business Partners for Development programme. In this role he acted as the broker or advisor of multi-sector partnerships involving RPG in India, Shell in Nigeria, BP in Colombia, Anglo American in Zambia and Placer Dome in Venezuela.

Michael has a PhD in Environmental Management from Imperial College, University of London and worked for a number of years in developing countries as a consultant with Environmental Resources Management, London. In the mid-1990s he joined the ODI, specialising in the adaptation of interest-based negotiation to resolve disputes and develop partnerships between communities, business, governments and NGOs. He now manages a new programme at ODI to improve the social and economic performance of corporate investment in developing countries.

Michael is the author of *Complex Problems . . . Negotiated Solutions* (ITDG Publishing, 2001) and of a novella on the art of partnership broking, *The New Broker: Brokering Partnerships for Development* (ODI, 2003). He is also Director of the consultancy company Sustainable Negotiation Services International (SNSⁱ) Limited.

Dr **Rory Sullivan** has been Director, Investor Responsibility with Insight Investment (the asset management arm of HBOS plc) since October 2002. In this role, he is responsible for leading Insight's engagement activities relating to climate change, human rights, and corporate social responsibility. He also contributes to Insight's broader work on corporate governance.

Rory has 15 years' experience in environmental management and public policy, having worked for the private sector and government agencies in Australia, South-East Asia, Africa and Europe. His experience includes evaluating development-focused partnerships (health, education, water) on behalf of the World Bank's Business Partners for Development programme, advising Environment Australia and the OECD on the design of pollution release and transfer registers, and assisting public- and private-sector organisations with the implementation of environmental and risk management systems.

Rory is the author (with Hugh Wyndham) of *Effective Environmental Management: Principles and Case Studies* (Allen & Unwin, 2001), and the editor of *Business and Human Rights: Dilemmas and Solutions* (Greenleaf Publishing, 2003). He has written over 100 articles, book chapters and papers on human rights, environmental policy and development issues.

Rory holds a first-class honours degree in electrical engineering (University College Cork, Ireland), masters' degrees in Environmental Science (University of Manchester, UK) and Environmental Law (University of Sydney, Australia), and a PhD in Law (Queen Mary, University of London, UK).

Contributors

The contributors to this book and their affiliations (at the time they contributed to the work of the Natural Resources Cluster of Business Partners for Development) are as follows:

Nicola Acutt, School of Environmental Sciences, University of East Anglia, UK

Assheton Carter, Corporate Citizenship Unit, Warwick Business School, University of Warwick, UK

Vicky Copeman, Environmental Resources Limited, UK

Rajat Das, Association of Social and Health Advancement, India

Aidan Davy, International Business Leaders Forum, UK

Edgardo Garcia Larralde, Living Earth, UK

Ralph Hamann, School of Environmental Sciences, University of East Anglia, UK

Paul Kapelus, Corporate Citizenship Unit, Warwick Business School, University of Warwick, UK

Aida Kiangi, Kahama Mining Corporation Limited, Tanzania

Nick Killick, International Alert, UK

Alex Mansutti, UNEG, Venezuela

Joydev Mazumdar, JayaPrakash Institute for Social Change, India

Jol Mitchell, Environmental Resources Management, UK

Amit Mukherjee, Integrated Coal Mining Limited, India

Santiago Porto, Natural Resources Cluster, Business Partners for Development, UK

Enrique Rivas, independent consultant, Venezuela

Jill Shankleman, Environmental Resources Management, UK

James Tull, Conflict Management Group, USA

Dom Verschoyle, Engineers Against Poverty (The Telford Challenge), UK

Abbreviations

ADM	Additional District Magistrate (India)
AIDS	acquired immunodeficiency syndrome
AMREF	African Medical and Research Foundation
APDF	African Project Development Facility (Zambia)
ASHA	Association for Social and Health Advancement (India)
BBZ	Barclays Bank Zambia
BDA	Business Development Alliance (Azerbaijan)
bopd	barrels of oil per day
BOT	build–operate–transfer
BPD	Business Partners for Development
BPXC	BP Exploration Company (Colombia)
CBE	Citizens for a Better Environment (Zambia)
CBPP	Construction Best Practices Programme
CIB	Construction Industry Board (UK)
CMSA	Cerro Matoso SA
CSSC	Centre for Strategic Studies in Construction
CSW	commercial sex worker
CVG	Corporación Venezolana de Guayana (Venezuela)
DFID	Department for International Development (UK)
DHMT	District Health Management Team (Tanzania)
DMO	District Medical Officer (Tanzania)
EIA	environmental impact assessment
EMP	environmental management plan
FDI	foreign direct investment
FSI	Foundation of San Isidro
GCS	Gulf Christian Services
GDP	gross domestic product
HIV	human immunodeficiency virus
HMRF	Humanitarian Medical Relief Foundation
HMTCUP	Her Majesty's Treasury Central Unit on Procurement
ICML	Integrated Coal Mining Limited (India)

ICRC	International Committee for the Red Cross
IDP	internally displaced person
IESC	International Executives Service Corps (Zambia)
IFC	International Finance Corporation (of the World Bank)
IFI	international financial institution
INVEST	Invest Trust (Zambia)
ISO	International Organisation for Standardisation
IT	information technology
KCM	Konkola Copper Mines plc (Zambia)
KDC	Kahama District Council
KEM	Kelian Equatorial Mining (Indonesia)
KMCL	Kahama Mining Corporation Limited (Tanzania)
LATM	livelihoods assessment and trust-building measures
LNG	liquefied natural gas
MCSC	Mine Closure Steering Committee (KEM, Indonesia)
MINCA	Minera Las Cristinas CA (Venezuela)
MOU	memorandum of understanding
MUZ	Mine Workers Union of Zambia
NGO	non-governmental organisation
NRC	Natural Resources Cluster (BPD)
ODI	Overseas Development Institute
OML	Oil Mining Licence
PR	public relations
PSDP	Private Sector Development Programme (EU)
SA	Social Accountability
SDP	social development programme
SME	small or medium-sized enterprise
SMP	social management plan
SPDC	Shell Petroleum Development Company Limited (Nigeria)
STD	sexually transmitted disease
STI	sexually transmitted infection
SWOT	strengths–weaknesses–opportunites–threats
UN	United Nations
USAID	US Agency for International Development
VSO	Voluntary Service Overseas
WMC	Western Mining Corporation
WWF	World Wide Fund for Nature
ZAMTIE	Zambian Trade and Investment Enterprise
ZCCM	Zambian Consolidated Copper Mines
ZCI	Zambian Copper Investments
ZCSMBA	Zambian Chamber of Small and Medium Business Associations

Index